P9-DXM-855

The
FAMILY CALENDAR
Cookbook

From Birthdays to Bake Sales, Good Food to Carry You Through the Year

KELSEY BANFIELD

WITHDRAWN

Running Press
PHILADELPHIA · LONDON

© 2015 by Kelsey Banfield
Published by Running Press,
A Member of the Perseus Books Group

All rights reserved under the Pan-American and International Copyright Conventions

Printed in China

This book may not be reproduced in whole or in part, in any form or by any means, electronic or mechanical, including photocopying, recording, or by any information storage and retrieval system now known or hereafter invented, without written permission from the publisher.

Books published by Running Press are available at special discounts for bulk purchases in the United States by corporations, institutions, and other organizations. For more information, please contact the Special Markets Department at the Perseus Books Group, 2300 Chestnut Street, Suite 200, Philadelphia, PA 19103, or call (800) 810-4145, ext. 5000, or e-mail special.markets@perseusbooks.com.

ISBN: 978-0-7624-5107-4
Library of Congress Control Number: 2014956344
E-book ISBN: 978-0-7624-5527-0
9 8 7 6 5 4 3 2 1
Digit on the right indicates the number of this printing

Cover and interior design by Ashley Haag
Edited by Kristen Green Wiewora
Typography: Adobe Caslon, Bodoni Antiqua, and Brandon Text

Running Press Book Publishers
2300 Chestnut Street
Philadelphia, PA 19103-4371

Visit us on the web!
www.offthemenublog.com

*To Daphne, Garner, and Duncan,
for filling our kitchen with love,
laughter, and joy all year long.
To Roger, Carla, and Will,
for the good food, kitchen memories,
and years of happiness in the garden.*

TABLE OF CONTENTS

Fall 141

Winter 227

INTRODUCTION

Do you dream of being the person who knows exactly what to make for PTA meetings, new moms, or the allergen-free school party? Are you tired of scrambling to find a good recipe every time you are asked to bring food to an event or entertain for the holidays? The secret is to make the same thing every time. All new moms will love you forever if you bring them baked chicken enchiladas or comforting tomato soup. The only birthday cake you'll ever need for your children is a moist vanilla layer cake with milk chocolate frosting. The holiday season is no time to try something new. With a roster of recipes from sparkling spiced shortbread, to the best-ever ham, to giftable homemade baking mixes and preserves, you'll be all set.

The Family Calendar Cookbook is a fresh and necessary look at all the cooking—New Year's Day brunch, birthday parties, homemade teacher gifts, dinners for new parents—required of parents throughout the year.

On-demand cooking requires a lot of recipes from a lot of sources. *The Family Calendar Cookbook* consolidates all of these recipes in one easy to use, practical guide on how to make and present easy, delicious, well-loved food for every occasion. This is the index card box you need if your mother did not pass one on to you. These are the recipes you will make every year.

When my daughter, Daphne, began preschool in 2009 I was introduced to a whole new cooking world. Not only did I cook daily meals for our family, I also cooked for birthday parties, picnics, teachers, and with the children in Daphne's classroom. I hosted large family holidays involving out-of-town guests with children. Every month had special occasions for which I was called upon to produce food above and beyond my everyday fare.

At first I tried to think of new recipes for every occasion. For birthday parties and bake sales I experimented with endless variations of cupcakes to make sure I always brought a new and interesting flavor. While I am an experienced home cook, coming up with all these new recipes was difficult and they didn't always work out perfectly. And every time I went somewhere, people just asked for my double chocolate cupcakes with vanilla bean frosting, beloved by children and adults. Why was I bothering to make up new variations when I already had a hit on my hands? I tossed the experiments and stuck with my tried and true. Now every time I arrive at an event, people are so excited I've brought their favorite. It has become the only cupcake recipe I need.

The best solution to on-demand cooking is a set of go-to recipes for every occasion. Having a repertoire is the easiest way to manage the ongoing cooking needs that send other parents scrambling.

Every spring for the past three years I've made the same scrumptious bacon and green chile quiche for the Teacher Appreciation Luncheon. In November I prepare the same make-ahead holiday gifts of vanilla extract, multigrain pancake mix, and spiced butterscotch sauce. Friends look forward to them so much, one mother told me she plans a few menu items around them for her holiday entertaining. No matter what time of year a new baby arrives, I have a cache of recipes for meals specifically geared toward new parents, such as my perfect braised chicken thighs and nourishing pesto soup. Every year Daphne's class asks me to come in and make mini baked banana bread muffins and decorate graham cracker gingerbread houses. I am the person everyone turns to for a recipe for a quiche that travels well, kid-friendly party food, or the perfect slow-cooker meal to serve a crowd.

In addition to building the ultimate recipe reserve, I've learned how to simply and beautifully present my food and gifts without employing complicated stencils, jigsaws, and glue guns. When I bring spiced chocolate bark to a hostess, I turn to my favorite packaging technique, a simple paper take-out box lined with polka-dot tissue paper and tied with matching ribbon. At the end of summer I always wrap the tops of apricot preserves jars in inexpensive gingham cloth and attach handwritten paper hanging tags so they are gift-ready in the pantry all winter long.

Whether it is entertaining a large crowd at home, carting portable snacks to school, or preparing sweets for a bake sale, there is no need to stress out about what to make.

The Family Calendar Cookbook covers the seasonal cooking needs of a typical household and includes from-scratch recipes for every event. In addition to birthday parties and portable potluck food, I tackle such prickly scenarios as allergy-friendly recipes for a classroom, meals for friends in need, and a summer potluck on the beach. This book will also elaborate on manageable and tasteful ways to present food for occasions without requiring any prior crafting skills or special equipment.

The Family Calendar Cookbook is your go-to source for no-fail, no-stress recipes to serve your family and community.

TIPS FOR NO-STRESS KITCHEN SUCCESS

When it comes to running my home kitchen, I don't subscribe to any hard-and-fast rules. Cooking for others should be a joyful way to show your love, not a rigid, stressful exercise. I believe recipes are meant to be tweaked and favorite dishes should be made time and again. It is fine if something doesn't look picture perfect, so long as it tastes amazing. Over time I've picked up little tricks here and there that have helped me achieve no-stress success and curate the go-to recipe repertoire. Before we get to the recipes, I want to share them with you.

COOKING

STOCK UP Inventory your kitchen regularly. Keep your pantry and refrigerator stocked with the basics, such as flour, spices, dried pasta, eggs, and butter. This way you'll always have on hand the essential base ingredients for many meals.

MAKE AHEAD Get in the practice of making dishes or preparing key components in advance. This will ease the chaos of preparing multiple things at once at mealtime.

USE YOUR FREEZER Most soups, meats, and baked goods can be frozen after they've been cooked. When baking for large parties, freeze your baked goods and defrost them the day of the event. Then all you have to do is frost them and you are out the door. Double recipes for such things as soups and casseroles and freeze half for nights when you are short on time.

PLAN IT OUT Before you entertain, spend some time on your strategy. Write out your menu, cooking times, ingredients, and courses. Plan a specific time for grocery shopping a couple of days before the event. Map out your oven times and temperatures to avoid a backlog of dishes to be cooked. Write down the times you want to serve each dish and lay out your pans in that order on the countertop. A well-thought-out approach will save you a world of trouble later on.

FOLLOW EACH STEP When cooking a recipe for the first time, follow all the instructions exactly. After you've made it once, you can tweak it the next time based on your observations.

MEASURE AHEAD Measure all the ingredients and place them all on the countertop before you start a recipe (you've probably heard the French term for this, *mise en place*). This way you won't forget anything or have to search for ingredients in your cabinet while you cook.

MAKE NOTES Make notes about your favorite dishes and tuck them away for future reference. Each time you make them, it will get a little easier and more fun.

SIMPLIFY Keep place settings, decorations, and beverages simple. People come to see you, not an elaborately decorated table.

THE CHILD FACTOR Do your best to stay in the kitchen while you cook, without multitasking childcare and chores. It is easy to get distracted with children running around. Engage them in an activity or ask someone else to watch them while you work.

TIPS FOR NO-STRESS CRAFTING SUCCESS

The crafts in this book are basic and accessible, which is how I craft at home. Their purpose is to not stress you out with complex techniques and expensive equipment. It is to experience the joy of creating from scratch and the satisfaction of sharing it with another person. Over time I've created a foolproof strategy for crafting success. These guidelines are meant to help you enjoy each craft project as you go. The more you make things, the more enjoyable the process will become.

START WITH THE BASICS Start with something you know you can handle. If you hope a complicated-looking project will magically become easy when you try it, it probably won't.

BE ORGANIZED When starting a new craft, place all the materials you'll need at the head of your craft table. This way you won't run around like crazy looking for something halfway through the project.

EXPECT A MESS Craft outdoors or in an area you don't mind being covered in paint, glue, and crayon. It is easier to craft in a place where you can make a mess without worry.

EXPECT IMPERFECTION Rarely is a craft project executed perfectly the first time around. Plan for error and embrace the lopsided wreath or too-thick paint. It is all about having fun as you go.

THE CHILD FACTOR The unexpected always occurs when crafting with children (think glitter explosions!). Concentrate on projects that are age appropriate for the youngest crafters, to keep them engaged and motivated.

FOOD STORAGE

Proper food storage is key for flavor and freshness. Wrap raw and cooked food tightly in plastic wrap, mark clearly with the contents and date, and store in the refrigerator or freezer. Vegetables should be stored in the vegetable crisper, where it is cold and humid. Store soups, dressings, and sauces in glass jars or containers with secure screw-top lids.

Refrigerated dough should be wrapped tightly in plastic wrap so that no air comes into contact with the dough. Frozen dough should be wrapped in a layer of plastic wrap and then an outer layer of aluminum foil for extra protection. If you are prescooping cookie dough into balls, freeze the balls on a cookie sheet, wrapped in plastic wrap, until they are frozen solid. Transfer the solid balls to plastic freezer bags and squeeze out as much air as possible before freezing.

ABOUT THE RECIPES

These recipes are my foolproof recipes for feeding and entertaining my family, friends, and community, and they can easily become yours, too. As with any home-cooked meal I expect you to tweak flavors over time to suit your tastes.

OVEN & STOVETOP These recipes were tested in home kitchens and every appliance works a little differently. What is medium-high heat on my stove may only require medium heat on yours. Adjust the heat accordingly if your food browns too quickly or doesn't cook fast enough.

MILK All the milk I cook with is whole milk unless noted.

BUTTER All the butter I cook with is unsalted butter unless noted.

EGGS All eggs are large eggs unless noted.

MEASUREMENTS Measure dry ingredients in cups and teaspoons, and measure wet ingredients in glass measuring cups. Butter is measured in ounces and sticks, or tablespoons. A standard-size stick is 4 ounces or 8 tablespoons.

MEASURING FLOUR When you measure flour, spoon the flour into the measuring cup. This will ensure you don't pack too much flour into the measuring cup, ending up with too much flour in your baked good.

COOKING TECHNIQUES

A key component to kitchen success is feeling comfortable with basic techniques. As with any skill, the more you do them, the easier they will become.

SAUTÉ A small amount of fat, such as olive oil or butter, is melted in a pan and the food is quickly moved around until softened or just cooked through. Sautéing is most commonly used for small pieces of meat or fish and chopped vegetables.

SIMMER Just below the boiling point, small bubbles rise to the surface and steam rises thickly from the top of the liquid. Simmering is most frequently used to slowly reduce sauces, thicken soups, and marry flavors.

BOIL When the surface of a liquid has multiple large bubbles popping at the surface and churns vigorously, allowing for rapid evaporation and fast cooking, you've reached the boiling point. Boiling is used for water to cook pasta and in short spurts when cooking soups or sauces to quickly marry flavors.

DEGLAZE An acid, usually a vinegar or wine, is poured into a pan where meat or vegetables have been sautéed. The acid lifts the flavorful browned bits of food off the bottom of the pan into a thin and rich liquid, which is stirred back into the food or used as the base for a flavorful pan sauce.

ROAST This technique uses dry heat to cook meat or vegetables while browning the exterior and cooking the interior. Roasting is most commonly used for large cuts of meat or whole vegetables.

BROIL Intense overhead heat quickly browns or caramelizes food. Broiling is most frequently used here to quickly melt cheeses or brown toppings.

FOLD IN This gentle mixing technique calls for broad scoop-and-lift strokes with a spatula to incorporate an ingredient into a light batter without deflating it. Folding in is most frequently used to keep specific batters for soufflés and delicate cookies light and airy. It is also use when incorporating vegetables and herbs into delicate salads, because it doesn't crush soft or delicate ingredients.

WHISK A wire whisk is used to rapidly beat or stir ingredients together. Whisking is most commonly used with egg dishes and thin sauces. A whisk is also used to aerate dry ingredients when baking.

EMULSIFY To vigorously mix liquids together to form a sauce or dressing. This is most frequently done when making salad dressings and light sauces.

Spring

When spring starts, clear out the remnants of winter from your kitchen, starting with the refrigerator. Empty out your jars of dribs and drabs of last year's preserves and return the washed jars to the basement (discard any used lids and buy new ones). Replace freezer-aisle produce on your grocery list with fresh and select seedlings from the nursery for your vegetable garden. It is time for meals that highlight fresh flavors and reflect the sunny mood.

GIVE YOUR TABLE CHARACTER To give your table a burst of spring, select flowers, produce, and decorative objects in shades of yellows, pinks, and whites. Arrange them in clean white containers and clear glass jars over pastel-hued linens. For Easter, include bowls of decoratively dyed eggs. Candles floating in low, shallow bowls illuminate the table.

Earth Day Gardening with Children

Starting a simple container garden with just two or three plants is an easy way to grow food for your family and introduce children to the concept of where food comes from. Bring your children to the garden center to choose some seedlings, even if it is just one or two, and plant them at home. Over the course of the spring and summer put the children in charge of regular watering and plant care. Teach them that this is how we tend the earth to grow the healthy food that we eat.

Planting a Container Garden

Outdoor container gardens can thrive anywhere there is direct sunlight, after the last frost date. Indoor container gardens can thrive on a sunny windowsill, in a sunroom, or in a room equipped with special growing lights.

Pots
Drainage dishes for the pots
Gardening gloves
Trowel
Hand rake
Watering can

1. Decide what to grow and plan the space: Make a list of the plants you would like to grow and consider whether the sunlight you get is sufficient for those plants. Assess your deck or wherever you plan to set your plants and make sure there is plenty of room for them. Make sure you can easily reach the pots with your hose or carry a large watering can out to them when necessary.

2. Inventory your containers: Herbs generally thrive in smaller containers, whereas vegetables and fruits have extensive root systems and need wider, deeper pots. All of the pots should have small holes in the bottom to allow for proper drainage and aeration. When buying seedlings, ask the grower or nursery manager the best size pot for each herb. Then match up what you are buying with the list of pots you have at home and pick up any extras that you might need. Once you have collected the right pots for each plant, you won't need to do this again the following year. Before you buy the soil, calculate the cubic feet or inches in each pot and have the number on hand. This will ensure that you buy the correct amount of soil to fill each one.

KITCHEN HERBS FOR A CONTAINER GARDEN

Basil	Mint
Chervil	Oregano
Chives	Parsley
Cilantro	Rosemary
Dill	Sage
Lemon thyme	Spearmint
Lemon verbena	Tarragon
Marjoram	Thyme

FRUITS & VEGETABLES FOR A CONTAINER GARDEN

Cherry tomatoes
Eggplant
Jalapeño peppers
Lemons
Limes
Raspberries
Strawberries
Sweet peppers

3. When your list is set, go to the nursery and buy seedlings. Living in the Northeast, I don't have time to grow everything from seed. If I planted basil seeds in April, I wouldn't have enough leaves for pesto until August! Starting with small plants is nice for small children as there is a little bit of instant gratification. Also, seedlings are hardier, so they can handle uncertain spring temperatures and little hands tugging at them. Make sure that you're buying plants that do well in containers. When in doubt, ask the grower to recommend a container-friendly variety.

4. Transplant the seedlings into the pots you have assigned them. And don't toss those plant markers! These little markers contain loads of helpful information concerning the ideal amount of sun, water, and heat for each plant. Continue to water each plant as needed while they grow. Be prepared to shift the pots around your garden space as the days lengthen, to allow them the right amount of shade and sun. (Using an old wheelbarrow or wagon to corral your containers makes moving them a cinch: You can wheel them into morning and afternoon sun as needed.)

5. Cook! Once your container garden is thriving, you can begin enjoying its fruits. Different fruits and vegetables will produce at different times, making for continuous gardening fun. With proper care, they should continue to thrive all season long.

Earth Day Gardening with Children 17

Painted Wooden Kitchen Utensils

Save painting projects for warm weather so you can do them outside. This way, you don't have to worry about tracking paint around the house. I was inspired to paint kitchen utensils after I saw similar ones for sale at a craft show. They make fun gifts for friends and are a great way to spiff up a kitchen when you are in the mood for a new look.

Tray or smooth platter

Parchment paper to spread on the painting space

Wooden utensils (I buy basic wooden spoons at our local kitchen store)

Masking tape

Craft paint

Small bowls or cups for the paint

Small foam brushes

1. Line the tray with parchment paper. Set aside.

2. Wrap a piece of masking tape tightly around the handle of the spoon about 3 inches from the base of the bowl of the spoon. Don't paint any nearer than that because you don't want the painted part to dip into the food you are cooking.

3. Squeeze one color of craft paint into a bowl. Dip the foam brush into the paint and work your way around the handle, painting it as you go. Once the entire handle is painted, place it on the prepared tray. Continue the process for additional spoons and paint colors. Allow the paint to dry for 1 hour. Then repeat the painting process for a second coat.

4. Once the handles are completely dry after the second coat, remove the masking tape and they are ready to be used or gifted. The paint should last a long time as long as the utensils are hand washed.

Idea For a fun gift, paint a cluster of utensils and tie them in a bow like a bouquet.

Paint Color Fun This is a great activity for children. Let them try mixing craft paints to make different colors.

Onion Skin Easter Eggs

I prefer this natural method of dyeing Easter eggs to the kits from the store. It creates a really cool mottled-looking egg. These look terrific gathered in a bowl as a centerpiece and are perfectly safe to eat.

MAKES 1 DOZEN EGGS

Large bunch of onion skins from 2 or 3 red
 onions
Large bowl
Cheesecloth
1 dozen eggs
Large pot
Rubber bands
Colander

1. Place the onion skins in a large bowl of water and let them soak for 10 minutes. Then carefully place the cheesecloth and eggs into the water so they are completely covered. While the onion skins, cheesecloth, and eggs are soaking, bring a large pot of water to a boil.

2. Working carefully, wrap each egg in onion skins until completely covered. Wrap the egg in the wet cheesecloth and secure it with a rubber band.

3. Place the wrapped eggs in the pot of boiling water and boil for about 11 minutes. Remove them from the pot and place them in a colander set over the sink. Run cool water over the eggs for 30 seconds to stop the cooking.

4. Working carefully, remove the cheesecloth and onion skins from each egg. They should be dyed all sorts of unique patterns in shades of red and purple from the onion skins. Allow the eggs to dry and cool. Set out as decoration. Refrigerate if they are not going to be eaten within 3 hours.

Note Freshly dyed and boiled eggs can easily be used for egg salad the next day!

Sleepover Party

Daphne started having sleepover parties the summer before kindergarten and she shows no signs of slowing down. At first I was a little daunted by hosting a group of children overnight, but once we figured out what the children liked, our sleepover parties ran smoothly. When children visit your house for a sleepover, they want to get in their jammies and spend the evening watching movies. Between shows, they want to chow down on homemade pizzas, ginger ale, and cookies. It is as simple as that. A few easygoing recipes to please all types of eaters are all you need to ensure everyone has a fun time and the parents get some sleep.

Your Sleepover Party Strategy

SNACKS Always have such snacks as cheese crackers, granola bars, popcorn, cheese sticks, yogurt sticks (also good when frozen!), chopped-up fruits and vegetables, and juice boxes at the ready for hungry children.

CANDY For movie time, set up a tray of treats. Allow each child to put together their own bowl of treats to keep in his or her lap and eat during the movie, just like at the theater.

GO CAMPING Outdoor sleepovers are always fun. Set up a tent in the backyard and send out the children with provisions. Pack a basket full of resealable plastic bags of their favorite snacks and a few water bottles. Don't forget to leave the porch light on (and the back door unlocked), and give them flashlights, too!

Homemade Ginger Ale

Like most children, Daphne loves soda. Mostly I try to limit sugary drinks to only very special occasions. For sleepovers, let the children indulge, but instead of buying it at the store, make this caffeine-free soda from scratch.

MAKES 2 QUARTS GINGER ALE

3 cups peeled and grated fresh ginger (8 to 10 ounces ginger)

2 cups granulated sugar

2 quarts unflavored sparkling water

1. In a large saucepan over medium-high heat, combine the ginger, sugar, and 4 cups of water, and stir until the sugar dissolves. Allow the mixture to simmer for about 40 minutes, or until it has reduced by two-thirds and gets slightly syrupy.

2. Remove the pan of syrup from the stovetop and allow it to cool to room temperature. Pour the mixture through a fine-mesh sieve to strain out the ginger pulp. (Dry the ginger pulp and use it for baking into scones or muffins.)

3. To make the ginger ale, pour the syrup into a large pitcher, add the sparkling water, and mix well.

4. Alternatively, pour the ginger syrup into standard 12-cube ice cube trays and freeze the cubes completely. It should make about twenty-eight ice cubes. To make an individual ginger ale, dissolve three ginger ice cubes per one cup of sparkling water and serve.

Tip Use a food processor to grate the ginger if you have one available.

Note My friend Char swears the most refreshing summer drink is to drop one ginger ice cube into her cup of iced green tea to make Gingered Green Tea. You can also drop two cubes into a tall glass of unsweetened lemonade to make Ginger Lemonade.

Simple Lemony Guacamole

Daphne prefers this simple guacamole over the kind that is loaded with tomatoes, onions, and jalapeño. Whip up this dip a few minutes before the party starts and the children can eat it with cheese quesadillas or tortillas chips.

MAKES 2 CUPS GUACAMOLE

6 ripe Haas avocados, halved and pitted
Juice of 1 large lemon
1 teaspoon kosher salt
1 tablespoon finely chopped fresh cilantro
    (optional)

1. Scoop the avocados into a large bowl. Immediately sprinkle the lemon juice over them.
2. Use a fork to mash the avocado, adding the salt as you go. Sprinkle the cilantro, if using, over the top of the avocado and fold it into the guacamole a few times. Serve immediately.

Note The cilantro is optional because I know there are many people who do not like it. If you leave it out, the guacamole will still taste great!

Easy Kid Pizzas

Have a whole bunch of dough balls ready with a variety of toppings the children can choose from. Set out everything on a low table and let them go crazy making the pizzas of their dreams! Preheat the oven so it is ready to go once the pizzas are completed; this way, they can be baked and on the table in just a few minutes.

MAKES 4 (10-INCH) PIZZAS

1½ cups warm (not hot) water, divided
2¼ teaspoons (1 packet) active dry yeast

4 tablespoons extra-virgin olive oil, divided
4 cups unbleached all-purpose flour
2 teaspoons kosher salt
Vegetable oil for dough bowl

1. Combine ¼ cup of the water and yeast in a small mixing bowl. Allow it to stand for 5 minutes. It should get a little foamy and start to expand. If you don't see any change after 5 minutes, the yeast might be dead. If so, discard the mixture and start over with fresh yeast. After 5 minutes, lightly stir the yeast and allow it to continue to bloom for 10 more minutes undisturbed. Then pour 1¼ cups of warm water and 2 tablespoons of the olive oil into the yeast mixture and mix well.

2. Place the flour and salt in a large bowl. While running on low speed a mixer fitted with a paddle attachment, slowly pour in the yeast mixture and remaining 2 tablespoons of olive oil. Once they are combined, switch the paddle for a dough hook. Knead the dough on medium speed for about 1 minute, or until a smooth dough ball forms.

3. Turn out the dough onto a floured surface and knead it a few more times. Then place it in a lightly oiled bowl to rise. Cover the bowl with a clean cotton towel and let it rise until it has doubled in size, about 2 hours.

4. When the dough has doubled in size, divide it into four equal pieces. Preheat the oven to 400°F. Place a pizza stone inside to warm, if using. If saving for later, wrap the dough balls individually in plastic and refrigerate. To use immediately, roll each ball of dough out into a 10-inch circle that is ⅛ inch thick. Top the crust with any toppings you would like, place on the heated pizza stone or an ungreased baking sheet, and bake for 15 to 18 minutes, or until the edges are golden brown.

Topping Ideas Pizza sauce, pesto, white cream sauce, shredded mozzarella cheese, goat cheese, ricotta cheese, pepperoni, sliced olives, sautéed spinach, halved cherry tomatoes, seeded and chopped green and red bell peppers, caramelized onions, cooked mushrooms, crumbled cooked sausage.

Broccoli Crunch Salad

I don't really enforce vegetable-eating during sleepovers, but this salad is always a hit. It is a classic from my childhood and it has stood the test of time for a reason. Use it to balance out all the sweet treats they enjoy during movie time.

MAKES 8 SERVINGS

½ cup mayonnaise

¼ cup sour cream

1 tablespoon granulated sugar

3 tablespoons cider vinegar

½ teaspoon kosher salt

⅛ teaspoon freshly cracked black pepper

1 cup dried cranberries

4 strips freshly cooked bacon (from 4 ounces uncooked bacon), crumbled

1 cup slivered almonds, lightly toasted

½ cup diced red onion (about ½ small red onion)

2 pounds broccoli florets, cut into bite-size pieces

1. Make the dressing by whisking together the mayonnaise, sour cream, sugar, cider vinegar, salt, and pepper in a large bowl until smooth.

2. Use a spatula to carefully fold in the cranberries, bacon, almonds, red onion, and broccoli.

Make sure everything is evenly coated with the dressing. Serve immediately. This salad can be made up to 2 hours in advance; store covered in the refrigerator until serving.

Peanut Butter Oatmeal Cookies

Ask anyone who knew me growing up, and they'll attest that peanut butter was my favorite food. I have passed this love on to my children, which is where these cookies come in. They are soft and peanut buttery, filled with tender oats, and are perfect for dunking in tall glasses of milk with friends.

MAKES 3½ DOZEN COOKIES

8 ounces (2 sticks) unsalted butter, at room temperature

1 cup packed light brown sugar

1 cup packed dark brown sugar

1 cup creamy peanut butter (not all-natural)

2 large eggs, at room temperature

2 teaspoons pure vanilla extract

2½ cups unbleached all-purpose flour

2 teaspoons baking powder

¾ teaspoon kosher salt

2 cups old-fashioned rolled oats (not quick-cooking)

1 (10-ounce) bag peanut butter chips

Granulated sugar for rolling

1. Preheat the oven to 350°F. Line two large baking sheets with parchment paper or silicone mats and set aside.

2. With an electric mixer, beat the butter, sugars, and peanut butter together at high speed in a large bowl until light and fluffy, about 3 minutes. Add the eggs and vanilla, beating well after each egg is added.

3. In a separate bowl, whisk together the flour, baking powder, and salt. With the mixer on low speed, slowly beat the flour into the butter mixture just until the flour is no longer visible. Stir in the oatmeal and peanut butter chips with a wooden spoon.

4. Use a 1½-inch cookie scoop to make balls of dough. Roll each ball in granulated sugar and place 2 inches apart on the lined baking sheets. Use your fingers to press down on the dough to flatten out the top slightly. Then make crosshatch marks with the tines of a fork.

5. Bake the cookies for 10 to 12 minutes, or until lightly browned around the edges. Allow them to cool on the baking sheet for 2 minutes; then transfer to a cooling rack to cool completely.

Spring Bake Sale

DARK CHOCOLATE CHUNK BLONDIES   26

—

MOIST VANILLA CUPCAKES
with CHOCOLATE BUTTERCREAM   27

—

DOUBLE CHOCOLATE CUPCAKES
with VANILLA BEAN FROSTING   28

The bake sale is the ubiquitous fund-raising idea that never gets old. The only problem with these events is deciding what to make! I used to try and come up with new recipes for every single bake sale until I realized I was just torturing myself. The best way to approach a bake sale is to have a foolproof cookie recipe and foolproof cupcake recipe you can easily make at a moment's notice. Once I nailed down these two desserts, I was never again tempted to try on the spur of the moment the latest Pinterest dessert circulating the Internet: When it's nine o'clock the night before the bake sale, these are my go-to desserts every single time I bake for any kind of fund-raiser. They are quickly becoming my signature desserts and can be yours, too!

Your Bake Sale Strategy

PORTABILITY Avoid heavy, tall cakes. Make items that can be easily moved from kitchen to vehicle to bake sale table without concern.

PACKAGING Keep it simple by packaging items in clear cello bags (page 262) with a ribbon and hanging tags (page 260).

SINGLE SERVING It is impractical to sell slices of cake or pie. On occasion, a whole pie or cake is for sale, but be sure it is packaged as one whole item and stays that way.

Dark Chocolate Chunk Blondies

These bar cookies are purposely thick and extra moist. I made them that way so they won't crumble when transported and can easily be eaten with one hand. You can make them with regular semisweet chocolate chunks if you want, but I think the dark chocolate makes them extra sophisticated. Make these for bake sales when cookies are requested. At casual bake sales, cut the bars right out of the pan. For bigger sales, stack them in groups of four in small cello bags (page 262).

MAKES 1 (13 X 9-INCH PAN)

- 8 ounces (2 sticks) unsalted butter, at room temperature, plus more for pan
- 2 cups unbleached all-purpose flour, plus more for dusting
- 1¾ cups packed light brown sugar
- ¾ teaspoon baking soda
- 1 teaspoon kosher salt
- 2 large eggs, at room temperature
- 1 tablespoon pure vanilla extract
- 12 ounces high-quality dark chocolate, cut into chunks

1. Preheat the oven to 325°F. Butter and flour the bottom and sides of a 13 x 9 x 2-inch pan and set aside.

2. Place the butter in a large heatproof bowl and melt it in the microwave at 50% power in 20-second intervals to make sure it doesn't explode. Once the butter is melted, whisk in the brown sugar until the mixture is completely smooth. Allow to cool for 5 minutes.

3. While the butter is cooling, whisk together the flour, baking soda, and salt in a small bowl and set aside.

4. Once the butter mixture has cooled, whisk in the eggs and vanilla until the mixture is smooth. Then use a spatula to fold in the dry ingredients until they are completely incorporated and no longer visible. Stir in the chocolate chunks.

5. Pour the batter into the prepared pan and bake for 40 to 42 minutes, or until a cake tester comes out clean. Allow the blondies to cool to room temperature in the pan. Slice and serve.

Moist Vanilla Cupcakes *with* Chocolate Buttercream

It is important to have the perfect chocolate cupcake and perfect vanilla cupcake in your bake sale repertoire. These two cupcake and frosting recipes can be mixed and matched as requested.

MAKES 24 CUPCAKES

FOR THE CUPCAKES

2¾ cups unbleached all-purpose flour

1½ cups granulated sugar

2 teaspoons baking powder

1 teaspoon kosher salt

6 ounces (1½ sticks) unsalted butter, at room temperature

3 large eggs

1 teaspoon pure vanilla extract

1 cup whole milk

FOR THE CHOCOLATE BUTTERCREAM

8 ounces (2 sticks) unsalted butter, at room temperature

4 ounces bittersweet chocolate, melted

1 teaspoon pure vanilla extract

¼ cup whole milk

1 pound confectioners' sugar

1. Preheat the oven to 350°F. Line two regular-size 12-cup muffin tins with paper liners and set aside. Mix the flour, granulated sugar, baking powder, and salt in a large bowl and set aside.

2. With an electric mixer, beat the butter at high speed in a large bowl until light and fluffy, then beat in the eggs one at a time, followed by the vanilla. With the mixer on low speed, alternate adding the flour and milk in three additions, ending with the milk. Scrape down the sides of the bowl as needed to ensure everything is incorporated.

3. Fill each lined muffin cup three-quarters full of the batter and bake for 20 to 22 minutes, or until the tops are lightly browned and spring back when touched. Allow the cupcakes to cool for 10 minutes in the tins, then transfer them to a cooling rack to cool completely.

4. To make the frosting: With an electric mixer, beat the butter at high speed in a large bowl until light and fluffy. Then beat in the melted chocolate, vanilla, and milk until completely incorporated. With a mixer on medium speed, carefully add the confectioners' sugar bit by bit until the frosting is light, fluffy, and spreadable.

5. To frost the cupcakes, you can place the frosting in a resealable plastic bag and snip off the corner to make a pastry bag, then pipe the frosting into the cupcakes. Or use an offset spatula to frost the cupcakes as desired.

Double Chocolate Cupcakes *with* Vanilla Bean Frosting

When Daphne turned three it seemed as if I was baking cupcakes nearly every week. Birthday parties, beach picnics, and school events all required at least a dozen or more! Instead of reinventing the wheel and trying a new flavor every time I worked on perfecting this recipe. These cupcakes have the perfect deep chocolate flavor and a soft, tender crumb, and they quickly became expected, and requested, wherever I went. I don't know who likes them more: the children or the adults!

MAKES 24 CUPCAKES

FOR THE CUPCAKES

2 cups plus 1 tablespoon unbleached all-purpose flour, divided

¾ cup granulated sugar

¾ cup unsweetened cocoa powder

2 teaspoons baking soda

½ teaspoon kosher salt

½ cup freshly brewed coffee

1 cup buttermilk

½ cup vegetable oil

3 large eggs

1 teaspoon pure vanilla extract

1 cup semisweet mini chocolate chips

FOR THE FROSTING

8 ounces (2 sticks) unsalted butter, at room temperature

1 vanilla bean, split and seeds scraped out

1 teaspoon pure vanilla extract

¼ cup whole milk

1 pound confectioners' sugar

1. To make the cupcakes: Preheat the oven to 350°F. Line two regular-size 12-cup muffin tins with paper liners and set aside.

2. In a small bowl, whisk together 2 cups of the flour and the granulated sugar, cocoa, baking soda, and salt and set aside. In a larger separate bowl, whisk together the coffee, buttermilk, oil, eggs, and vanilla until smooth. Slowly pour the dry ingredients into the wet ingredients, stirring as you go, until the flour is no longer visible.

3. Toss the chocolate chips with the remaining 1 tablespoon of flour and gently stir them into the batter.

4. Divide the batter evenly among the lined 24 muffin cups, filling each one about three-quarters full. Bake the cupcakes for 22 to 25 minutes, or until the tops spring back when lightly touched and a cake tester comes out clean.

Allow the cupcakes to cool in the tins for about 5 minutes, then transfer them to a cooling rack to cool completely before icing.

5. To make the frosting: With an electric mixer, beat the butter at high speed in a large bowl until light and fluffy. Then beat in the vanilla seeds, vanilla, and milk until completely incorporated. With a mixer on medium speed, carefully add the confectioners' sugar bit by bit until the frosting is light, fluffy, and spreadable.

6. To frost the cupcakes, you can place the frosting in a resealable plastic bag and snip off the corner to make a pastry bag, then pipe the frosting into the cupcakes. Or use an offset spatula to frost the cupcakes as desired.

Note This recipe makes a large batch and can be halved if you want fewer cupcakes. For bake sales, it works well to sell the cupcakes individually or in groups of four, six, or eight. I've found disposable cupcake boxes at baking supply stores, which have little compartments for each cupcake and plenty of overhead space for icing. It keeps the cupcakes looking nice on the bake sale tables.

Road Trip Snacks

HANDHELD ROAD TRIP SNACK FOOD IDEAS   31

Whether we are driving to Cooperstown to visit my parents or going on our annual family trip to Charleston, South Carolina, I am a big fan of piling the family in the car and hitting the highway. To prepare for our trips, my jobs include packing clothes, roads games, and snacks. Although it can be fun to stop at roadside joints, we generally try to avoid fast food and stick with homemade goodies instead.

Your Road Trip Snack Strategy

PLAN AHEAD Skip the guessing game of planning stops for snacks along the way. Pick two or three family favorites and pack them in one cooler. This way, everyone knows what is available and you don't have to worry about buying overpriced junk you'd rather your children didn't eat.

MELT-PROOF Pack a flexible insulated bag with a few cold packs for snacks that need to stay cool. Don't pack frozen foods, such as Popsicles, Italian ices, or ice cream. No cooler I've ever met will keep them cold enough to survive a road trip without turning into a melted sticky mess.

EASY HANDLING Skip foods that need straws, spoons, or forks, so you don't have to pack utensils.

EASY CLEANUP Bring one or two plastic bags to use as garbage bags. Collect any leftover juice boxes or food scraps and dispose of them at your next stop.

CLEAN HANDS Pack hand wipes. Lots of them.

HANDHELD ROAD TRIP SNACK FOOD IDEAS

WRAPS Make a large wrap and cut it into 1-inch rolls for easy eating. Here are some ideas for fillings:

Turkey & Swiss with Hummus on Whole Wheat Swipe a whole wheat wrap with 1 tablespoon of hummus. Layer with two slices of turkey and two slices of Swiss cheese. Roll and cut.

Garden Vegetable Pesto Swipe a whole wheat wrap with 2 teaspoons of pesto and layer on leaves of baby romaine, three thin slices of tomato, six slices of cucumber, two slices of provolone cheese, and one half of a sliced avocado. Roll and cut.

Chicken Caesar Spread 2 teaspoons of Caesar dressing on a whole wheat wrap, layer on two thick leaves of iceberg lettuce, one thinly sliced cooked or grilled chicken breast, and a pinch of shredded Parmesan. Roll and cut.

VEGETABLES & DIP Pack a small plastic container or jam jar of dip and chopped vegetables in a resealable plastic bag on the side. Here are some dip ideas:

Hummus (page 202), Buttermilk Ranch Dressing (page 163), Peach Tomato Salsa (page 41), Simple Lemony Guacamole (page 22).

Vegetables: Carrots, Cucumbers, Peppers, Broccoli, Cherry Tomatoes, Celery

DRY PORTABLE FOODS Peeled hard-cooked eggs (keep cool), bagels with cream cheese (ditto), Dried Cherry & Ginger Granola (page 52), popcorn, Fruity Oat Bars (page 210), Mini Banana Bread Muffins (page 215), Zucchini Applesauce Bread (page 88), Apricot Almond Shortbread Squares (page 122), Chocolate Chunk Pretzel Cookies (page 319), mixed bag of sliced fruits and berries, Roasted Chickpea Crunchies (page 208)

INSTANT SWEET & SALTY TRAIL MIX Combine 1 cup of roasted salted cashews, 1 cup of dried cranberries, ½ cup of dark chocolate chips, and 1 cup of roasted salted sunflower seeds.

YOUR FAVORITE ROAD TRIP CANDIES!

Last year, I took a fun poll on Facebook and my blog, asking you to share your favorite road trip candies. These are the sweets you love to stock up on before you travel. In many cases, these treats are things you only buy when you travel and, therefore, really look forward to! I love all of these ideas and can totally see myself stocking up some of these the next time my family takes off on an adventure!

Clark Bars
Frozen peppermint patties
Frozen Snickers bars
Gummy bears
Jelly beans
M&M's

Mike & Ikes
Mini peanut butter cups
Shoestring licorice
Swedish Fish
Tootsie Rolls
Yogurt-covered pretzels

Egg Hunt Brunch

LEMON-SCENTED SOUR CREAM WAFFLES   34

—

EASY PAIN AU CHOCOLATE   35

—

ASPARAGUS SCRAMBLED EGGS   35

—

CHOW MEIN EGG "NESTS"   36

Easter often coincides with the start of spring, so plan an easy brunch to match the mood. Set out a buffet of fresh asparagus with eggs, lemon waffles, and light pastries with a pitcher of freshly squeezed blood orange juice. Let the kids nibble and hunt down all the eggs from the Easter bunny, while the adults enjoy their second cup of coffee. It is all about lightness, fun, and the good weather to come.

Lemon-Scented Sour Cream Waffles

The bright citrus scents of these waffles evoke the freshness of spring. For an Easter egg hunt brunch, make large batches and pile them on plates for everyone to enjoy. Set a pitcher of warm maple syrup and fresh berries alongside so people can top the waffles however they choose.

MAKES 8 LARGE WAFFLES

Vegetable oil for waffle iron, if necessary

5 large eggs

⅔ cup granulated sugar

1 tablespoon freshly grated lemon zest (from 1 medium-size lemon)

1 cup sour cream

1 cup unbleached all-purpose flour

1 teaspoon kosher salt

4 tablespoons (½ stick) unsalted butter, melted and cooled

1. Preheat the oven to 200°F. Preheat and grease the waffle iron according to the manufacturer's directions.

2. In a large bowl, whisk together the eggs, sugar, lemon zest, and sour cream until the mixture is slightly frothy. Fold in the flour and salt until just combined, then lightly stir in the melted butter so the batter is evenly moistened.

3. Cook the waffles in batches until golden brown. To keep the waffles warm, place them on a large baking sheet and place them in the preheated oven as they come off the waffle iron.

4. When all the waffles are ready, pile them on a plate and top as desired with warm maple syrup and fresh berries.

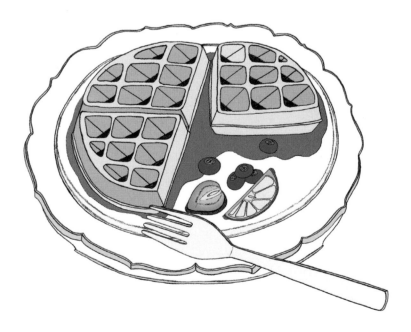

Easy Pain au Chocolate

There are many days when I think I could live on pastries alone. A bag of croissants is the first thing my husband brought me in the hospital after Garner was born! The only catch is that preparing puff pastry from scratch is a pain in the neck. Make it easy on yourself and buy the puff pastry already made. The pastries can be frozen once they are cut and the chocolate folded in. Bring back to room temperature, brush with egg wash, and bake right before guests arrive.

MAKES 8 PASTRIES

1 large sheet frozen all-butter puff pastry, thawed and rolled out to make a 10-inch square

8 ounces semisweet chocolate squares (I use Ghirardelli chocolate bars and break them into the stamped 1-ounce squares)

1 large egg, beaten

1. Preheat the oven to 350°F and line a baking sheet with parchment paper.

2. Use a sharp knife or pizza cutter to cut the pastry into eight 5-inch squares.

3. Place a 1-ounce chocolate square in the center of a pastry square and pull two diagonally opposite corners over the chocolate, layering the flaps as if you are covering the chocolate with a blanket. Brush a little bit of the beaten egg onto the bottom flap of the pastry so that the top flap sticks to it. Then lightly brush the remaining egg all over the top of the pastry. Repeat with the remaining squares.

4. Line up the pastries 3 inches apart on the prepared baking sheet and bake for 15 to 18 minutes, or until the tops turn golden brown. Allow them to cool on the baking sheet for 5 minutes, then transfer to a cooling rack until they are cool enough to eat.

Asparagus Scrambled Eggs

This egg dish is perfect for serving on a platter to family and friends. It is the best way to take advantage for the first asparagus of the season and it will always get rave reviews.

MAKES 4 SERVINGS

1 pound asparagus, trimmed

1 tablespoon olive oil

1½ teaspoons kosher salt, divided

1 teaspoon freshly cracked black pepper, divided

8 large eggs

¼ cup whole milk

1 tablespoon unsalted butter

1. Preheat the oven to 400°F. Line a large, rimmed baking sheet with parchment paper.

2. Arrange the asparagus in one even layer on the baking sheet, drizzle the olive oil over it, and sprinkle with 1 teaspoon of the salt and ½ teaspoon of the pepper. Roll the asparagus with your fingertips so it is evenly coated. Roast the asparagus for 18 to 20 minutes, or until browned and softened. Remove from the oven and transfer the warm asparagus to a large platter.

3. While the asparagus is cooling, whisk together the eggs, milk, and remaining ½ teaspoon of salt and ½ teaspoon of pepper in a large bowl. Melt the butter over medium heat in a large skillet and add the eggs. Stir them gently with a wooden spoon until just cooked, about 2 minutes. Spoon the eggs on top of the cooked asparagus and serve.

Chow Mein Egg "Nests"

Children dive for these Easter treats the moment they see them. Make them the day before brunch and fill them with candy eggs right before everyone arrives. They are primarily for the children, but it is not unusual to see adults eating them, too!

MAKES 30 NESTS

2 cups semisweet chocolate chips

¼ cup creamy peanut butter

1 teaspoon kosher salt

10 ounces chow mein noodles

60 chocolate eggs or jelly bean eggs

1. Line a large, rimmed baking sheet with waxed paper and set aside.

2. In a large, microwave-safe bowl, heat the chocolate chips on high at 30-second intervals for 1 to 2 minutes, stirring well after each interval. Once the chips are melted, stir in the peanut butter until the mixture is completely smooth. Then stir in the kosher salt.

3. Carefully fold in the noodles, being carefully not to break them. Turn the mixture with a spatula until the noodles are completely coated. Use clean hands to pinch off pieces of the mixture and form them into 2-inch rounded mounds. Place the mounds on the prepared baking sheet and use two fingers to press a nestlike indentation into the center of each mount. Place the sheet of nests in the freezer until they have hardened completely, at least 12 hours.

4. To serve, remove the nests from the freezer and fill them with the candy eggs.

Passover

FIVE-SPICE BRISKET   38

—

ARUGULA & FENNEL SALAD   39

—

MATZO CRUNCH   39

Use this modern Passover menu to entertain with ease. It is full of flavor and you'll be able to pull off your seder without a hitch.

Five-Spice Brisket

Brisket is a classic seder dish. My friend Phoebe had the best idea for giving it a twist: add sweet and hot spices. The simple change instantly freshens up the dish and makes it new again.

MAKES 6 TO 8 SERVINGS

3 pounds beef brisket, fat cap trimmed

6 garlic cloves, crushed

2 cups beef stock

2 tablespoons extra-virgin olive oil

2 sweet onions, sliced

½ cup ketchup

½ cup dark brown sugar

1 tablespoon kosher salt

2 teaspoons Chinese 5-spice powder

¼ teaspoon cayenne pepper

1 stick cinnamon

1. Preheat the oven to 500°F. Place the brisket in a 13 x 9-inch baking dish (preferably metal). Brown the meat in the oven, 10 minutes per side.

2. Remove the pan from the oven, add the garlic, and carefully pour in the beef stock. Lower the heat to 350°F, cover the dish with foil, and braise the brisket in the oven for 1 hour.

3. In the meantime, heat the olive oil in a large skillet. Sauté the onions over medium-high heat until soft and beginning to brown, 8 minutes. Lower the heat to medium-low and slowly cook the onions until caramelized, about 12 minutes more, stirring occasionally.

4. Whisk together the ketchup, sugar, salt, 5-spice powder, and cayenne and add to the brisket pan along with the cinnamon stick. Whisk until the new flavorings are dissolved in the broth. Arrange the caramelized onions on top of the meat. Cover the pan again with foil, and return to the oven for 2 hours, until the meat is fork-tender but not falling apart.

5. Transfer the brisket to a cutting board and allow to rest until cool enough to touch. Thinly slice the meat against the grain. Arrange the sliced brisket on a serving platter and ladle the sauce over the top.

Arugula & Fennel Salad

This bitter green salad is a welcome burst of brightness on your table. You don't have to plan ahead to make it: Just toss the ingredients together quickly before guests arrive.

MAKES 4 SERVINGS

8 ounces baby arugula, rinsed and dried

½ fennel bulb, cored and thinly sliced

1 tablespoon finely chopped shallot

1 tablespoon freshly squeezed lemon juice

1 teaspoon Dijon mustard

3 tablespoons extra-virgin olive oil

½ teaspoon kosher salt

¼ teaspoon freshly cracked black pepper

1. In a large bowl, toss the arugula and fennel together. Set aside.

2. In a small bowl, whisk together the shallot, lemon juice, and mustard. Pour the olive oil into it in a steady stream, whisking constantly until emulsified. Add the salt and pepper and mix well.

3. Drizzle the dressing over the salad and toss well until evenly coated. Serve immediately.

Matzo Crunch

This recipe was adapted from the original cracker bark that has been passed around since what seems like the beginning of time. It is fun to make with kids and is completely addictive to eat. Serve in shards on a big platter so everyone can help themselves.

MAKES 30 PIECES

5 sheets matzos

8 ounces (2 sticks) unsalted butter

1 cup dark brown sugar

12 ounces semisweet chocolate chips

1. Preheat the oven to 350°F. Line a large, rimmed baking sheet with parchment paper or a silicone mat. Line up the matzos so they are just touching on the baking sheet, breaking the pieces as necessary so they fit.

2. In a large saucepan, heat the butter and sugar over medium heat until melted. Stir it together until smooth, then pour it over the matzo. The crackers will float a little bit, which is fine.

3. Bake for 8 to 10 minutes, or until the mixture bubbles. Drop the chocolate chips on top and carefully smooth them with a spatula as they begin to melt. Spread the chocolate over the entire pan.

4. Allow the pan to cool to room temperature, then move it to a refrigerator to chill for at least 4 hours. Once it is cold, break the bark into pieces and serve.

Cinco de Mayo

When I was young, my aunt and her family lived in Mexico City. Every other year we would travel from Cooperstown to Mexico to visit my cousins and enjoy a generous dose of Mexican culture. Although I was a little too young to truly understand the amazing cuisine, I loved immersing myself in the landscape and history. Every trip we would explore a different part of the country, climbing temples, swimming in the Pacific, and walking the cobblestone streets of San Miguel. The colors were shockingly vivid and the people so warm and loving. Although I haven't traveled to Mexico in years, there is still a special place for it in my heart.

Whipping up a Mexican feast to celebrate Cinco de Mayo is simple. A few popular Mexican-style dishes, a giant picture of sangria (a traditionally Spanish beverage that is beloved in Mexico, too), and condiments set out in tortilla bowls are all you need to throw your own fiesta.

Peach Tomato Salsa

This simple salsa is your new all-purpose summer condiment. It tastes best with peaches, but it also works well with many sweet fruits, such as nectarines and apples.

MAKES 2 CUPS SALSA

1 small red onion, peeled and finely chopped

2 large tomatoes (heirloom or Roma work well), cored, seeded, and finely chopped (1½ to 2 cups)

1 jalapeño pepper, seeded and finely chopped

3 tablespoons finely chopped fresh cilantro

2 large peaches, pitted and chopped into ¼-inch dice (about 1 cup)

Juice from 2 medium-size limes

Pinch of kosher salt

1. In a large bowl, combine the onion, tomatoes, jalapeño, cilantro, and peaches. Stir them well, then stir in the lime juice and salt. Allow the mixture to sit for a few minutes so the flavors can combine. Serve with chips!

Tip Swap out this homemade peach salsa for regular salsa in your favorite seven-layer dip recipe.

Tortilla Chip Chilaquiles Mash

This nontraditional take on the classic tortilla-based egg dish first came about on a lazy Sunday morning when I was craving chilaquiles but only had a bag of tortilla chips on hand. I fudged the classic recipe a bit and came up with this: a cheesy, salty, egg mash that it is supersatisfying even when it isn't Cinco de Mayo. Serve it with fresh salsa, slices of avocado, and a spicy Bloody Mary on the side.

MAKES 4 SERVINGS

1 tablespoon unsalted butter

6 large eggs, lightly beaten

3 cups tortilla chips (it is okay to measure them in handfuls; use 3 big handfuls)

1½ cups shredded Mexican cheese blend

½ cup salsa

2 teaspoons hot pepper sauce, or more if desired

1. In a large, nonstick skillet, melt the butter over medium heat and swirl the pan so it coats the entire bottom. Then add the eggs and stir them lightly with a wooden spoon so they begin to scramble.

2. After 30 seconds, add the chips, cheese, salsa, and hot sauce and cook until the eggs are just set, 30 seconds to 1 minute. Carefully fold the eggs once or twice with a spatula. Divide among four plates and serve.

Add-in Ideas If you want to add meat to this dish, crumble in some freshly cooked bacon. Additional garnishes for serving are dollops of guacamole and sour cream or fresh sliced avocado.

Baked Vegetable Stacked Enchiladas

One of my favorite parts about Mexican cuisine is the liberal use of vegetables. This easy main course is a hearty and satisfying Tex-Mex dish, perfect for feeding a crew. It also translates well to an easy weeknight meal. When serving this, have bowls of sour cream, guacamole, sliced scallions, and salsa nearby so people can garnish their enchiladas as desired.

MAKES 4 TO 6 SERVINGS

1 large zucchini, chopped into 1½-inch pieces

1 large yellow summer squash, chopped into 1½-inch pieces

1 medium eggplant, chopped into 1-inch pieces

1 medium-size yellow onion, chopped into 1½-inch pieces

1 large jalapeño pepper, seeded and coarsely chopped

2 to 3 tablespoons olive oil

1 teaspoon kosher salt

1 (14-ounce) can black beans, drained and rinsed

½ teaspoon chili powder

Vegetable oil

2 (10-ounce) cans red enchilada sauce

9 (6-inch) corn tortillas

1½ cups shredded Mexican cheese blend, divided

1 cup sour cream, for serving

1 cup guacamole, for serving

¼ cup thinly sliced scallions (white and light green parts), for serving

1 cup salsa, for serving

1. Preheat the oven to 425°F.

2. Line a baking sheet with parchment paper and spread out the chopped vegetables in one even layer. Use a second sheet, if needed, to avoid crowding and steaming the vegetables; they'll brown more easily if they have plenty of breathing room. Drizzle with the olive oil and toss so they all have a light coating of oil. Sprinkle the salt on top.

3. Roast the vegetables for 35 to 40 minutes, or until they are softened and lightly browned, turning them once or twice with a wooden spoon while they cook to ensure even browning. When they are finished, remove them from the oven and lower the heat to 350°F.

4. In a large bowl, toss the vegetables with the beans and chili powder. Set aside.

5. Grease the inside of a 13 x 9 x 2-inch pan with vegetable oil, then pour a small amount of enchilada sauce on the bottom so it just coats the bottom of the dish. Place three corn tortillas, overlapping, on the bottom of the dish. Pour another thin layer of enchilada sauce over the tortillas. Layer with ½ cup of the shredded cheese and half of the roasted vegetables. Top the vegetables with another layer of tortillas and pour half of the remaining enchilada sauce over the tortillas. Layer again in this order: another ½ cup of cheese, all the remaining vegetables, and all the remaining tortillas. Pour the remaining enchilada sauce over the tortillas and sprinkle the top with the remaining ⅓ cup of cheese.

6. Bake the casserole for about 30 minutes, or until the sauce is hot and bubbling. Serve warm!

Note If you prefer more protein, add 2 cups of cooked shredded chicken to the bowl with the vegetables in step 4.

Grilled Shrimp Tacos

No fiesta is complete without tacos. Please your guests by wrapping grilled shrimp in a tortilla and topping it with all kinds of fresh ingredients.

MAKES 4 TO 6 SERVINGS

20 large shrimp, shelled and deveined

¾ cup olive oil

¼ cup freshly squeezed lemon juice

6 garlic cloves, minced

½ teaspoon cayenne pepper

½ teaspoon kosher salt

Vegetable oil

1 large ear corn

12 flour tortillas

1 cup tomato salsa or fresh Peach Tomato Salsa
(page 41)

1 avocado, peeled, pitted, and diced

¼ cup cotija cheese or crumbled goat cheese

1 tablespoon coarsely chopped fresh cilantro
(optional)

1. Place the shrimp in a large resealable plastic bag. In a small bowl, whisk together the olive oil, lemon juice, garlic, cayenne, and salt. Pour the mixture into the bag with the shrimp and shake gently so the shrimp are evenly coated. Place the bag on a flat plate or in a pan and refrigerate for at least 4 hours or up to overnight.

2. Light the grill and bring it to medium heat. Once it is hot, brush a small amount of vegetable oil on the corn and grill it over medium heat until the kernels char, but don't burn to a crisp. Rotate the ear as necessary to it cooks evenly, 6 to 8 minutes. Allow the ear to cool slightly; then cut off the kernels into a bowl.

3. Place the shrimp in a grill basket and cook them for 2 to 3 minutes per side, or until they are bright pink. Then remove the basket from the grill and allow them to cool slightly.

4. While they are cooling, quickly grill the tortillas on each side, about 30 seconds per side. Place them on a platter for taco assembly.

5. To assemble your tacos, place two or three shrimp on a tortilla and top it with some charred corn, a dollop of salsa, a few cubes of avocado, a pinch of cheese, and a pinch of cilantro, dividing all the garnishes evenly among the tacos and serving on a large platter. Or you can plate the shrimp, tortillas, and garnishes separately and allow everyone to assemble their tacos as desired.

Slow-Cooker Chipotle Tortilla Soup

My friend, Ellise Pierce, wrote the coolest cookbook about her native Texan cuisine, titled Cowgirl Chef. *Her recipe for authentic tortilla soup is one of my favorites. The only problem is that it took too long for me to make from start to finish with two kids underfoot. I adjusted the recipe so I could make it in my slow cooker and now it is a cinch to pull together.*

MAKES 8 SERVINGS

8 garlic cloves, unpeeled

1 medium-size yellow onion, peeled and cut into 8 wedges

1 teaspoon olive oil

6 (6-inch) corn tortillas

1 (28-ounce) can whole tomatoes with juices

2 chipotle peppers in adobo sauce

4 cups low-sodium chicken stock

1 teaspoon kosher salt

½ teaspoon freshly cracked black pepper

1 ripe avocado, cut into cubes, for garnish

2 cups shredded Mexican cheese blend, for garnish

2 cups tortilla chips, for garnish

1. Turn the broiler to the high setting and adjust two oven racks to 6 to 12 inches underneath the broiler. Line a baking sheet with parchment paper. Toss the garlic and onion with the olive oil and spread them evenly on the pan. Broil them until the onion begins to char around the edges, 10 to 15 minutes.

2. Meanwhile, place the tortillas on a baking sheet and place on the oven rack beneath the onion and garlic pan. Broil the tortillas for 10 to 15 minutes, turning halfway through, or until they crisp up and turn golden brown. Remove them from the oven and allow them to cool slightly.

3. Allow the garlic cloves and onion wedges to cool, then squeeze the garlic out of its skins and into the slow cooker. Add the onion, tomatoes, chipotle peppers, chicken stock, salt, and pepper. Break the tortillas into small pieces and stir them into the soup.

4. Cook the soup on low for 5 to 6 hours. Then place an immersion blender in the soup and purée it until it has a semichunky consistency. If you don't have an immersion blender, place the mixture in batches in a regular blender and process, being careful of the hot steam. Scoop into serving bowls and garnish with chunks of fresh avocado, a sprinkle of cheese, and fresh tortilla chips.

Note For spicier soup, add one or two additional chipotle peppers!

Fruity White Sangria

This fresh and fruity sangria is a nice change from heavier red wine sangria. Pile in the citrus to give each sip a bright zing. Any other chopped fresh fruit you want to add would taste great, too.

MAKES 6 TO 8 SERVINGS

½ cup apricot brandy

¼ cup granulated sugar

2 (750 ml) bottles dry white wine

1 small Granny Smith apple (or other tart apple), peeled, cored, and thinly sliced

1 medium-size lemon, chilled, thinly sliced

1 medium-size lime, chilled, thinly sliced

1. In a small saucepan over medium-low heat, combine the apricot brandy and sugar. Bring the mixture to a low simmer, gently swirl the pan, and continue to simmer until it the sugar is completely dissolved. Remove the mixture from the heat and allow it to cool.

2. Meanwhile, pour the white wine into a large pitcher, add the sweetened brandy, and stir well. Place the pitcher in the refrigerator to cool for at least 4 hours, or until chilled. Stir the fruit slices into the pitcher and serve in tall glasses.

Mexican Chocolate Cake

This recipe is inspired by a cake recipe in Park Avenue Potluck, *the first cookbook I ever worked on. It is spiced with cinnamon and covered with a rich boiled chocolate frosting. It is the best way to cap off a Mexican fiesta. Serve it with vanilla ice cream or lemon gelato.*

MAKES 8 TO 10 SERVINGS

FOR THE CAKE

6 ounces (1½ sticks) unsalted butter, plus more for pan

2 cups unbleached all-purpose flour, plus more for dusting pan

1¾ cups granulated sugar

1 teaspoon baking soda

½ cup Dutch-processed cocoa powder

½ cup buttermilk

2 large eggs

1 teaspoon ground cinnamon

1 teaspoon pure vanilla extract

FOR THE FROSTING

6 tablespoons unsalted butter, plus more for pan

2 tablespoons plus 2 teaspoons Dutch-processed cocoa powder

½ cup buttermilk

2 cups confectioners' sugar

½ teaspoon ground cinnamon

⅛ teaspoon kosher salt

1. Preheat the oven to 375°F. Butter and flour a 13 x 9 x 2-inch baking dish and set aside.

2. To make the cake: In a large bowl, whisk together the flour, granulated sugar, and baking soda and set aside.

3. In a medium saucepan, combine ½ cup of the cocoa powder, 6 ounces (1½ sticks) of the butter, and 1 cup of water, and bring to a simmer over medium-low heat just until the butter has melted. Whisk to blend, remove from the heat, and allow to cool slightly.

4. In a separate bowl, whisk together the buttermilk, eggs, cinnamon, and vanilla and set aside.

5. Fold the cooled butter mixture into the flour until evenly combined, then whisk in the egg mixture until a smooth batter forms.

6. Pour the batter into the prepared pan and bake for 25 to 30 minutes, or until the top springs back when touched and a cake tester inserted into the center comes out clean. Remove the pan from the oven and allow to cool for 10 minutes.

7. To make the frosting: Combine the butter, cocoa powder, buttermilk, confectioners' sugar, cinnamon, and salt in a saucepan. Bring it to a simmer over medium heat just until the butter melts, and whisk until smooth. Let the frosting cool at room temperature for 10 minutes. Pour it over the warm cake and use a spatula to spread over the whole cake until the thick frosting is smooth. Allow the cake to continue to cool for 15 minutes. Serve warm or at room temperature.

Teacher Appreciation Luncheon

BACON & CHILE QUICHE   49

—

HOT CHICKEN SALAD   50

—

SNAP PEAS *with* GOAT CHEESE & MINT   51

—

DRIED CHERRY & GINGER GRANOLA   52

—

MINT BROWNIE TART   53

When Daphne started preschool, she immediately became attached to her wonderful teachers. To demonstrate my gratitude for their guidance, I started cooking for the luncheon held for them during Teacher Appreciation Week each spring. Making a meal hardly seemed like enough, given all they did for her, but they were grateful for the sentiment.

Bacon & Chile Quiche

Cooking for the teachers means transporting fresh food from my kitchen to the school. This is one of the main reasons I always make quiche. It tastes great and can easily be taken from one place to the next without concern! This is adapted from an old Bon Appétit *recipe and I make it every single year. I've even handed out the recipe to the teachers on several occasions.*

MAKES 1 (9-INCH) PIE

FOR THE CRUST

4 ounces (1 stick) cold unsalted butter, cut into small pieces

1½ cups unbleached all-purpose flour, plus more for rolling

Pinch of kosher salt

¼ cup ice water

FOR THE FILLING

8 strips bacon, cooked and roughly chopped

1 (4-ounce) can diced green chiles

4 scallions, coarsely chopped (white and green parts)

1½ cups shredded sharp Cheddar cheese

½ cup shredded Monterey Jack cheese

1¼ cups whole milk

4 large eggs

½ teaspoon kosher salt

½ teaspoon freshly cracked black pepper

1 teaspoon chopped chives

1. To make the crust: Combine the butter, flour, salt, and ice water in the bowl of a food processor and give it a few quick pulses until a crumbly dough forms. Scoop out the mixture and place it on a lightly floured surface. Gather the dough in your hands and knead it a few times to form it into a tight ball. Flour a rolling pin and roll it into a circle 12 inches in diameter.

2. Press the dough into a 9-inch pie plate and use kitchen scissors to trim any excess off the sides. Use your fingers or fork tines to make a decorative pattern or crimp around the edge. Prick the crust all over with the fork tines. Cover the dish with plastic wrap and chill it for 1 hour in the refrigerator.

3. Preheat the oven to 375°F. Line the bottom and side of the chilled crust with parchment paper and fill it with pie weights or dried beans, then bake it for 15 minutes, or until lightly golden.

4. Once the crust has baked, remove the weights. Increase the oven temperature to 400°F.

5. To make the filling: Sprinkle the bacon, peppers, and scallions over the bottom of the warm crust. Combine the cheeses and sprinkle them evenly over the top of the bacon mixture.

6. In a large bowl, beat together the milk, eggs, salt, and pepper until fully combined. Pour the egg mixture over the cheeses. Sprinkle the chopped chives on top.

7. Bake the quiche for 42 to 45 minutes, or until the top is set and a knife inserted into the center comes out clean. Remove the quiche from the oven and allow it to cool slightly. Cut into wedges and serve warm.

Note To transport this quiche to school, allow it to cool completely after baking. Then cover it with plastic wrap and then a layer of aluminum foil. Refrigerate it if you are not going to serve it right away. To reheat: Heat the oven to 350°F. Remove the plastic wrap and recover the quiche with the aluminum foil. Place the quiche in the oven and allow it to warm for 5 to 10 minutes, or until heated through.

Hot Chicken Salad

This hot chicken salad is a delicious hefty meal that was a hit with the teachers. It is warm and creamy so it is perfect for serving in a cool spring day. To complete the presentation, serve a big basket of soft rolls on the side.

MAKES 8 TO 10 SERVINGS

1 tablespoon unsalted butter, melted, plus more for pan

3 cups cooked chicken, shredded

2 celery stalks, finely chopped

½ cup slivered almonds

1 small yellow onion, finely chopped

1 teaspoon kosher salt

½ teaspoon freshly cracked black pepper

1 cup mayonnaise

¼ cup sour cream

1½ cups sharp Cheddar cheese, coarsely grated

¾ cup panko breadcrumbs

1. Preheat the oven to 350°F. Butter the bottom and sides of a 9-inch square baking dish and set aside.

2. In a large bowl, mix together the chicken, celery, almonds, onion, salt, and pepper. In a separate bowl, fold together the mayonnaise, sour cream, and Cheddar cheese. Then stir the mayonnaise mixture into the chicken until combined. Spread the mixture in the prepared baking dish.

3. In a small bowl, mix together the melted butter and panko until the breadcrumbs are evenly coated, then spread the breadcrumbs over the chicken mixture. Bake the casserole for 20 minutes, or until bubbly along the edges. Remove from the oven and allow to cool for about 15 minutes before serving.

Snap Peas *with* Goat Cheese & Mint

Fresh spring snap peas are perfect for the spring luncheon. I love how the tangy cheese and fresh mint taste so fresh. The bright green color is a cheerful addition to the table.

MAKES 6 TO 8 SERVINGS

1 tablespoon olive oil

16 ounces sugar snap peas, rinsed and trimmed

2 tablespoons coarsely chopped fresh mint

⅛ teaspoon freshly cracked black pepper

¼ teaspoon fine sea salt

⅓ cup crumbled goat cheese

1. Heat the olive oil over medium-high heat in a large skillet. Add the peas and sauté until they are just tender enough that a fork is just able to pass through them, 3 to 4 minutes.

2. Stir the mint, pepper, and salt into the peas and transfer them to a serving platter or shallow bowl. Top with the crumbled goat cheese and serve.

Dried Cherry & Ginger Granola

A jar of fresh granola is an all-purpose homemade gift for the teachers. Package the jar in a small wooden box or basket with a tin of tea and honey to make a special breakfast bin.

MAKES 6 CUPS GRANOLA

⅓ cup plus 1 teaspoon vegetable oil, divided

3 cups old-fashioned rolled oats

1 cup coarsely chopped pecans

1 teaspoon fine sea salt

1 teaspoon ground cinnamon

¼ teaspoon ground ginger

1 teaspoon pure vanilla extract

½ cup pure Grade A maple syrup

¼ cup apple cider

1 cup dried cherries

½ cup finely chopped crystallized ginger

1. Preheat the oven to 350°F. Rub the bottom and sides of an 18 x 13-inch rimmed baking sheet with 1 teaspoon of the vegetable oil and set aside.

2. In a large mixing bowl, combine the oats, pecans, salt, cinnamon, and ground ginger. Fold these together with a wooden spoon so the oats and spices are evenly incorporated.

3. In a separate bowl, whisk together the remaining ⅓ cup of oil, vanilla, maple syrup, and apple cider. Pour this evenly into the oat mixture and fold everything together, working carefully so the oats are not crushed. The mixture will be sticky.

4. Spread the mixture in an even layer onto the prepared baking sheet and bake for 15 minutes without disturbing. Remove the baking sheet from the oven and use a long-handled wooden spoon to stir the granola a few times so it will toast evenly. Return it to the oven for an additional 12 minutes, or until it is golden brown and fragrant. Remove the pan from the oven and place it on the counter to cool. Immediately stir in the dried cherries and crystallized ginger.

5. The granola will crisp and harden as it cools on the countertop for an hour or more. Once it has completely cooled to room temperature, pour the granola into gift bags or store in glass jars to eat.

Idea To make this granola part of a breakfast bin, wrap it in a cello bag (page 262) with a bright ribbon. To gift it on its own, pour it into a mason jar and tie a wooden scooper or breakfast spoon to the side.

Mint Brownie Tart

This brownie tart tastes like a giant Junior Mint. I like to think the midday chocolate treat gives the teachers a little extra energy for an afternoon on the playground.

MAKES 1 (10-INCH) TART

FOR THE BROWNIES

6 tablespoons unsalted butter, plus more for pan

½ cup unbleached all-purpose flour, plus more for dusting pan

1 pound semisweet chocolate, finely chopped (do not use chocolate chips), divided

3 large eggs

¾ cup granulated sugar

1 teaspoon pure vanilla extract

¼ teaspoon baking powder

1 teaspoon kosher salt

FOR THE FROSTING

3 tablespoons unsalted butter, melted and cooled

2 cups confectioners' sugar

3 tablespoons crème de menthe

1. To make the brownies: Preheat the oven to 350°F. Generously butter and flour the inside of a 10-inch tart pan and set aside.

2. Combine 14 ounces of the chocolate and the butter in a large, microwave-safe bowl. Heat in the microwave at 50% power in 30-second bursts until the butter and chocolate have melted completely together. Stir them until they form a smooth chocolate sauce. Set aside and allow to cool.

3. Meanwhile, in a separate bowl, whisk together the eggs, granulated sugar, and vanilla. Stir this into the cooled chocolate mixture.

4. In a small bowl, stir together the baking powder, flour, and salt. Fold this into the chocolate mixture until no white streaks are visible. Pour the batter into the prepared tart pan and use a spatula to spread the top evenly.

5. Bake the brownies for 25 to 30 minutes, or until the top is set and a cake tester comes out clean. Allow to cool completely before serving or frosting.

6. To make the frosting: Whisk together the butter, confectioners' sugar, and crème de menthe. It should get fairly thick and turn a light shade of green. If it still seems a little runny, pop it in the freezer for about 10 minutes to firm up. Spread it evenly on top of the brownie tart.

7. Finely chop the remaining 2 ounces of chocolate and scatter it over the mint frosting. Slice and serve.

Mother's Day

COCONUT CHAI LATTE 55

—

DOUBLE CINNAMON ROLLS 56

—

FRUITY CAIPIRINHA 58

—

ARUGULA & CAMEMBERT SALAD
with PEAR VINAIGRETTE 58

—

EASY SPICY CRAB CAKES 59

—

CHOCOLATE PEANUT BUTTER CAKE 60

If there is one day you should give Mom a break from the kitchen, it is Mother's Day. This your chance to create delicious food for her all day long, much as she does for her family the rest of the year. Don't worry if you don't have mad kitchen skills. Cooking for Mom doesn't have to mean getting overly fancy. A delicious hot tea, skillfully assembled salad, and rich chocolate dessert will suit her just fine. More than anything, she just wants to be with her family, and the sentiment of a lovingly homemade meal is what will mean the most.

Coconut Chai Latte

I often use coconut milk in lieu of cow's milk in my morning beverages because I love the tropical-like flavor. The light, creamy taste pairs particularly well with chai tea. This warm mug of comfort is perfect for serving Mom during her breakfast in bed. It is a welcome break from regular coffee.

MAKES 4 CUPS CHAI LATTE

4 chai tea bags

4 teaspoons wildflower honey, plus more to taste

¼ cup light canned coconut milk, plus more to taste

1 teaspoon ground cinnamon

1. Bring 4 cups of water to a rapid boil. Place the four tea bags each in individual coffee mugs or heatproof glasses. Pour 1 cup of hot water over each of them and allow the bags to steep for about 4 minutes, or until the tea is rich dark brown color. Remove the tea bags and discard.

2. Stir 1 teaspoon of honey and 1 tablespoon of coconut milk, plus more to taste, into each mug of tea. Top each with a pinch of cinnamon. Serve immediately.

Note If you don't have coconut milk on hand, almond, rice, or soy milk would also work well.

Double Cinnamon Rolls

When I lived in Manhattan, I treated myself to a cinnamon roll at Oren's once a week. I loved how the cinnamon was actually in the dough instead of just rolled inside the pinwheel. This sophisticated pastry is deceptively simple to make. They are perfect for serving to Mom for breakfast in bed.

MAKES 15 ROLLS

FOR THE ROLLS

3¾ cups unbleached all-purpose flour, plus more
   for rolling

½ cup granulated sugar

1 tablespoon ground cinnamon

1 teaspoon kosher salt

2¼ teaspoons active dry yeast

1 cup buttermilk, warmed

3 tablespoons unsalted butter, melted and
   cooled, plus more for pan

1 large egg

Vegetable oil for dough bowl

FOR THE FILLING

4 tablespoons (½ stick) unsalted butter, melted

¾ cup light brown sugar

1 teaspoon ground cinnamon

FOR THE GLAZE

1½ cups confectioners' sugar

2 teaspoons pure vanilla extract

¼ cup whole milk

1. To make the rolls: With an electric mixer on low speed, mix together the flour, granulated sugar, cinnamon, salt, and yeast once or twice so they are evenly incorporated. Switch out the beater blade for the dough hook.

2. In a small bowl, whisk together the buttermilk, butter, and egg. Pour it into the dry ingredients and mix the ingredients on medium-low speed until a dough forms and is completely smooth and begins to pull away from the sides of the mixing bowl, about 3 minutes.

3. Lightly oil the inside of a large mixing bowl and turn the dough into it. Cover the bowl with a clean cotton kitchen towel and place it in a warm, dry place away from direct sunlight. Allow the dough to rise for at least 3 hours, or until it has doubled in size.

4. Once the dough has risen, turn it out onto a floured surface. Brush some flour onto a rolling pin and roll the dough out to a 14 x 12-inch rectangle.

5. To fill the rolls: Brush the dough with the cooled butter, leaving a 1-inch border around the edges. Sprinkle the dough with the brown sugar and cinnamon. Use your hands to roll the dough into a log that is 14 inches long, starting with one of the long edges. Use a serrated knife to cut the rolls in 1-inch rolls.

6. Brush the inside of a 13 x 9 x 2-inch pan with butter and nestle the rolls into it in one even layer, they will be touching but should not overlap. There should be three rows of five rolls. Cover this dish with a clean cotton kitchen towel and place in a warm, dry place away from direct sunlight. Allow the dough to rise for 2 more hours.

7. Preheat the oven to 375°F. Place the pan in the oven and bake for 22 to 25 minutes, or until the rolls are golden brown on top. Remove the pan from the oven and allow them to cool for at least 20 minutes before glazing.

8. To make the glaze: Whisk together the sugar, vanilla, and milk. For a thinner glaze, add more milk in 1-teaspoon increments until the desired consistency is reached. Drizzle the glaze over the cooled rolls and enjoy.

Note   These rolls are best when served fresh from the oven. As they cool, they will begin to harden. If you're serving them later, warm them in the microwave at 50% power for 30 seconds to soften.

Fruity Caipirinha

Let's not forget the importance of cocktail hour on Mother's Day. Try this easy fruit drink when Mom deserves a little more than her usual glass of wine!

MAKES 2 SERVINGS

12 ripe strawberries, washed, hulled, and sliced

1 tablespoon plus 2 teaspoons granulated sugar

1 lime, cut into 4 wedges

½ cup white rum

1¼ cups ice cubes, plus more for serving

1. Place the berries in a cocktail shaker and mash them with the sugar and half of the lime wedges, using the end of a wooden spoon or something similar. Pour in the rum and ice cubes, cover, and shake well.

2. Fill two cocktail glasses half-full with ice cubes. Pour the rum mixture evenly between each glass and remove the lime wedges. Use the remaining lime wedges to garnish. Serve.

Arugula & Camembert Salad *with* Pear Vinaigrette

To really impress Mom with your gourmet cooking skills, throw together this luxurious salad for lunch alongside crab cakes. She'll love the bites of rich Camembert tossed with the aromatic dressing.

MAKES 4 TO 6 SERVINGS

1 medium-size pear (about 4 ounces), peeled, cored, and diced

½ shallot, finely chopped

¼ teaspoon kosher salt

⅛ teaspoon freshly cracked black pepper

¼ cup extra-virgin olive oil

2 tablespoons Champagne vinegar

8 ounces arugula, washed and stems removed

¾ cup pecan halves, lightly toasted

4 ounces Camembert cheese, sliced thinly

1. Make the vinaigrette by combining the chopped pear, shallot, salt, oil, and vinegar in a blender or food processor and puréeing until smooth.

2. Place the arugula and pecans in a large salad bowl and toss them with the vinaigrette. Top the salad with the slices of cheese. Serve.

Easy Spicy Crab Cakes

Homemade crab cakes are an impressive dish that is easier to make than you think. Serve them over salad or on toast with a few slices of bacon, tomato, and lettuce to make a crab cake BLT.

MAKES 8 CRAB CAKES

4 cups panko breadcrumbs

1 pound jumbo lump crabmeat, picked over

2 large eggs, lightly beaten

5 tablespoons light mayonnaise

2 teaspoons Old Bay seasoning

2 teaspoons red pepper hot sauce (we use Cholula)

Pinch of kosher salt

4 tablespoons (½ stick) unsalted butter, plus more as needed

2 lemons, cut into wedges

Tartar sauce

1. Pour the breadcrumbs into a large bowl and add the crabmeat, eggs, mayonnaise, Old Bay, hot sauce, and salt. Mix well with a wooden spoon until everything is completely incorporated.

2. Use eight 4-ounce ramekins to mold your crab mixture into eight crab cakes: Stuff each ramekin with enough of the crab mixture that it is tightly packed but still flat on the top. Cover each ramekin with plastic wrap. If you don't have ramekins on hand, use your hands to gently form the crab cakes into 4-inch rounds that are about 1-inch thick and place on a plate topped with waxed paper. Cover the plate with plastic wrap. Refrigerate the crab cakes for at least 4 hours, or until firm.

3. When ready to cook, carefully run a knife around the edge of each ramekin to release its crab cake onto a plate or platter. To cook the crab cakes, melt the butter in a large skillet over medium heat and place the cakes in the melted butter. You may have to cook them in batches, depending on the size of your skillet; add a little more butter to the pan for the second batch if necessary. Cook the crab cakes for 4 minutes per side, or until lightly browned on the bottom. Transfer to a plate and serve with lemon wedges and tartar sauce for dipping.

Chocolate Peanut Butter Cake

This recipe is based on my friend Hilary's. It is rich and dense, and I top it with a generous swath of peanut butter buttercream to make it taste like the grown-up version of my favorite peanut butter cup candy. Mom will love indulging in a decadent slice to cap off her delicious day.

MAKES 10 TO 12 SERVINGS

4 ounces (1 stick) unsalted butter, at room temperature, plus more for pan

1½ cups unbleached all-purpose flour, plus more for dusting pan

⅓ cup unsweetened cocoa powder

1 teaspoon baking soda

1⅓ cups granulated sugar

1⅛ teaspoon kosher salt, divided

1 cup freshly brewed strong black coffee, cooled to room temperature

5 tablespoons vegetable oil

2 teaspoons pure vanilla extract

¼ cup whole milk

1 tablespoon white wine vinegar

⅔ cup creamy peanut butter (not all-natural)

1 cup confectioners' sugar

1. Preheat the oven to 350°F. Butter and flour the inside of a 9-inch round cake pan. In a large bowl, combine the flour, cocoa powder, baking soda, granulated sugar, and 1 teaspoon of the salt and set aside.

2. In a small bowl, whisk together the coffee, oil, vanilla, milk, and vinegar. Carefully fold the wet ingredients into the dry ingredients and stir until completely smooth. Pour the batter into the prepared cake pan and bake for 20 to 25 minutes, or until the top springs back when touched and a cake tester comes out clean. Allow the cake to cool for 10 minutes in the pan, then invert it onto a cooling rack to cool completely.

3. To make the frosting: With an electric mixer, beat the peanut butter and butter at high speed in a large bowl until light and fluffy. Slowly beat in the confectioners' sugar and remaining salt until completely smooth. Use an offset spatula to generously frost the top of the cake. Slice and serve!

Graduation Parties

GRILLED MANGO CHICKEN   62

—

PESTO CAPRESE TORTELLINI SALAD   63

—

LOADED VEGETABLE KEBABS   64

—

PEANUT BUTTER CUP GRADUATION CAPS   65

—

VANILLA FUNFETTI SHEET CAKE
with LEMON BUTTERCREAM   65

Graduation parties are another occasion when you need a standby menu of entertaining recipes for a crowd. In Connecticut, our weather is usually perfect for an outdoor celebration by the end of May. To celebrate Daphne's educational milestones, we like to fire up the grill, invite friends to the backyard, and toast the graduates.

Grilled Mango Chicken

The fresh, fruity flavor of this grilled chicken is perfect for kicking off summer. Cook the barbecue sauce well in advance. Marinate the chicken the night before so you are all set to grill when everyone arrives.

MAKES 4 SERVINGS

2 medium-size mangoes, peeled and cubed
   (about 1 cup)
4 garlic cloves, peeled
1 tablespoon freshly squeezed lemon juice
1 teaspoon soy sauce
½ cup ketchup
1 teaspoon kosher salt
4 large boneless skinless chicken breasts

1. In a medium saucepan, combine the mangoes, garlic, lemon juice, soy sauce, ketchup, and salt. Simmer for about 10 minutes, stirring occasionally. Remove from the heat and use an immersion blender to purée the sauce until smooth. Allow the sauce to cool for about 10 minutes before using, or refrigerate overnight.

2. Place the chicken in a shallow baking dish and add half of the sauce. Turn the chicken twice to coat it well. Cover the dish with plastic wrap and refrigerate for a minimum of 2 hours. Then remove it from the refrigerator and light the grill to a medium flame.

3. Place the chicken over the heat and grill it for about 5 minutes per side, until cooked through. Brush both sides with the remaining sauce and cook for another 6 minutes. Remove from the heat, slice, and serve.

Pesto Caprese Tortellini Salad

This features fresh pesto from the outdoor garden. It is perfect for outdoor parties and it stands up well to the heat, as it is mayonnaise-free!

MAKES 4 TO 6 SERVINGS

24 ounces fresh cheese tortellini

½ cup fresh (page 86) or store-bought pesto

1 cup grape tomatoes, halved

4 ounces fresh mozzarella cheese, cut into
    ½-inch cubes

1 tablespoon toasted pine nuts

1. Cook the tortellini according to the package instructions and drain well. Return it to the pot and stir in the pesto until the tortellini is evenly coated.

2. Pour the tortellini into a large serving bowl and toss with the tomatoes, mozzarella, and pine nuts. Serve warm or at room temperature.

Loaded Vegetable Kebabs

Marinated grilled vegetables are a snap to make and you can use all kinds of vegetables. They smell and taste like summer and are much easier to eat standing up than leafy salads.

MAKES 8 TO 10 SKEWERS

1 red bell pepper, cored, seeded, and sliced

1 green or yellow bell pepper, cored, seeded, and sliced

2 large zucchini, cut into 1-inch pieces

1 pint cremini mushrooms, cut into 1-inch slices

1 pint cherry tomatoes

1 red onion, peeled and cut into wedges

1 cup Easy Italian Dressing (page 164)

1. In a large mixing bowl, combine the peppers, zucchini, mushrooms, tomatoes, and onion with the dressing. Stir the vegetables a few times and place them in the fridge to marinate for 2 hours, or up to overnight, to let them soak up all the flavors.

2. Light your grill and begin to heat it to a medium flame. Carefully thread the vegetables onto the skewers (see note), packing them in so they just barely touch.

3. Place the vegetables on the grill and cook for 6 to 8 minutes, rotating at least once to ensure even browning. The vegetables should be lightly charred and cooked through.

Note If using wooden or bamboo skewers, be sure to soak them in water at least 20 minutes to prevent burning.

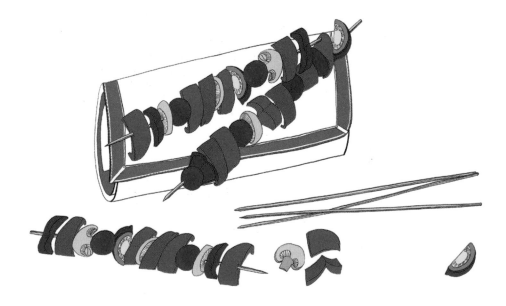

Peanut Butter Cup Graduation Caps

Have the children help you make these and scatter them around the table for the little ones to nibble on.

MAKES 12 CAPS

12 miniature peanut butter cups

3 tablespoons store-bought chocolate buttercream frosting

12 large chocolate squares (such as Ghirardelli)

12 brown M&M's

1 (24-inch-long) strand black licorice, divided

1. To assemble the graduation caps, unwrap and invert a peanut butter cup and place a dollop of chocolate buttercream on the bottom. Place a square of chocolate, logo side down, on top of the peanut butter cup and press down firmly to make the cap.

2. To make the cap tassel, snip off 2 inches of licorice and dip the end in buttercream. Stick the creamy end in the center of the top of the chocolate square and allow it to loosely hang off the side of the chocolate. Top it with an M&M, dipping the M&M in a little extra buttercream to secure it to the licorice.

Note If you can't find chocolate squares, chocolate graham cracker squares will also work.

Vanilla Funfetti Sheet Cake *with* Lemon Buttercream

A big party calls for a big ole cake. This easy sheet cake harkens back to funfetti cake, the classic white cake filled with sprinkles, always a childhood favorite. The size feeds a crowd with ease. Skip the fancy decorations, and top it with fluffy yellow frosting and loads of rainbow sprinkles.

MAKES 1 CAKE, ABOUT 36 SERVINGS

FOR THE CAKE

8 ounces (2 sticks) unsalted butter

2 cups granulated sugar

2 large eggs, lightly beaten

1 teaspoon pure vanilla extract

½ cup buttermilk

2 cups plus 1 tablespoon unbleached all-purpose flour, divided

1 teaspoon kosher salt

1 teaspoon baking powder

¼ teaspoon baking soda

⅓ cup (1 [1.75-ounce] container) multicolored sprinkles, plus more for decorating

FOR THE FROSTING

4 ounces (1 stick) unsalted butter, at room
temperature, cubed

8 ounces cream cheese, at room temperature

1 teaspoon freshly grated lemon zest

2 teaspoons freshly squeezed lemon juice

½ teaspoon salt

3 cups confectioners' sugar

¼ cup whole milk, plus more if needed

Yellow food coloring paste (optional)

1. To make the cake: Preheat the oven to 375°F. Line a rimmed half sheet pan (18 x 13 x 1-inch) with parchment paper and set aside.

2. In a large saucepan, bring the butter and 1 cup of water just to a boil over medium heat. Remove it from the stovetop, pour it into a large mixing bowl, and allow it to cool for 10 minutes.

3. Once the butter has cooled, whisk in the granulated sugar, eggs, vanilla, and buttermilk until completely smooth. Use a spatula to fold in 2 cups of the flour, and the salt, baking powder, and baking soda. Toss the sprinkles with the remaining tablespoon of flour and stir into the batter.

4. Pour the batter into the prepared baking pan and spread it evenly with a spatula. Bake for 23 to 25 minutes, or until the top is golden brown and a cake tester inserted into the center comes out clean. Allow the cake to cool in the pan completely before frosting.

5. To make the frosting: With an electric mixer fitted with a paddle attachment, beat the butter, cream cheese, lemon zest and juice, and salt on high speed in a large bowl until completely incorporated. Then slowly add the confectioners' sugar and beat until smooth, about 3 minutes. With the mixer on medium speed, slowly add the milk until light and fluffy. If the frosting is still too thick, add more milk by the teaspoonful until the desired spreadable consistency is reached. For yellow frosting, beat in two or three drops of yellow food coloring paste. Spread the fresh frosting on the cake. To make a sprinkle border: Place a 16 x 11-inch sheet of parchment paper or cardboard on the center of the cake. Shake the sprinkles all over the exposed frosting around the edges. Then remove the paper, retouch the frosting, and the border is set. Slice and serve!

Summer

The summer kitchen revolves around the bounty of the garden and the farmers' market. It is time to savor the intense flavors of eating fresh from the stalk and preserving everything you can. Streamline your recipes and keep your cooking simple. Don't worry about complicated recipes or fancy presentations. Take time to enjoy your garden, walk the children through the markets, and craft on the front steps.

GIVE YOUR TABLE CHARACTER Bring nature inside with fresh cut flowers, wild grasses, and produce from the garden. Fill glass jars with fresh bouquets and line them up the length of the table on top of a neutral-colored table runner. Pour sand into hurricane vases and nestle the candles in the middle for an easy, beachy candlelight dinner.

THE FARMERS' MARKET

The availability of locally produced food differs greatly from place to place. If you have a farmers' market in your area, pile the children in the stroller and shop at it each week. Talk about the variety of produce they see, and enjoy the samples and any activities taking place. This not only helps parents get their shopping completed efficiently, but also teaches children about food sources.

Your Farmers' Market Shopping Strategy

BRING BAGS Bring many reusable bags for carrying purchases. Pack an insulated bag if you intend to buy meats or dairy products. Bring a small bag or backpack for young children. They can pick out a few treasures and be responsible for carrying them home.

REMEMBER REFRESHMENTS Pack a bag with water bottles and snacks for children if you plan to be there for more than thirty minutes. Shopping for food inevitably makes everyone hungry. Refuel your trusty shopping companions with quick bites to avoid a midmarket meltdown.

COME PREPARED Bring a shopping list and a pen. Children can help you correctly identify the foods you are looking for and check them off the list. It's a fun game, and it also helps them learn what food looks like in baskets or crates, not just when it has been gussied up for the supermarket shelves.

NEW FOOD CHALLENGES Let the children touch and taste whatever they are allowed to. Challenge them to pick out one new food to try each week. This is a great way to expand their palates and teach them about seasonal eating.

LEARN NEW RECIPES Farmers have great recipe ideas for their own produce. Ask your children what they want to eat and chat with a farmer to find a new, exciting way to prepare it at home.

Summer Beverages

In the summer, keep your refrigerator stocked with pitcher full of iced tea and carafe of fresh chilled coffee concentrate. This way, you always have a refreshing sip at the ready.

Cold-Brewed Coffee

I didn't start drinking coffee until Garner was born. There was something about having two children that pushed me over the edge! In the winter, I usually use our simple coffeemaker, but in the summer, I like to make it using this cold brewing method I adapted from the New York Times. *It is so simple and it makes a very strong coffee. For an afternoon treat, I serve it over ice with a touch of milk and drizzle of vanilla simple syrup.*

MAKES 3 CUPS COFFEE CONCENTRATE

FOR THE CONCENTRATE
1 cup coarsely ground coffee beans
3 cups cold filtered water

FOR SERVING
Cold water
Ice cubes (optional)
Cold milk (optional)
Sweetener of choice (optional)

1. To make the concentrate: Scoop the coffee grounds into the bottom of a clean quart-size glass jar with a lid. Fill the jar to the brim with the filtered water and seal tightly with the lid. Chill the jar in the refrigerator for at least 12 hours, or up to overnight.

2. Remove the lid of the jar and secure a coffee filter over the mouth, using rubber bands. Then, holding the rubber bands, pour the coffee concentrate into a pitcher that you will use to serve it. The coffee filter should strain out all of the coffee grounds so that none escape into the pitcher.

3. To make a glass of coffee: Pour equal parts coffee concentrate and cold water into a glass and add ice cubes, if desired. Add milk and sweetener to your iced coffee as you would normally do.

Note A popular thing to do is stir together one part concentrate with two parts water and pour the contents into an ice cube tray to make coffee ice cubes. Use these ice cubes to chill your iced coffee so your beverage never gets diluted with water.

THREE WAYS TO MAKE ICED TEA

In the summer months, iced tea is my beverage of choice. I start off with a tall glass filled with lemon slices every morning and drink more throughout the day. There are many ways to make iced tea, each one yielding a slightly different tasting beverage. Once you get the method down, you can make any flavor you want.

Cold-Brewed Iced Tea

This method yields the iced tea with the strongest flavor and, I think, the highest caffeine content.

MAKES 2 QUARTS ICED TEA

5 tea bags
2 quarts cool filtered water

1. Place the tea bags in a 2-quart pitcher. Add the water and chill the pitcher in the refrigerator for 12 hours, or overnight. Remove the tea bags and enjoy.

Note To secure the tea bags in the pitcher overnight, clip the strings the side of the pitcher with a clothespin.

Sun Tea

Sun tea is a personal favorite. The mellow heat of the sun produces a milder, sweeter tea. This method is a little bit controversial since some say that the sun encourages bacterial growth in the tea pitcher. I make sure my pitcher is freshly washed and dried before I begin and I have never had any trouble.

MAKES 2 QUARTS ICED TEA

5 tea bags
2 quarts filtered water, at room temperature

1. Place the tea bags in a 2-quart pitcher. Fill the pitcher with room-temperature filtered water and place a lid on top. Place the pitcher in direct sunlight outdoors for one hour. Keep an eye on it. It should turn a dark golden color. After 1 hour, remove the tea bags and place the pitcher in the refrigerator to cool down.

Traditional Iced Tea

If you don't have time to make cold-brewed ice tea and don't have a place to make sun tea, then regular brewed tea always works beautifully.

MAKES 2 QUARTS ICED TEA

5 tea bags
2 quarts boiling water

1. Place five tea bags in a heatproof 2-quart pitcher. Add the boiling water and allow the tea to steep for 5 minutes. The tea should turn a dark brown color. Remove the tea bags and place the pitcher in the refrigerator to cool down.

SERVING ICED TEA

Any of the three iced teas are delicious when served with:
- **Sliced fruits:** Lemons, oranges, peaches, mango, or watermelon
- **Herbs:** Sprigs of mint, basil, lavender, rosemary, or thyme

To vary the flavors of your iced teas, try combining herbal teas with black teas as follows:
- **Raspberry Tea:** Two raspberry herbal tea bags, three black tea bags

- **Peach Tea:** Two peach herbal tea bags, three black tea bags
- **Mint Tea:** Two mint tea bags, three black tea bags, one small handful of clean fresh mint leaves

Roasted Peach Lemonade

One year, I decided to roast peaches before adding them to lemonade, after tasting a similar drink in Atlanta, Georgia. Roasting the fruit concentrates its flavor and makes the drink even more intense. This is particularly great for outdoor parties. It also makes a tasty cocktail with a little rum mixed in!

MAKES 4 CUPS LEMONADE

4 medium-size peaches, pitted and sliced in half
1 tablespoon granulated sugar
4 cups fresh lemonade of choice

1. Preheat the oven to 400°F.

2. Place the peach halves skin-side down in a baking dish and sprinkle the tops with the sugar. Roast them for about 25 minutes, or until the tops of the peaches are moist and juicy and the skins begin to shrivel slightly.

3. Remove the pan from the oven and allow the peaches to cool until they are comfortable to handle, about 10 minutes. Use your fingers to pinch the skins off the fruit.

4. Drop the peaches into a blender and fill it with just enough lemonade to cover them. Purée the fruit completely. The liquid will look foamy and bubbly, which is normal.

5. Pour the remaining lemonade into a large pitcher and stir in the peach lemonade purée. Stir the mixture vigorously to incorporate the pulp and serve immediately over ice. Always be sure to stir the mixture well before pouring to draw the flavorful pulp off the bottom.

Note If you prefer your lemonade pulp-free, strain it once or twice through a fine-mesh sieve lined with cheesecloth before serving.

Fruit Vodkas

In the summer, infuse your vodka with the flavors of fresh fruits. They taste so much better than the artificially flavored vodkas from the store. Mix your flavored vodkas with sparkling water or fresh lemonade for awesome refreshing summer cocktails! These vodkas also make great hostess gifts or party favors for summer gatherings.

MAKES 2 PINTS FRUIT VODKA

2 pints fresh strawberries, washed, hulled, and quartered
2 tablespoons sugar
1 (750 ml) bottle good-quality vodka

1. Divide the strawberries equally between two glass pint-size jars. They should reach the brim of the jars and be packed tightly. The number of strawberries you use per jar will vary a little depending on their size.

2. Add 1 tablespoon of sugar to each jar and divide the vodka equally between the jars, filling them to the brim. Screw the lid tightly on and gently shake the jar to agitate the berries and the sugar.

3. Place the jars in a cool, dry area away from sunlight and gently agitate them every day for 7 days.

At the end of 7 days the berries will be leached of most of their color and the vodka will be red.

4. Strain out the berries and loose seeds by setting a strainer lined with cheesecloth over a glass bowl. Pour the contents of the jar through the strainer and discard the seeds and berries. The remaining liquid in the bowl is ready to drink. The vodka can be stored in any clean glass bottle. It is best stored in the refrigerator or freezer and should be used within 1 month.

Notes

This method works for many juicy fruits. For example, to make raspberry vodka, substitute 2 pints of raspberries for the strawberries. For peach vodka, use 2 pints of sliced, peeled peaches.

Be sure to choose the freshest, organic berries you can find and wash them well before use.

Sparkling Cherry Lemonade

This reminds me of the fancy French lemonade in glass bottles at the store. Have your children help you make this. They can pulse the food processor and stir in the cherries.

MAKES 6 CUPS LEMONADE

1 tablespoon lemon zest

¾ cup granulated sugar

1 cup freshly squeezed lemon juice

4 cups sparkling water

½ cup sliced cherries, pitted, stems removed

1. Make a simple syrup by combining 1 cup water with the lemon zest and sugar in a small saucepan over medium heat. Heat the mixture just until the sugar dissolves.

2. Fill a pitcher with the lemon juice and sparkling water and stir in the syrup.

3. In a food processor, pulse the cherries two or three times. They should be finely chopped but not completely shredded. Pour the cherries and all the juices into the lemonade. Stir well and serve!

Half-and-Half Tea Lemonade

To give your iced tea a twist, stir in lemon simple syrup to make it a half ice tea/half lemonade, similar to the popular Arnold Palmer. The bright zing of citrus adds just the right amount of sweetness without being overwhelming.

MAKES 2 QUARTS LEMONADE

5 black tea bags

7 cups boiling water

1 tablespoon lemon zest

1 cup granulated sugar

1 cup freshly squeezed lemon juice

1. Place the tea bags in a heatproof pitcher and add the boiling water. Allow the bags to steep for 15 minutes before removing and discarding.

2. While the bags are steeping, place the lemon zest, sugar, and 1 cup of water in a small saucepan and bring to a simmer over medium heat. Heat until the sugar is dissolved. Remove the pan from the heat and stir in the lemon juice.

3. Stir the warm lemon syrup into the tea. Place a lid on the pitcher and refrigerate for at least 6 hours, or until the tea is chilled. Serve over ice.

Dark and Stormy

In the heat of the summer, try this gingery rum cocktail. The heavily spiced ginger beer mixed with dark rum is our standby cocktail for drinking on the boat or by the campfire.

MAKES 4 SERVINGS

Ice

8 ounces dark rum

4 (10-ounce) bottles ginger beer

1 lime

1. Fill four pint glasses with ice cubes. Pour 2 ounces of rum into each glass, followed by 10 ounces of the ginger beer.

2. Squeeze a lime wedge into each glass and stir once or twice with a swizzle stick.

Frozen Treats

Classic Vanilla Ice Cream Base

You only need one ice cream base recipe; once you get the hang of it, you can dream up nearly any flavor you want. The possibilities are endless, and making ice cream is a great activity for children during the summer.

MAKES 2½ CUPS ICE CREAM

2 cups heavy whipping cream
½ cup half-and-half
¾ cup granulated sugar
1 tablespoon pure vanilla extract
Pinch of fine sea salt

1. Place the cream, half-and-half, sugar, vanilla, and salt in a small saucepan over medium-low heat. Heat the mixture until small bubbles start to appear around the sides. Remove the mixture from the heat and stir it gently until all the sugar dissolves. Allow the mixture to cool to room temperature, then refrigerate for 2 hours.
2. Pour the mixture into an ice-cream maker and churn according to the manufacturer's directions. Scoop the ice cream into a freezer-proof container with a lid and freeze for 5 hours before serving.

FLAVORING IDEAS

CHOCOLATE CHIP Add ½ cup of mini chocolate chips 5 minutes before the end of churning.

MINT CHOCOLATE CHIP Add ¼ teaspoon of peppermint extract instead of vanilla. Add ½ cup of mini chocolate chips 5 minutes before the end of churning.

CHOCOLATE Add 4 ounces of the finely chopped chocolate of your choice to the saucepan in step 1. Proceed to step 2 once the chocolate melts completely.

PEACH WITH CANDIED GINGER Peel and chop two small ripe peaches and macerate them in 2 teaspoons of sugar for 4 hours to extract their juices. Add the peach chunks and peach syrup 2 minutes before the end of churning. Stir in 1 tablespoon of finely chopped candied ginger once the machine has been turned off.

STRAWBERRY SWIRL Macerate 1 cup of chopped strawberries in 2 teaspoons of sugar for 4 hours. Add the strawberry pieces and syrup 2 minutes before the end of churning.

LEMON VERBENA Add 6 coarsely chopped fresh lemon verbena leaves to the cream mixture while it is simmering. Allow them to infuse the cream mixture until it has cooled to room temperature. Pluck out the leaves before churning.

Quick Chocolate Sauce

When composing a sundae, you need chocolate sauce. This rich, fudgy ganache comes together in seconds. To make it more sophisticated, you can make it with dark chocolate.

MAKES 1½ CUPS SAUCE

1 cup heavy whipping cream
1 pound semisweet chocolate, finely chopped
Pinch of salt
1 tablespoon pure vanilla extract

1. In a medium saucepan over medium heat, heat the cream until it just begins to simmer. Remove the pan from the heat, and immediately add the chocolate, salt, and vanilla and stir until completely smooth. Drizzle over ice cream and enjoy.

Note To make peppermint chocolate sauce, add ½ teaspoon of peppermint extract and omit the vanilla.

Ice Pops

Once you master the technique for making ice pops, you can make nearly any flavor you want. We like to improvise new flavors by using up fresh fruit and herbs we have in the fridge. Here are a few of our favorites. For each variation, blend all its ingredients together until smooth, pour into a set of eight 3-ounce ice pop molds, and freeze.

MAKES 8 ICE POPS

STRAWBERRY-LEMONADE 1½ cups of washed and hulled fresh strawberries, ¼ cup of confectioners' sugar, 1 cup of lemonade.

CHERRY-LIME 1 cup of cherry juice, 1 cup of frozen pitted cherries, ⅓ cup of plain yogurt, 2 tablespoons of freshly squeezed lemon juice.

BLUEBERRY-MINT YOGURT 1 cup of fresh blueberries, 1¼ cups of plain yogurt, three large mint leaves, 2 tablespoons of confectioners' sugar.

PEACH-BASIL 2 cups of puréed fresh peaches (about four peaches), four large fresh basil leaves, 2 tablespoons of confectioners' sugar, 1 tablespoon of freshly squeezed lemon juice.

COCONUT WATER-PINEAPPLE 1½ cups of cubed pineapple, 2 tablespoons of agave nectar, 1 cup of coconut water.

Homemade Sprinkle Cones

Every child I know goes nuts for the sprinkle cones at the ice-cream shop. Make them at home by dipping the cones in melted chocolate and rolling them in sprinkles.

MAKES 6 SPRINKLE CONES

6 standard flat-based ice-cream cones
½ cup small sprinkles of your choice
8 ounces semisweet chocolate chips

1. Place a sheet of parchment paper on a large dinner plate or similar size platter and line up the cones, open side down, on top of the paper. Fill a ramekin with the sprinkles and set them next to the plate with the cones.

2. In a microwave-safe bowl, melt the chocolate chips in 30-second bursts at 50% power just until they are melted and can be stirred until smooth.

3. To make the cones: Carefully dip each cone into the melted chocolate by about 1 inch. Turn the cone once or twice in the chocolate to make sure it is evenly coated. Then immediately dip the cones in the ramekin of sprinkles and turn once or twice to help the sprinkles stick well. Stand up the finished cone on the parchment paper. Repeat with the remaining cones.

4. Once the cones are all dipped, place the plate in the refrigerator to chill for 2 hours so the chocolate will harden. When ready to use, remove from the fridge, scoop ice cream into the cone, and enjoy!

Easy Peanut Butter Toffee Sauce

If you like peanut butter sauce over chocolate ice cream, you need to try this. This comes together in a snap and tastes amazing over all kinds of flavors.

MAKES 1½ CUPS SAUCE

1 cup creamy peanut butter

¼ cup chopped roasted salted peanuts

¼ cup toffee bits, or a chopped toffee bar (such as Heath Bar)

1. In a small saucepan over low heat, melt the peanut butter and stir in the chopped peanuts and toffee. Drizzle over ice cream and serve!

Peach Sherbet

Once I discovered Mark Bittman's technique for making fruit sherbet, I never looked back. It could hardly be easier and has worked with every single fruit I have ever tried. This is a terrific recipe to make with children, too. Try having fun and making different flavors, such as peach-strawberry or raspberry-mango—the sky's the limit!

MAKES 4 TO 6 SERVINGS

1 pound frozen peach slices

½ cup crème fraîche

⅓ cup sugar, or less if you don't want it too sweet

1. Place all the ingredients into the bowl of the food processor fitted with a blade and process until completely smooth. It should be the same texture as a thick buttercream frosting. If it is too thick, add a tablespoon or two of water to loosen it up. But don't add so much that the mixture becomes liquid.

2. Serve right away, or scrape the purée into a bowl that will fit in your freezer, cover with plastic wrap, and freeze. Bring to room temperature for about 10 minutes before serving.

Tip If you want to make this look fancy, save a few pieces of whole fruit to use as a garnish.

Cherry-Lime Slushies

Growing up in Cooperstown, one of my favorite summer treats was a bright green slushie from the Red Nugget Ice Cream Shop. The syrup was dispensed into a cup of crushed ice from a machine in the back and I am 100 percent sure there was nothing natural about it. These days I love making slushies at home with the children with somewhat healthier ingredients!

MAKES 4 SLUSHIES

2 cups frozen sweet pitted cherries

2 cups crushed ice

1 (6-ounce) can frozen limeade concentrate

1. Place the cherries in a food processor and process until puréed. Strain them through a fine-mesh sieve into the large pitcher. Stir in the crushed ice, 4 cups of water, and the limeade concentrate. Divide among four glasses and serve.

Tip This recipe will work with frozen strawberries, blueberries, or peach slices, or a mixture of them all!

Best-Ever Strawberry Graham Cracker Icebox Cake

When it is too hot to bake but you still need a dessert to feed a crowd, this is the dessert for you. I picked up the method for this dessert from my friend Faith Durand's book Bakeless Sweets. *It takes minutes to assemble and can chill out in the fridge for up to a day before you serve it.*

MAKES 8 TO 10 SERVINGS

3¼ cups chilled heavy whipping cream

⅓ cup confectioners' sugar

1 teaspoon pure vanilla extract

⅛ teaspoon salt

4 cups thinly sliced strawberries (about
    1½ pounds)

28 graham crackers (whole rectangles,
    not squares)

1. With an electric mixer fitted with the whisk attachment, whip the cream, confectioners' sugar, vanilla, and salt at high speed in a large bowl until soft peaks form. Very gently fold in the strawberries, being careful not to deflate the whipped cream.

2. Smear a little bit of the whipped cream on the bottom of a 13 x 9 x 2-inch dish and layer the graham crackers along the bottom so they are touching but not overlapping. Spoon about 1 cup of the strawberry whipped cream on top of the graham crackers and gently spread it evenly over them. Repeat this layering three more times, finishing with the whipped cream. You'll have four layers of graham crackers and four layers of whipped cream.

3. Refrigerate the cake for at least 2 hours. The graham crackers will soften as the cake chills. Do not let it sit for more than 24 hours or it will get too soggy. Remove the cake from the refrigerator when you are ready to serve it. Cut into squares with a sharp knife and enjoy immediately.

Lawn Party

PESTO CHICKEN SALAD   86

—

CORN & TOMATO SALAD   87

—

ZUCCHINI APPLESAUCE BREAD   88

—

PEACH SLAB PIE   88

—

NO-BAKE S'MORE CRUNCH BARS   90

Nothing says summer like setting up a buffet on the picnic table and having a casual lawn party with friends. For daytime, follow a simple game plan to prepare easy foods that can be served at room temperature. Let people fill up their plates and plop down on the lawn for some easier conversation and laughs.

Pesto Chicken Salad

In the summer, I use pesto in as many dishes as possible. This easy chicken salad is great for a summer party because it can be served cold or at room temperature. Set a sliced baguette on the side so people can make sandwiches if they want.

MAKES 4 CUPS

FOR THE PESTO

1 cup packed fresh basil leaves

1 large garlic clove

¼ cup pine nuts, lightly toasted

2 ounces freshly grated Parmesan cheese

⅓ cup extra-virgin olive oil

FOR THE SALAD

¼ cup plain Greek yogurt

¼ cup low-fat mayonnaise

2½ pound rotisserie chicken, meat removed and shredded

Salt and freshly cracked black pepper

1. To make the pesto: Combine the basil and garlic in a food processor and process to a fine paste. Add the pine nuts and process again until the mixture is smooth. Add the cheese and process until a thick paste forms. With the machine running, pour the olive oil down the feeder tube and process until the pesto loosens up and becomes smooth and creamy.

2. To assemble the salad: In a large mixing bowl, combine the fresh pesto, yogurt, and mayonnaise until smooth. Fold in the chicken until it is evenly coated. Taste for seasonings. Serve.

Corn & Tomato Salad

A light corn salad tastes like summer. It is perfect for serving outdoors as a side dish. Be sure to use the freshest local corn you can find for maximum flavor.

MAKES 8 SERVINGS

6 ears corn, shucked

1 small red onion, peeled and finely chopped

1 pint cherry tomatoes, halved

3 tablespoons cider vinegar

3 tablespoons extra-virgin olive oil

½ teaspoon kosher salt

¼ teaspoon freshly cracked black pepper

⅓ cup fresh basil leaves, cut in chiffonade

1. Bring a large pot of salted water to a boil and add the corn. Cook it for 4 minutes, then drain and run it under ice cold water to stop the cooking. Pat the corn dry and cut the kernels off the cob, placing them in a large bowl.

2. Stir in the onion, tomatoes, vinegar, olive oil, salt, and pepper. Scatter the basil on top and stir it in right before serving.

Zucchini Applesauce Bread

This is your new forever zucchini bread recipe. It is moist and sweet with subtle fruity undertones from the applesauce. For parties, arrange slices on a platter for people to nibble on.

MAKES 1 LOAF

Cooking spray

1 large zucchini (about 8 ounces), coarsely shredded

1½ cups unbleached all-purpose flour

1 teaspoon baking powder

⅛ teaspoon baking soda

¼ teaspoon ground nutmeg

½ teaspoon kosher salt

1 large egg

½ cup granulated sugar

¼ cup light brown sugar

¼ cup vegetable oil

¼ cup plain applesauce

1. Preheat the oven to 350°F. Spray an 8 x 4-inch loaf pan with cooking spray and set aside.

2. In a large bowl, combine the zucchini, flour, baking powder, baking soda, nutmeg, and salt. Set aside.

3. In a smaller bowl, whisk together the egg, sugars, vegetable oil, and applesauce until smooth. Pour the wet ingredients into the dry ingredients and stir well until a smooth batter forms.

4. Pour the batter into the prepared loaf pan and bake for 45 to 50 minutes, or until a cake tester comes out clean and the top springs back lightly when touched. Allow the bread to cool in the pan for 10 minutes, then invert it onto a cooling rack and allow to cool completely.

Peach Slab Pie

This pie effortlessly serves a crowd. It is so much easier to make one large one than several small ones!

MAKES 10 TO 12 SERVINGS

FOR THE CRUST

5 cups unbleached all-purpose flour, plus more for dusting

2 teaspoons kosher salt

2 tablespoons granulated sugar

12 ounces (3 sticks) cold unsalted butter, cut into small pieces

1 cup ice water, or more as needed

FOR THE FILLING

8 cups fresh peeled peach slices, (about 11 peaches), or 5 (10-ounce) bags frozen peach slices, thawed

3 tablespoons cornstarch

½ cup granulated sugar

Zest and juice of 2 medium-size lemons

1 large egg, beaten

1. To make the crust: In a large food processor, combine the flour, salt, sugar, and butter and pulse until small crumbs form. Remove the tube of the processor and pulse while slowly adding the ice water. Stop adding the water the second the dough comes together and forms one big ball.

2. Remove the dough from the processor and divide it into two equal pieces. Press them into disks and wrap them with plastic wrap. Refrigerate them for at least 1 hour, or up to overnight.

3. Preheat the oven to 375°F. Remove the dough from the fridge and allow it to warm slightly.

4. While it is warming, make the filling: Place the peach slices, cornstarch, sugar, and lemon zest and juice in a large mixing bowl and toss everything together with your hands. Let it sit while you roll out the dough.

5. On a heavily floured surface, roll out one piece of dough to a 12 x 16-inch rectangle. Drape it on a 15 x 10 x 1-inch rimmed baking sheet and trim the edges so there is 1 inch of overhang all around. Roll out the second piece of dough to an 11 x 15-inch rectangle.

6. Gently spread the filling into the dough so it is in one even layer. Place the second sheet of dough over the filling. Brush the edges with water and pinch it together with the overhang from the bottom layer of dough. Use a knife or pie cutters to slice a few slits in a decorative pattern on the top of the pie. This will allow it to vent while it bakes.

7. Brush the top of the pie evenly with the beaten egg and bake it for 40 to 45 minutes, or until the crust is golden brown on top. The filling should be hot and bubbly.

8. Remove the pie from the oven and allow it to cool for about 20 minutes. Then slice and serve!

No-Bake S'More Crunch Bars

These crunchy milk chocolate treats are like portable s'mores. They are always a hit with children at lawn parties, though, truth be told, the adults enjoy them just as much. They can be made far in advance and refrigerated until the event. They also transport well as long as they are kept cool.

MAKES 1 (13 X 9-INCH) PAN

24 ounces milk chocolate (don't use chocolate chips)

4 ounces (1 stick) unsalted butter, cut into pieces

½ cup light corn syrup

16 graham cracker rectangles, broken into 1-inch pieces

1½ cups mini marshmallows

1. Coarsely chop the chocolate and place it in a microwave-safe bowl with the butter pieces. Microwave the bowl at 50% power at 30-second intervals until the chocolate and butter have melted. Stir them until smooth and glossy. Stir in the corn syrup until the mixture is completely smooth. Scoop out 2 cups of the chocolate mixture and set aside.

2. Stir the graham crackers and marshmallows into the remaining chocolate mixture and fold a few times until they are evenly coated with chocolate. Press the mixture into a lightly oiled 13 x 9-inch pan and make sure it is as smooth on top as possible.

3. Pour the reserved chocolate mixture over the bars and smooth it over the top of the bars all the way to the edges, pressing down to make sure everything is packed in. Cover the dish with plastic wrap and refrigerate for at least 6 hours, or until the bars are completely solid.

4. When ready to serve, use a sharp knife to break up the bars and cut them into bite-size pieces.

Note These bars are about 1 inch thick. For thicker bars, pack the warm chocolate-graham cracker batter into a 9-inch square pan.

Variation For some extra fun, use 2 cups of a breakfast cereal, such as Cinnamon Toast Crunch Cereal or Golden Grahams, in lieu of the graham crackers.

Summer Small-Batch Canning

My father and I have always enjoyed canning together. The first recipe he taught me was my grandmother's famous bread & butter pickle recipe, and we've steadily worked our way through jams, pickled vegetables, and sauces over the years. Each summer with my parents in Cooperstown, we'll tackle a few large canning projects together, such as making ten quarts of blueberry pie filling and a triple recipe of Apricot Lemon Thyme Jam to give away at Christmas. However, when I am at home in Connecticut, I pare down my canning ambitions. It is far easier, and more practical, for me to make two or three pints of something instead of dozens. I can accomplish all of these recipes with the children at home.

Your Small-Batch Canning Strategy

Choose two or three preserving recipes each summer, depending on how much time you have. Plan ahead by calculating the number of jars and equipment you'll need. Set aside the appropriate amount of time for each recipe. Tackle a batch or two a day until your pantry is full.

To increase the variety of food in your pantry, host a jam swap. It is a great way to share the summer's bounty and try new and interesting flavors. It can be organized the same way as a cookie swap in December. Each person brings one jar preserves per guest to swap and goes home with a whole new selection of preserves for winter.

A FEW SMALL-BATCH CANNING BASICS

PRESERVING EQUIPMENT You'll need a nonreactive saucepan or specialized stainless-steel canning pan, a long-handled spoon for stirring brines and jams, a ladle for scooping hot liquid into jars, a pot deep enough to hold a single layer of a few pint-size jars with 1 inch of boiling water covering the top, tongs for removing jars from boiling water, and a stack of clean kitchen towels. For large projects, it is helpful to have a large canning pot with a cooling rack insert that can process up to eight pint-size jars at a time.

STERILIZING JARS You can use any style of glass jar that you like for canning. Just make sure they have been sterilized thoroughly before you begin. My preferred method for sterilizing them is to run them through a hot dishwasher cycle, with nothing else in the dishwasher, without soap. Dry the jars with the heated drying cycle. If there are any water droplets remaining on the jars, remove them from the machine with tongs and place them face-up on a tray lined with a clean kitchen towel to dry completely before use. Sterilize the lids and rims by placing them in a pan of boiling water for 5 minutes. Remove and allow to cool on a clean kitchen towel until ready to use.

WATER BATH PROCESSING The term *processing* refers to submerging the filled and closed jars in a bath of boiling water for an allotted amount of time. A proper water bath must be at a rolling boil with enough water to cover the tops of the jars by 1 inch. This creates a vacuum seal that makes the jar shelf-stable for the pantry. If you do not process your jars, they must be stored in the refrigerator to prevent spoilage (no matter how many decades your grandparents stored and ate their preserves after just flipping the hot filled jars upside down on the countertop to seal!).

TIMING If you plan to process your jars, start bringing your hot water bath to a boil while you are cooking your brines, jams, or sauces. It takes a long time to bring such large volumes of water to a boil and it is imperative that the process of transferring the filled, sealed jars with the hot contents to the hot water bath goes quickly so the contents don't cool. I've added a step in each recipe when you should ready the water bath to boil to ensure your timing works.

TESTING THE SEALS When you've finished processing your jars and they have been resting for 12 hours, test the top of each jar with your finger. If the seal in the lid moves up and down, it hasn't sealed. Place the jar in the refrigerator immediately to store.

Apricot Lemon Thyme Jam

Patricia Wells's book The Provence Cookbook *gave me the idea to include the apricot kernel in the jam while it cooks. It lends the jam a distinct almondlike note that elevates the flavor. I add lemon thyme to our jam because it adds a subtle earthy lemony flavor.*

MAKES 6 HALF-PINTS JAM

2 pounds apricots, roughly chopped (reserve the pits)

1½ cups granulated sugar

1½ teaspoons fresh lemon thyme leaves (or regular fresh thyme leaves if lemon thyme isn't available)

1. Use a small hammer or heavy object to crack open the apricot pits and remove the kernels in the center. Reserve these kernels and discard all the remaining pit pieces. Place the kernels in a sheet of cheesecloth and tightly tie all the sides together with kitchen twine to form a bundle.

2. In a large stockpot, combine the apricots, bundle of kernels, sugar, and lemon thyme. Stir everything together, place a clean kitchen towel over the top, and let the pot sit at room temperature for an hour.

3. Place the pot on a large burner over medium heat. Bring the apricots to a simmer, uncovered, and stir continuously for 1 hour, or until the fruit has dissolved into a thick stew and the volume of the pot has reduced by half. Remove the pot from the heat and cover it with a clean kitchen towel. Allow it to sit for at least 12 hours in a cool, dry place in your kitchen, or up to 24 hours.

4. The next day, first start your hot water bath in a large, deep pot that will hold six half-pint jars (or three pint-size jars) with an inch of water covering them, and sterilize your jars, lids, and rims.

5. Place the pot back on the heat and bring the apricots to a low boil. Stir for an additional 15 minutes, or until you are able to drag a spatula through and it leaves an open track behind it for a few seconds before filling back in. Use a pair of kitchen tongs to pluck out the bundle of kernels and discard.

6. Place the sterilized jars in the sink to catch any hot drips while they are being filled. Ladle the jam into each jar, leaving a ½-inch headspace at the top. Carefully wipe the rims of the jars with a clean kitchen towel. Top each jar with a sterilized lid and rim. Only tighten each jar as much as you can twist with your fingertips; do not force it.

7. If you are not using a canning rack to hold your jars, place a clean kitchen towel on the bottom of the pot so the jars don't touch the bottom. Place the jars carefully in the boiling water, using tongs, and process them for 10 minutes, starting the timer only when the water has returned to a boil.

8. When the jars are done processing, use the tongs to transfer the jars to a cool, dry place away from direct sunlight and do not disturb for 12 hours. Throughout the day you'll hear the pop-pops of the seals on the jars forming. After the jars have finished resting, remove the rim and check to see the seal has formed: You should be able to lift the jar by the lid. Any jars that don't seal should be immediately transferred to the refrigerator for storage.

Honey Peaches

To preserve the flavor of peaches, pack them at home in sweet honey syrup. You'll be grateful midwinter when some soft, syrupy peaches stirred into vanilla yogurt brighten your mood and your palate!

MAKES 4 PINTS PEACHES

1¼ cups wildflower honey
4 pounds ripe peaches, rinsed and patted dry

1. In a large saucepan, combine the honey with 3 cups water and bring to a simmer. Stir a few times and let it simmer until the honey is dissolved. Remove from the heat and set aside while you prepare the peaches.

2. Bring a second large pot of water to a boil to blanch and peel the peaches. Set a large bowl of ice water next to the stovetop. Halve each peach and remove the pit. Drop the peach halves into the boiling water for 1 minute. Scoop the halves out with a spider or sieve and immediately transfer it to the bowl of ice water. Once the peaches have cooled enough to touch, peel off the skins with your fingers and discard.

3. Start your hot water bath, and sterilize four pint-size jars and their lids and rims.

4. Pack the peeled peach halves, cut-side down, into the sterilized jars. Use a wooden skewer to gently position the peaches so you can pack them as tightly as possible without damaging them.

5. Once the peaches are packed in, place the jars in the sink in case of hot drips. Ladle the honey syrup over them, leaving a ½-inch headspace at the top. Carefully wipe the rims of the jars with a clean kitchen towel. Top each jar with a sterilized lid and rim. Only tighten each jar as much as you can twist with your fingertips; do not force it.

6. If you are not using a canning rack to hold your jars, place a clean kitchen towel on the bottom of the pot so the jars don't touch the bottom. Place the jars carefully in the boiling water, using tongs, and process them for 30 minutes, starting the timer only when the water has returned to a boil. **7.** When the jars are done processing, use the tongs to transfer the jars to a cool, dry place away from direct sunlight and do not disturb for 12 hours. Throughout the day you'll hear the pop-pops of the seals on the jars forming. After the jars have finished resting, remove the rim and check to see the seal has formed: You should be able to lift the jar by the lid. Any jars that don't seal should be immediately transferred to the refrigerator for storage.

Ruby Razz Jam

Rhubarb is my favorite plant in the garden. I incorporate it into everything I make all summer long. This sweet, tart jam means you can even enjoy rhubarb in the winter, too!

MAKES 5 HALF-PINTS JAM

8 cups chopped rhubarb (about 3 pounds)
4 cups granulated sugar
2 tablespoons bottled lemon juice
3 pints fresh raspberries, rinsed and patted dry

1. Place the rhubarb, sugar, and lemon juice in a large mixing bowl and toss to coat. Cover the bowl and chill it in the refrigerator for at least 8 hours, or up to 12, stirring occasionally.
2. Place a ceramic plate in the freezer. Start your hot water bath, and sterilize five half-pint jars and their lids and rims.
3. Pour the rhubarb mixture into a heavy-bottomed stockpot or Dutch oven, bring it to a simmer over medium heat, and stir until the sugar dissolves. Then raise the heat to high and boil it for 5 minutes, using a long-handled spoon to stir the mixture as it thickens. Add the raspberries, lower the heat to medium-high so the jam maintains a gentle boil, and cook, stirring, for 8 to 10 more minutes. As you stir the raspberries and rhubarb will break down into small, tender pieces.
4. To test whether the jam is done, drop a teaspoonful on the chilled plate. Draw a quick line through it with your fingertip. If the line stays for a few seconds before filling back in, it is ready. If there is no trace of the line, continue to stew the jam for 2 more minutes before repeating this process.
5. Place the sterilized jars in the sink in case of hot drips. Ladle the jam into them, leaving a ½-inch headspace at the top. Carefully wipe the rims of the jars with a clean kitchen towel. Top each jar with a sterilized lid and rim. Only tighten each jar as much as you can twist with your fingertips; do not force it.
6. If you are not using a canning rack to hold your jars, place a clean kitchen towel on the bottom of the pot so the jars don't touch the bottom. Place the jars carefully in the boiling water, using tongs, and process them for 10 minutes, starting the timer only when the water has returned to a boil.

7. When the jars are done processing, use the tongs to transfer the jars to a cool, dry place away from direct sunlight and do not disturb for 12 hours. Throughout the day you'll hear the pop-pops of the seals on the jars forming. After the jars have finished resting, remove the rim and check to see the seal has formed: You should be able to lift the jar by the lid. Any jars that don't seal should be immediately transferred to the refrigerator for storage.

Pickled Jalapeños

If your jalapeños proliferate as quickly as mine do, throw together this simple pickle to use them up. Pickled jalapeños last for up to a year and can be used in everything from guacamole and quesadillas to mixing into chicken casseroles and spreading over nachos.

MAKES 4 HALF-PINTS JALAPEÑOS

1 pound fresh green jalapeño peppers

2 cups cider vinegar

3 tablespoons granulated sugar

4 tablespoons kosher salt

2 garlic cloves, peeled

2 tablespoons whole black peppercorns

1. Remove and discard the stems and slice the jalapeños into ⅛-inch-thick slices. If you want your jalapeños less spicy, remove the seeds. Place the slices in a small bowl next to the stovetop.

2. Start your hot water bath, and sterilize four half-pint jars and their lids and rims.

3. In a large, nonreactive saucepan, bring the vinegar, 2 cups of water, sugar, salt, garlic, and peppercorns to a boil for 1 minute. Scrape the jalapeños into the brine, lower the heat to medium-low, and cook for 5 minutes.

4. Place the sterilized jars in the sink in case of hot drips. Ladle the jalapeños and brine into them, leaving a ½-inch headspace at the top. Carefully wipe the rims of the jars with a clean kitchen towel. Top each jar with a sterilized lid and rim. Only tighten each jar as much as you can twist with your fingertips; do not force it.

5. If you are not using a canning rack to hold your jars, place a clean kitchen towel on the bottom of the pot so the jars don't touch the bottom. Place the jars carefully in the boiling water using tongs and process them for 10 minutes, starting the timer only when the water has returned to a boil.

6. When the jalapeños are done processing, use the tongs to transfer the jars to a cool, dry place away from direct sunlight and do not disturb for 12 hours. Throughout the day you'll hear the pop-pops of the seals on the jars forming. After the jars have finished resting, remove the rim and check to see the seal has formed: You should be able to lift the jar by the lid. Any jars that don't seal should be immediately transferred to the refrigerator for storage.

Blood Orange Bourbon Marmalade

My mother is the marmalade maker in our house and now she has gotten me into it, too. We love making this thick, citrusy spread in winter when blood oranges are in season. I added a little bourbon to it one year to counter the sweetness of the oranges, and now we love dark, smoky notes it lends to the jam.

MAKES 3 PINTS MARMALADE

1½ pounds blood oranges
4 cups granulated sugar
⅓ cup bourbon or bourbon extract

1. Use a mandoline to cut the oranges into horizontal slices ⅛ inch thick. Keep them stacked in the shape of the orange and cut the slices into quarters. Place them in a 5-quart stockpot with 4 cups of water. Cover the pot and let it sit in a cool, dry place for 24 hours.

2. Place a ceramic plate in the freezer. Start your hot water bath, and sterilize three pint-size jars and their lids and rims.

3. Bring the orange mixture to a boil over a medium-high heat, then lower the temperature to medium-low and simmer until the mixture is reduced to 4 cups, about 45 minutes. Stir in the sugar and bring the mixture back to a boil over medium-high heat, skimming off any foam, for about 15 minutes.

4. To test for doneness, drop a tablespoon of marmalade on the chilled plate and drag your finger through it. If it leaves a trail it is finished. If not, it still needs to simmer more.

5. Pour in the bourbon and stir well. Place the sterilized jars in the sink in case of hot drips. Ladle the marmalade into them leaving a ½-inch headspace at the top. Carefully wipe the rims of the jars with a clean kitchen towel. Top each jar with a sterilized lid and rim. Only tighten each jar as much as you can twist with your fingertips; do not force it.

6. If you are not using a canning rack to hold your jars, place a clean kitchen towel on the bottom of the pot so the jars don't touch the bottom. Place the jars carefully in the boiling water, using tongs, and process them for 10 minutes, starting the timer only when the water has returned to a boil.

7. When the jars are done processing, use the tongs to transfer the jars to a cool, dry place away from direct sunlight and do not disturb for 12 hours. Throughout the day you'll hear the pop-pops of the seals on the jars forming. After the jars have finished resting, remove the rim and check to see the seal has formed. You should be able to lift the jar by the lid. Any jars that don't seal should be immediately transferred to the refrigerator for storage.

Boozy Bourbon Cherries

Make these in the summer when cherries are in season and save them to give out all year. This is a great gift for cocktail lovers. It is a snap to make and the sharp boozy cherries taste so delicious in Manhattans, stirred into seltzer, or drizzled over a slice of cheesecake!

MAKES ABOUT 6 HALF-PINTS CHERRIES

6 cups bourbon

1 cup granulated sugar

6 cups fresh sweet cherries, washed, pitted, and stems removed

1. In a saucepan over low heat, bring the bourbon and sugar to a simmer. Continue to simmer until the sugar dissolves. Turn off the heat and allow the syrup to cool for at least 15 minutes.

2. Meanwhile, pack 1 cup of cherries into a clean half-pint jar. Position a funnel over the mouth of the first jar and pour the syrup over the cherries until it covers the fruit. Use a clean wooden spoon to push the fruit down and make sure it is submerged, taking care not to crush the cherries. Repeat this process with five additional half-pint jars. You should have enough syrup to fill each one. If there is any leftover syrup, use it to make a cocktail.

3. Seal the jars with their lids and place the cherries in the refrigerator. They should be used within 1 year.

Note As the cherries macerate in the bourbon syrup, they will shrink in size. This is normal and they will still taste delicious.

Berry Harvest Recipes

Every summer I take Daphne and her friend Emma strawberry picking. They get such a kick out of picking and eating the fresh fruit straight from the source, remarking on the intense redness and sweetness of the berries compared to the pale-centered fruit they find in the shops in midwinter. In under an hour, we usually come home with more than a dozen pounds!

Your Berry-Picking Strategy

PLAN Once picked, most berries only stay fresh for a day or two, so plan what you want to make with them before you go. Having essential ingredients, sterilized jars, or even premade piecrusts on hand when you return with your fresh berries will save you a lot of time. This way you can wash and hull the berries and get straight to cooking. Set aside at least two pounds of berries to freeze for winter.

RESEARCH Look up the pick-your-own, also called U-Pick, berry crops in your area. In spring and summer around the United States you can typically find strawberries, raspberries, and blueberries. On occasion you also find farms with blackberry or huckleberry bushes.

GET CHILDREN INVOLVED Berry picking is a great activity for everyone from toddlers to older children. Bring a little sand pail or something they can easily fill up while you concentrate on the heavier basket. Show them how the berries are weighed at the counter after you pick. Keep a little record of how much they pick each year. I'll bet the weight gets heavier each year!

Berry Syrups

I first made strawberry syrup after I read about it in Marisa McClellan's book Food in Jars: Preserving in Small Batches Year-Round. *The recipe is so simple and the syrup is such a treat to have around all summer. Apply her syrup-making method to any of the berries in your harvest and you'll have a fridge full of strawberry, raspberry, and blueberry syrups. Use them all summer long for stirring into sparkling water to make berry soda, drizzling over ice cream, flavoring lemonade, and pouring over pancakes (thicken them with cornstarch to make a slow-moving syrupy topping).*

MAKES 2 PINTS SYRUP

2 pints raspberries, strawberries, or blueberries
2 cups granulated sugar

1. Place the berries and 3 cups of water in a large saucepan and bring the mixture to a boil for 1 minute. Lower the heat and simmer until the berries are soft and leached of most of their color, about 15 minutes.

2. Start your hot water bath, and sterilize two pint-size jars and their lids and rims.

3. Position a fine-mesh sieve lined with one layer of cheesecloth over a large mixing bowl. Pour the berries and their juice into the sieve and strain it undisturbed for about 15 minutes. Do not force or press the berries while they are draining.

4. Discard the solids, return the strained liquid to the pot, and add the sugar. Bring it to boil and skim away any foam that appears on top. Boil until all the sugar has dissolved and the liquid is clear.

5. Remove the pot from the heat and place your sterilized jars in the sink in case of hot drips. Pour the hot syrup into the jars and close with the lids and rims. Store in the refrigerator for up to 6 months.

Tip If you are using strawberries, they should be hulled and chopped. If you are using raspberries or blueberries, lightly mash them with a potato masher so they soften.

Note I usually don't preserve this syrup because we use it so quickly. If you want to seal it, then follow the water bath instructions on page 92 and process for 10 minutes, starting the timer only when the water has returned to a boil.

Easy Blender Buttermilk Crèpes *with* Berries

As soon as Daphne was old enough to stand at the stovetop with me, I taught her how to make crepes. Hers were somewhat thick at first, but the older she gets the more adept she becomes. Get your children to make these with you. Then they can fold them up with whipped cream and berries for breakfast or a rich dessert. Last summer we gave this recipe to Emma and now she likes to make them, too!

MAKES 10 CRÈPES

1 cup strawberries, washed, hulled, and chopped

2 teaspoons granulated sugar

1 cup unbleached all-purpose flour

1 tablespoon granulated sugar

¼ teaspoon kosher salt

1½ cups buttermilk

4 large eggs

3 tablespoons unsalted butter, melted and slightly cooled, plus more butter for pan

Whipped cream, for serving

1. Combine the berries and sugar in a small bowl and stir well. Allow the berries to macerate while you make the crepes.

2. Combine the flour, sugar, salt, buttermilk, eggs, and 3 tablespoons of butter in a blender and blitz until completely smooth and a little frothy on top, about 45 seconds.

3. Place a 9-inch nonstick skillet over medium heat and melt a teaspoon of butter in it so that it just coats the entire pan. When the pan is hot, pour in ⅓ cup of the batter and gently tilt the pan in a circle so that the batter almost entirely covers the bottom. Allow the crème to cook for 2 to 3 minutes, or until you can just lift the edge with a rubber spatula and the bottom is golden brown. Slide the spatula underneath the crêpe to lift the edge away from the pan. Pinch the edge with your fingers and flip the crêpe completely. Cook the second side for about 1 minute.

4. Remove the crêpe from the pan and immediately fill it with some of the berry mixture. Fold the crêpe once or twice and serve with whipped cream. Repeat, using more butter for the pan as needed.

More Sweet Filling Ideas Sliced bananas, dollops of chocolate nut spread (such as Nutella), chocolate chips, softened sliced apples with cinnamon, pastry cream.

Berry Spinach Salad

Berries give wonderful dimension to dark green salads. Reserve this particular salad recipe for the days you pick them fresh from the field. Throw this together for a side dish or a colorful main course with grilled shrimp on top.

MAKES 4 TO 6 SERVINGS

4 cups fresh baby spinach, stems removed and coarsely chopped

½ cup packed fresh mint leaves

1 cup fresh blueberries, washed and patted dry

1 cup fresh strawberries, washed, hulled, and sliced

½ cup fresh feta cheese, crumbled

½ cup walnuts, lightly toasted

2 tablespoons granulated sugar

5 tablespoons buttermilk

1 tablespoon poppy seeds

1 tablespoon white wine vinegar

1. In a large bowl, toss the spinach and mint leaves. Add the blueberries and strawberries and toss well. Top the salad with the crumbled feta and walnuts.

2. Combine the sugar, buttermilk, poppy seeds, and vinegar in a mason jar or container with a lid and shake vigorously. Pour the dressing into the salad bowl and toss well.

Blueberry Maple Syrup

This recipe combines the two best pancake toppings—fresh fruit and maple syrup—into one amazing syrup you'll want to pour over everything from pancakes to cheesecake!

MAKES 3 CUPS SYRUP

2 cups blueberries, washed and thoroughly patted dry

2 cups pure Grade A maple syrup

1. In a small saucepan, combine the berries and syrup over medium-low heat. Heat the mixture for about 5 minutes, allowing it to bubble slowly, stirring occasionally. The berries will just begin to collapse, but they shouldn't fully burst.

2. Remove the mixture from the stovetop and allow it to cool for 5 minutes. Then place a funnel over a couple of glass jars with lids and pour in the maple syrup mixture. Allow the syrup to cool completely before sealing with the lids.

Note Hulled and chopped strawberries, blackberries, or cranberries would also work beautifully in this recipe.

Blueberry Snack Cake

My friend Barbara introduced me to Laurie Colwin's Nantucket Cranberry Pie recipe years ago. Since then, I have adapted it many times over using all kinds of fruit. In June, I make this with a mix of our berry harvest. It is the best kind of spongy sweet cake for summer that can be made with nearly anything you have on hand. It comes together in one bowl and begs to be snacked on all day long.

MAKES 1 (10-INCH) CAKE

6 tablespoons unsalted butter, melted, plus
    more for pan

2 cups fresh blueberries

1½ cups granulated sugar, divided

2 large eggs, at room temperature

1 cup unbleached all-purpose flour

1 teaspoon almond extract

Confectioners' sugar for dusting

1. Preheat the oven to 350°F. Butter the bottom and sides of a 10-inch pie plate.

2. Scatter the fresh blueberries and ½ cup of the granulated sugar on the bottom of the pie plate and set aside.

3. In a large bowl, whisk together the remaining cup of granulated sugar, and the eggs, melted butter, flour, and almond extract until smooth. Pour the mixture over the berries and smooth the top with a spatula.

4. Bake the cake for 35 to 40 minutes, or until the edges are golden brown and the center is set. Remove from the oven and allow to cool completely. Lightly dust the top with confectioners' sugar, slice, and serve.

Father's Day

On Father's Day, give Dad a day to remember with a roster of his favorite foods. Start the day with an awesome Bloody Mary and meaty egg wrap, and finish it with a juicy burger, cheesy potatoes, and a cold beer. With some simple planning, everything will come together in a snap and you can all spend the day with him, not in the kitchen.

Spicy Chorizo Breakfast Wraps

My kids' Uncle Will came up with this awesome breakfast recipe during his days as a bachelor. It is the perfect man food to kick off Father's Day. It contains enough protein to carry anyone through to lunch, and just enough cheese and egg to combat any trace of a hangover lingering from the previous evening.

MAKES 4 WRAPS

4 large eggs

½ teaspoon ancho chili powder

½ teaspoon garlic salt

2 fresh spicy chorizo sausages (about 6.5 ounces total), casings removed

6 slices bacon, cut into 1-inch pieces

1 heaping cup frozen hash browns

4 large flour tortillas

½ cup shredded Mexican cheese blend

1. In a small bowl, whisk together the eggs, chili powder, and garlic salt and set aside.

2. In a large, nonstick skillet over medium-low heat, combine the sausage and bacon. Use a large wooden spoon to break up the sausage into small pieces. Stir the mixture a few times to ensure the meats cook evenly.

3. After the meat has cooked for about 3 minutes, pour off some of the grease so there is 1 tablespoon remaining, and add the frozen hash browns to the pan. Stir them into the meat and continue cooking everything until the meats are cooked through and the hash browns are hot and crispy, about 5 more minutes.

4. Pour the egg mixture into the pan and use a wooden spoon to cook the eggs until just set, about 1 minute. Turn them once to finish cooking and remove the pan from the heat so they don't overcook.

5. While you are cooking the eggs, wrap the tortillas in a paper towels and microwave them for 10 seconds at 50% power, just enough to warm them and make them flexible. Divide the mixture evenly among the four tortillas and sprinkle with cheese. Tuck in the ends, roll them up, and slice in half. Serve!

Bloody Marys

I used to buy expensive Bloody Mary mixes until I learned how easy it is to make them at home. We make this cocktail a lot, but it is especially fitting on Father's Day. If you like spice, feel free to add more hot sauce and pepper to suit your taste.

MAKES 4 SERVINGS

3 large limes, divided

Celery salt for rimming

4 cups tomato juice

1½ cups good-quality vodka

1 tablespoon Worcestershire sauce

2 teaspoons hot sauce, or more to taste

Freshly cracked black pepper

4 celery stalks, for garnish

1. Cut one of the limes into four wedges and rub the juicy part around the rims of four glasses. Dip the rims in the celery salt to coat.

2. Place the juice of the second lime (about 1 tablespoon), tomato juice, vodka, hot sauce, and Worcestershire in a pitcher and stir well.

3. Fill each glass with ice and divide the Bloody Marys among them. Sprinkle each cocktail with a pinch of black pepper. Cut the remaining lime into wedges and garnish each cocktail with a wedge of lime and a celery stalk.

Dad Burgers

There is nothing Duncan loves more than a great Father's Day meal fresh from the grill. We've experimented with many kinds of homemade burgers and this is the best. To give the meat a kick, we add a few ground chipotle peppers. If you want the patties extra spicy, add another pepper or two and keep some napkins nearby for wiping your brow.

MAKES 6 LARGE PATTIES

1¾ pounds ground beef (80% lean)

2 tablespoons Worcestershire sauce

2 canned chipotles in adobo, very finely chopped

2 teaspoons onion powder

2 teaspoons kosher salt

6 thick slices sharp Cheddar cheese

6 hamburger buns

Lettuce for topping

Tomato slices for topping

1. Light a charcoal grill and heat to medium-high heat.

2. Place the beef in a large bowl and make a well in the middle. Add the Worcestershire, chopped chipotles, onion powder, and kosher salt to the well. Use clean hands to gently distribute these ingredients throughout the beef.

3. Shape the meat into six equal-size burger patties. Do not pack the meat too tightly or the burgers will be tough.

4. Grill the burgers over direct heat for about 6 minutes, then turn them and cook for 3 to 4 minutes longer, topping the burgers with the cheese for the last 2 minutes, to achieve medium doneness. For medium well- or well-done burgers, continue to cook for a few minutes more, until the desired doneness is achieved.

5. Carefully remove the burgers from the grill and transfer them to the buns, topping each with lettuce and tomato. Serve.

Wedge Salad

Keep it simple when it comes to salads for Dad. There is nothing quite like a wedge salad with crisp lettuce and rich blue cheese, sprinkled with bacon and tomatoes. If you are in the mood for a lighter meal, this can serve as an entrée.

MAKES 6 SERVINGS

1 tablespoon olive oil

8 ounces slab bacon, cut into ½-inch cubes

1 cup mayonnaise

¾ cup sour cream

2 teaspoons Worcestershire sauce

1 garlic clove, finely chopped

1 teaspoon kosher salt

4 ounces crumbled blue cheese

3 hearts of romaine

1 cup cherry tomatoes, washed and halved

1. Heat the olive oil to a large skillet over medium heat. Add the bacon and cook until golden brown and crispy, about 10 minutes. Transfer the bacon to a paper towel–lined plate and allow to cool.

2. Whisk together the mayonnaise and sour cream together in small bowl, then stir in the Worcestershire, garlic, and salt until well combined. Fold in the crumbled blue cheese.

3. Remove any wilted outer leaves from the hearts of romaine and cut each heart in half lengthwise. Set the halves on six plates and drizzle 1 to 2 tablespoons of the dressing over each wedge. Sprinkle each with the cooked bacon and halved cherry tomatoes. Serve.

Sour Cream & Chive Potato Skins

When I was pregnant with Garner, I could chow down a plate of these just as easily as my husband did. The salty crisp potatoes with the tangy sour cream and chives were my pregnancy craving's dream come true! They are perfect for Father's Day because they are truly hearty man food and pair perfectly with burgers.

MAKES 6 SERVINGS

6 medium-size baking potatoes, well scrubbed

Olive oil

1 cup sour cream

½ cup mayonnaise

1 garlic clove, finely chopped

1 tablespoon fresh parsley, finely chopped

1 tablespoon fresh chives, plus more for garnish

1 teaspoon kosher salt

½ teaspoon freshly cracked black pepper

1. Preheat the oven to 400°F. Prick each potato a few times with a fork and rub the skins all over with olive oil. Place them directly on the top oven rack with a baking sheet lined with parchment paper on the bottom rack to catch any drippings. Bake for 1 hour.

2. While the potatoes are baking, combine the sour cream, mayonnaise, garlic, parsley, chives, salt, and pepper in a bowl. Taste the mixture and add another pinch of salt if needed. Set aside.

3. When the potatoes are done baking, allow them to cool until they are comfortable to handle, about 30 minutes. Cut them in half and scoop out the insides, leaving a ¼-inch layer of flesh on the potato skin. Rub each half all over with more olive oil and place skin-side up in an ovenproof baking dish. Sprinkle the potatoes with a little kosher salt and bake for 10 minutes. Then remove the dish from the oven, flip the potatoes to skin-side down, and bake for an additional 10 minutes, or until the edges are browned and crispy.

4. Remove the potatoes from the baking dish and fill each with a dollop of the dressing. Garnish each with chives and serve.

Note There will be dressing left over. Save it to serve with cut-up vegetables or chips the next day!

Guinness Bundt Cake

Duncan isn't usually a chocolate fanatic like me, but he loves this rich chocolate cake. The beer gives it smooth, creamy undertones and a velvety, melt-in-your-mouth texture.

MAKES 1 BUNDT CAKE

FOR THE CAKE

8 ounces (2 sticks) unsalted butter, at room temperature, plus more for pan

⅔ cup Dutch-processed cocoa powder, plus more for dusting the pan

1 cup stout beer, Guinness preferred

1 cup granulated sugar

1 teaspoon kosher salt

2 cups unbleached all-purpose flour

1¼ teaspoons baking soda

2 large eggs, at room temperature

½ cup sour cream, at room temperature

FOR THE GLAZE

4 ounces bittersweet chocolate, coarsely chopped

½ cup heavy whipping cream

1 tablespoon light corn syrup

2 tablespoons granulated sugar

1. Preheat the oven to 350°F. Butter the inside of a 9½-inch Bundt pan and dust with cocoa powder. Set aside.

2. In a heavy-bottomed saucepan, heat the butter, cocoa powder, beer, and sugar over medium heat, until the butter has completely melted and the sugar is dissolved. Whisk the mixture until all the ingredients are smooth. Remove from the heat and allow to cool for 5 minutes.

3. While the beer mixture is cooling, with an electric mixer fitted with the paddle attachment, whisk together the salt, flour, and baking soda on low speed in a large bowl. Add the cooled beer mixture and beat for 1 minute on medium speed. Add the eggs and sour cream and beat for 2 minutes on medium speed, stopping to scrape down the sides of the bowl as needed.

4. Pour the batter into the prepared pan and bake for 45 to 50 minutes, or until a cake tester comes out clean. Let cool the cake in the pan for 10 minutes, then turn it out onto a cooling rack to cool completely.

5. Once the cake is at room temperature, prepare the glaze: Place the chopped chocolate and cream in a heatproof bowl and microwave at 50% power at 30-second intervals until the chocolate has melted. Stir together until smooth. Stir in the corn syrup and sugar until the sugar has completely dissolved. Drizzle the cooled cake with the glaze and serve.

Beach Picnic

Between living so close to the ocean in Connecticut and growing up on Lake Otsego in Cooperstown, beach picnics have always been a regular part of my life. When packing for the beach, keep it simple and light. Handheld sandwiches, lots of fruit, and ice-cold drinks are all you need to sustain your family during a hot day in the sun.

Your Beach Picnic Strategy

FOOD Picnic food must transport well. Skip foods that melt or turn to mush easily. Concentrate on packing foods that can stand up to the hot summer sun and won't be ruined if a little sand gets on your plate.

GEAR Use an airtight insulated cooler layered with ice packs to keep food cold. For additional cooling, fill stainless-steel water bottles with lots of ice water and nestle them among the food. Pack an old cotton quilt or blanket for sitting. Don't forget to bring a garbage bag to carry off any remnants from your meal.

BEACH SANDWICHES

These sandwiches are hearty enough to satisfy you after a busy morning at the beach and are enhanced by bright sunshine and salty air. Keep these three in heavy rotation all summer long and you'll always have an awesome picnic. To keep them cool before eating, wrap the sandwiches in aluminum foil and place them directly on top of the ice packs lining the bottom of the cooler. Each baguette makes three sandwiches.

CHICKEN, MOZZARELLA, TOMATO, & BASIL Slice one large baguette that is about 24 inches in length into three equal 8-inch sections. Slice each section in half horizontally and drizzle one side with 2 teaspoons of balsamic vinegar whisked together with 1 tablespoon of olive oil. Top with ½ cup of shredded cooked chicken, four ¼-inch-thick slices of mozzarella cheese, four thick slices of ripe tomato, and six coarsely chopped basil leaves. Slice and serve.

ARUGULA & PROSCIUTTO WITH FIG JAM Slice one baguette that is about 24 inches in length into three equal 8-inch sections. Slice each section in half horizontally and spread one side with 2 tablespoons of fig jam. Top with ½ cup of packed baby arugula, and three slices of prosciutto. Slice and serve.

TURKEY, BRIE, & MANGO CHUTNEY Slice one large baguette that is about 24 inches in length into three equal 8-inch sections. Slice each section in half horizontally and layer on four or five thin slices fresh roast turkey. Top with 2 tablespoons of mango chutney (Major Grey's preferred) and three thin slices of Brie cheese. Slice and serve.

Variation For a change from baguettes—and plain old PB&J—spread 1 tablespoon of almond butter on one slice of soft whole wheat bread and sprinkle it with the tiniest pinch of sea salt. Spread another slice of bread with your fruit jam of choice. Press the bread slices together. Slice and serve. Makes one sandwich.

Watermelon Fruit Skewers

Cold fresh watermelon is, hands-down, the best picnic sweet treat. You can make these skewers before you head to the beach. They are easier to eat than watermelon wedges and there is no rind left over to dispose of. You can also add whatever chopped fruit you have on hand.

MAKES 10 TO 12 (10-INCH) SKEWERS

1½ to 2 pounds watermelon, cut into 2-inch chunks

1 pint strawberries, washed and hulled

1 large honeydew melon, cut into 2-inch chunks

1 bunch green grapes, washed

1. Assemble each 10-inch skewer by arranging the fruit in the following pattern two times: watermelon chunk, strawberry, honeydew chunk, green grape.

Tip Place the skewers in a long, shallow plastic container with a lid. Pop the container in the freezer until you are ready to leave for the beach. The fruit will thaw but still be cool by the time you are ready to eat.

Salted Caramel Brownies

Brownies are the best way to cap off a beach picnic with rich, fudgy bang. Here, we lend a new twist to an old favorite with a dollop of salted caramel sauce.

MAKES 1 (13 X 9-INCH) PAN

- 8 ounces (2 sticks) unsalted butter, plus more for pan
- 4 ounces semisweet chocolate, coarsely chopped
- 1½ cups granulated sugar
- 4 large eggs, at room temperature, lightly beaten
- 1 teaspoon pure vanilla extract
- 1 cup unbleached all-purpose flour
- ½ teaspoon kosher salt
- ¼ cup salted caramel sauce (or ¼ cup caramel sauce with 1 teaspoon fine sea salt stirred in)

1. Preheat the oven to 350°F. Butter the inside of a 13 x 9 x 2-inch pan and set aside.

2. Place the butter and chocolate in a microwave-safe bowl and melt on high in 30-second bursts until the butter is melted. Stir together until smooth and glossy. Stir in the sugar, followed by the eggs and vanilla, until smooth. Fold in the flour and salt until the flour is just incorporated and no longer visible.

3. Pour the batter into the prepared pan. Drizzle the caramel sauce over the batter. Use a butter knife to lightly swirl the caramel sauce into the batter. Do not overstir because you want the caramel to make visible streaks in the brownies.

4. Bake for 35 to 40 minutes, or just until a cake tester comes out clean and the top is set. Allow the brownies to cool in the pan for at least an hour; they will firm up as they cool. Slice and serve.

Ladies' Lunch

CRUDITÉS *with* GREEN GODDESS DIP   117

—

MINI SPICED TURKEY SLIDERS   118

—

ZUCCHINI TART   119

—

ARUGULA SALAD *with* HERBED PAN-ROASTED TOMATOES   120

—

ASPARAGUS & COUSCOUS SALAD   121

—

APRICOT ALMOND SHORTBREAD SQUARES   122

—

LAVENDER BISCOTTI   123

A ladies' luncheon in the garden should be casual and fun. Ask everyone to wear sundresses and flip-flops instead of formal hats and heels. Keep the fare light and the conversation lively by focusing on a vegetable-centric menu with some spiced turkey sliders for protein and a sweet nibble at the end.

Crudités *with* Green Goddess Dip

When summer vegetables are at their peak, they practically beg to be eaten raw. They are so full of flavor it is almost a crime not to. To accompany your veggies, make this bright green dip full of fresh herbs from the garden.

MAKES 6 TO 8 SERVINGS

FOR THE DIP

1½ cups packed fresh parsley leaves

½ cup packed fresh basil leaves

2 tablespoons light packed fresh tarragon leaves

4 scallions, roughly chopped (white and light green parts only)

1 cup low-fat sour cream

⅔ cup low-fat mayonnaise

1 teaspoon freshly squeezed lemon juice

1 teaspoon kosher salt

¼ teaspoon freshly cracked black pepper

FOR THE VEGETABLES

2 large zucchini, trimmed and cut into 3-inch sticks

4 large carrots, trimmed and cut into 3-inch sticks

1 bunch radishes, washed and thinly sliced

2 red bell peppers, seeded and sliced

1 pint cherry tomatoes, washed and served whole

1. To make the dip: Place the parsley, basil, tarragon, and scallions in the bowl of a food processor and pulse until everything is minced. Add the sour cream, mayonnaise, lemon juice, salt, and pepper and pulse for three or four 10-second bursts, or until the creamy dip forms. You should have about 2 cups.

2. To assemble the platter: Place the fresh vegetables in a decorative arrangement on a large platter with the bright green dip in a bowl in the center.

More Vegetable Crudité Ideas Snap peas, blanched pencil asparagus, green bell peppers, yellow or orange bell peppers, yellow squash, cucumber slices, cauliflower florets.

Mini Spiced Turkey Sliders

Turkey sliders are a fun alternative to heavy summer burgers. They fill you up without feeling like a weight in your stomach. Because tomatoes are always so fresh this time of year, they are my topping of choice, along with a little cheese.

MAKES 8 SLIDERS

1½ pounds fresh ground light turkey meat

2 tablespoons freshly grated Parmesan cheese

2 garlic cloves, minced

1 teaspoon crushed red pepper flakes

½ teaspoon dried basil

½ teaspoon kosher salt

¼ teaspoon freshly cracked black pepper

8 thin slices Gruyère cheese, for serving

8 slider-size buns

Tomato slices for serving

Pickles, lettuce, ketchup, and mustard, for serving (optional)

1. Heat a charcoal or gas grill to medium-high heat.

2. While the grill is heating, lightly mix together the turkey, Parmesan, garlic, red pepper flakes, basil, salt, and black pepper. Divide the mixture into eight equal portions and form them into 1-inch-thick patties.

3. Brush the grill with olive oil and grill the burgers for 4 to 6 minutes total, flipping halfway through, until completely cooked through. About 1 minute before the end of cooking, place a slice of Gruyère on the top of the slider and allow it to melt. Transfer the sliders to the slider buns and top with tomato slices. Serve warm with a spread of toppings, as desired.

Zucchini Tart

This simple tart is like pizza with a sophisticated twist. It is unexpected way to eat zucchini in the summer, a time when there is plenty of squash on hand.

MAKES 6 TO 8 SERVINGS

1 sheet frozen puff pastry, thawed

1 cup coarsely grated Gruyère cheese

1 cup coarsely grated Parmesan cheese

8 ounces herbed goat cheese, at room temperature, crumbled

2 large egg yolks

¼ cup light cream

½ teaspoon kosher salt

1 small zucchini, sliced into ⅛-inch-thick rounds

2 ounces crumbled plain goat cheese

1 tablespoon olive oil

1. Preheat the oven to 400°F. Roll out the puff pastry on a floured surface until ⅛ inch thick and place on a baking sheet lined with parchment paper or a silicone mat. Prick it all over with fork tines and bake it for about 10 minutes, or until golden brown but not fully done. Remove from the oven and allow to cool.

2. While the pastry is baking, whisk together the Gruyère, Parmesan, herbed goat cheese, egg yolks, cream, and salt in a large bowl. Spread this mixture evenly over the cooled pastry, leaving a 1-inch border around the side. Layer the zucchini slices on top of the cheese mixture, allowing them to overlap as necessary.

3. Dot the top of the zucchini with the plain goat cheese, drizzle with olive oil, and bake for about 20 minutes, or until the crust is deep brown but not burned, and the cheese mixture is puffed and set. Allow to cool slightly, cut into squares, and serve.

Arugula Salad *with* Herbed Pan-Roasted Tomatoes

This laid-back salad is wonderful for serving all those delicious tomatoes from the garden. Serve it alongside turkey burgers as a light, summery side.

MAKES 6 TO 8 SERVINGS

¼ cup olive oil

2 garlic cloves, finely chopped

2 cups cherry tomatoes

12 large basil leaves, finely chopped

2 teaspoons fresh thyme leaves

1½ teaspoons kosher salt, divided

8 cups fresh arugula

¼ teaspoon freshly cracked black pepper

2 tablespoons red wine vinegar

¼ teaspoon granulated sugar

1. In a large, wide skillet, heat the olive oil over medium heat and cook the garlic for 1 minute. Then add the tomatoes, basil, thyme, and 1 teaspoon of the salt. Lower the heat to medium-low and cook for 8 to 10 minutes, turning occasionally until the tomatoes collapse but don't burn.

2. While the tomatoes are cooking, place the arugula in a salad bowl and set aside.

3. Fill a mason jar or dressing shaker with pepper, red wine vinegar, sugar, and remaining salt.

4. Remove the tomatoes from the heat. Use a slotted spoon to scatter the cooked tomatoes over the arugula. Drizzle the pan drippings into the jar with the vinegar mixture and shake well to combine. Toss the arugula and tomatoes with the tomato dressing and serve.

Asparagus & Couscous Salad

This salad is lemony, bright, and perfect for setting on your table. Because it is completely mayonnaise-free, it is safe to leave out in the warm weather and serve at room temperature.

MAKES 4 TO 6 SERVINGS

1 (10-ounce) box uncooked plain couscous

12 ounces thin asparagus, trimmed and cut into
  1-inch pieces

1 pint grape tomatoes, halved

1 teaspoon freshly grated lemon zest

1 teaspoon freshly squeezed lemon juice

¼ cup extra-virgin olive oil

1½ tablespoons red wine vinegar

½ teaspoon kosher salt

¼ teaspoon freshly cracked black pepper

4 ounces crumbled feta cheese

1 tablespoon minced fresh parsley

1. Prepare the couscous according to the package instructions, fluff well, and set aside.

2. Meanwhile, bring water to a boil in a wide skillet and add the asparagus. Cook for about 2 minutes, or until the asparagus can easily be speared with a fork, but is not soft. Remove the pan from the heat and drain the asparagus in a colander. Then run the asparagus under very cold tap water, rinsing well, to stop the cooking.

3. Pat the asparagus dry and place in a large bowl. Add the tomatoes and top them with the fluffed couscous.

4. Whisk together the lemon zest and juice, olive oil, vinegar, salt, and pepper. Pour over the couscous slowly, tossing the asparagus mixture as you dress the salad until everything is lightly coated. Toss in the feta and parsley and serve warm or at room temperature.

Apricot Almond Shortbread Squares

At your garden party, serve sweets that are light and fruity. These simple shortbread bites hit all the marks. They are made with fresh, summery jam and can be cut into small bite-size pieces.

MAKES 16 SQUARES

4 ounces (1 stick) unsalted butter, at room temperature

¾ cup granulated sugar

1 teaspoon pure vanilla extract

2¼ cups unbleached all-purpose flour

1 teaspoon kosher salt

12 ounces apricot jam

¾ cup sliced almonds

1. Preheat the oven to 350°F.

2. With an electric mixer and beat the butter and sugar on high speed in a large bowl until fully combined, about 1 minute. Lower the mixer speed to low and beat in the vanilla. Beat in the flour and salt just until the dough comes together and forms a ball.

3. Remove the dough from the bowl and pat three quarters of it into a 9-inch square baking pan, allowing ¼ inch of dough to climb up the sides. Spread the jam onto the dough in the pan, leaving a ⅛-inch border around the edge.

4. Break up the remaining dough into small pieces and use your hands to roll it together with the sliced almonds. Scatter the mixture evenly over the top of the jam. Bake the bars for 45 minutes, or until they are lightly browned and cooked through. Allow the bars to cool in the pan for 1 hour. Use a sharp knife to slice and serve.

Lavender Biscotti

These summery biscotti are perfect for nibbling during late summer afternoons. They are filled with the floral scent of lavender and pair beautifully with a tall glass of iced tea.

MAKES 30 TO 35 BISCOTTI

6 tablespoons unsalted butter, at room temperature

⅔ cup granulated sugar

½ teaspoon kosher salt

2 teaspoons pure vanilla extract

¼ teaspoon almond extract

1½ teaspoons baking powder

2 large eggs

2 teaspoons dried food-grade lavender blossoms

2 cups unbleached all-purpose flour

White sanding sugar

1. Preheat the oven to 350°F. Line a baking sheet with parchment paper or a silicone mat.

2. With an electric mixer fitted with the paddle attachment, beat the butter, granulated sugar, salt, vanilla, almond extract, and baking powder on medium speed in a large bowl until smooth, about 2 minutes. Then beat in the eggs one at a time. Lower the mixer speed to low, and beat in the lavender blossoms and flour until just combined.

3. Transfer the dough to the lined baking sheet and shape it into two smooth loaves that are 9½ inches long, 2 inches wide, and about 1 inch thick. Sprinkle the top of each log with sanding sugar as desired.

4. Bake the dough for 25 minutes, or it just begins to turn golden brown. Remove it from the oven and lower the temperature to 325°F.

5. Transfer the logs to a cutting board to cool slightly. Use a serrated knife to cut the logs into ½-inch-thick slices. Separate the slices so they are evenly distributed on the baking sheet about 1 inch apart. Return them to the oven and allow them to bake for 25 to 30 minutes, or until they are golden brown and dry in the center. Transfer the biscotti to a cooling rack to cool completely. They will continue to harden up as they cool. Store in a closed container at room temperature.

Note For a summery hostess gift, place the biscotti in a cloth-lined basket alongside a selection of tea bags.

Fourth of July

Every year we celebrate the Fourth of July by riding in my dad's Model A Ford in the Springfield Center Parade in Springfield Center, New York. It is rumored to be one of the oldest Independence Day parades in America and recently celebrated its hundredth anniversary. After our outing we have a huge family picnic filled with all sorts of summery foods set out on a long, rustic table. For our family, this is the official start of high summer and we celebrate with an easy feast full of traditional American flavor.

Peach Caprese Salad

This simple salad is great for summer because it is easy to prepare ahead and highlights all the best flavors of the season. The brilliance is in its simplicity; all you need are the ripest summer tomatoes, juiciest summer peaches, a splash of olive oil, and some salt, and you've got summer on a plate.

MAKES 4 TO 6 SERVINGS

3 ripe tomatoes (about 1 pound), halved and sliced ¼ inch thick

2 ripe peaches, pitted and sliced ¼ inch thick

½ pound fresh mozzarella cheese, sliced ¼ inch thick

6 fresh basil leaves

3 tablespoons extra-virgin olive oil

¼ teaspoon fine sea salt

⅛ teaspoon freshly cracked black pepper

1. Select a large platter and arrange the tomatoes, peaches, and mozzarella in a pattern, allowing them to overlap slightly.

2. Tear the basil leaves with your hands and scatter them over the top of the salad. Drizzle the olive oil over everything and sprinkle it with the salt and pepper. Allow to sit for 5 minutes to let the flavors combine before serving.

BURGERS & HOT DOGS ON A GRILL

No matter how inventive I try to get with grilled foods, we always make hamburgers and hot dogs on the Fourth of July. The recipes are simple and mouthwatering; the trick is not to make them too complicated. If available, use a charcoal grill because of the smoky flavor it imparts.

Hamburgers

MAKES 8 HAMBURGERS

3 pounds ground round (85% lean)

2 tablespoons Worcestershire sauce

1 tablespoon garlic powder

2 teaspoons onion powder

1 teaspoon kosher salt

½ teaspoon freshly cracked black pepper

8 thick slices sharp Cheddar cheese

8 soft hamburger buns

Red onion slices, lettuce, tomato slices, and ketchup, for serving

1. Bring the grill to a medium flame.
2. In a large bowl, combine the beef, Worcestershire, garlic powder, onion powder, salt, and pepper with your hands just until fully combined.
3. Form eight equal-size burger patties and grill the burgers over medium heat until cooked to desired doneness, 8 to 10 for medium-rare, 10 to 15 minutes for medium, or 15 to 18 minutes for well-done. About 1 minute before the end of cooking, add a slice of cheese to the top of each burger. Allow the cheese to melt onto the burger. Transfer the burgers to the hamburger buns, top with your desired toppings, and serve.

Hot Dogs

MAKES 8 HOT DOGS

8 organic all-beef hot dogs

8 soft split-top hot-dog buns

Mustard, ketchup, relish, and coleslaw for serving

1. Bring the grill to a medium flame and grill the dogs slowly, about 5 minutes per side, until cooked through. Serve on the hot-dog buns with your desired toppings.

Turtle S'Mores

These s'mores are one of my favorite treats from my childhood. It all came from the idea to use Rolo candy in our favorite campfire dessert, instead of the regular plain chocolate bar. You will love this new twist.

MAKES 8 S'MORES

4 large graham cracker rectangles, split in two

8 chocolate-covered caramels (such as Rolo candies)

8 large marshmallows

1. Take two graham cracker halves and put them on a plate. Then select a branch from a tree that is living. The branch should be green inside or else it might catch fire. (If you have long metal skewers, you can use those.)

2. Spear the marshmallow with the tree branch and hold it over a bonfire or grill. Turn it slowly to allow it to warm through to the core without getting burned on the exterior.

3. When the marshmallow is done, smear it off the stick and right onto one of the graham cracker halves. Top it with a candy and close it with a second graham cracker. Make additional s'mores with the remaining ingredients. Eat immediately!

Berry Rhubarb Crisp

For the perfect red, white, and blue dessert, use nature's natural palette. Mix ripe in-season berries and rhubarb, top them with crumbly butter topping, and finish them off with a scoop of vanilla ice cream. It is a sweet and refreshing summer dessert that fits the festive mood.

MAKES 1 (9-INCH-SQUARE) PAN

6 ounces (1½ sticks) cold unsalted butter, cut into small cubes, plus more for pan

2 cups fresh blueberries, washed and patted dry

3 cups fresh raspberries, washed and patted dry

2 cups chopped rhubarb stalks, cut into 1-inch pieces (about 4 stalks)

1 cup granulated sugar

1 teaspoon grated orange zest

1 tablespoon cornstarch

½ cup freshly squeezed lemon juice

1 cup unbleached all-purpose flour

½ cup light brown sugar

1 teaspoon kosher salt

1 cup quick-cooking oats

1. Preheat the oven to 350°F. Butter the bottom and sides of a 9-inch square pan and set aside.

2. Toss the blueberries, raspberries, and rhubarb with the granulated sugar and orange zest in a large bowl. Dissolve the cornstarch in the lemon juice and stir it into the fruit mixture. Pour the fruit into the baking dish and use a spatula to even out the top.

3. With an electric mixer fitted with the paddle attachment, combine the flour, brown sugar, salt, and oats at low speed in a large bowl. Slowly add the butter. Beat just until the mixture forms small crumbs, about 4 minutes.

4. Pat the crumb mixture on top of the fruit, going all the way to the edge of the pan. Place the baking dish on top of a baking sheet lined with parchment and bake it for 50 to 55 minutes, or until the fruit is hot and bubbly and the top is golden brown. Allow to cool slightly before serving with vanilla ice cream.

Campfire Cooking

Most of my camping knowledge is based on what I learned in the Girl Scouts in elementary school. Every so often, our troop used to venture into the woods of upstate New York and spend a night roasting s'mores and singing songs under the stars. Back then, we didn't care much about cooking great food. In fact, I am fairly sure we mostly ate sandwiches our mothers had packed. But these days I am all about cooking interesting food over a campfire. Since our children are young, most of our camping takes place in our backyard or at our local state park. With these simple dishes we still are able to embrace the fun of an outdoor adventure and enjoy a little family time off the grid.

TOOLS FOR CAMPFIRE COOKING

- Swiss Army knife
- Bottle opener with corkscrew
- Plastic cutting board with knife
- Tongs
- Wooden spoon
- Stainless-steel spatula
- Camping pot for water

- Camping skillet
- Stainless-steel seating utensils
- Aluminum foil
- Plastic pail for washing dishes
- Biodegradable soap
- Cotton kitchen towel
- Wooden clothespins for hanging towels to dry

Your Campfire Cooking Strategy

PLANNING Before going camping, sit down and thoroughly plan your menu. Then follow it with a list of ingredients. Take into consideration what will last in your cooler, whether you will have refrigeration, and how you'll access clean water for drinking and cooking. Try to plan portions so there won't be leftovers.

EASY CLEANUP Foil cooking is terrific for camping because the foil can double as a plate and doesn't need to be washed afterward. Keep things environmentally friendly by using stainless-steel utensils that can be washed and reused easily: They create less trash, which you'll have to pack out of your campsite.

SEASONINGS Instead of packing dozens of herbs, I usually elect to bring a container of salt and a dried herb blend. This seasoning should be versatile enough to season everything from eggs to vegetables to meat. If I need other seasonings, I measure them out ahead of time and label each plastic bag with the dish.

Sausage & Eggs in Foil

This simple breakfast recipe is ideal for waking up on cold mornings. If you don't have sausage patties, you can always use vegetables or a tortilla to line the bottom of the bag.

MAKES 4 SERVINGS

4 frozen precooked sausage patties

4 large eggs, lightly beaten

Salt and freshly cracked black pepper

1 cup shredded Cheddar cheese

1. Allow the fire to burn down to hot coals.

2. Lay out four squares of aluminum foil and roll up the sides to contain the egg when it is added. Place a sausage patty on each foil square. Carefully distribute equal amounts of the beaten eggs over the sausage patties and sprinkle with some salt and pepper. Add a layer of aluminum foil on top and seal the sides well.

3. Use a spatula to slide the foil packets over the coals and allow to cook for at least 15 minutes. Rotate the packet as needed to ensure even cooking. After cooking, open up each packet and sprinkle the cooked egg with ¼ cup of cheese. Allow it to melt and then eat.

Feta in Foil

This recipe is one of our favorite splurges when cooking over an open fire. It is a simple, delicious appetizer that Duncan and I love. Sometimes we make this at home over the grill.

MAKES 4 SERVINGS

8 ounces feta cheese

2 garlic cloves, finely chopped

1 teaspoon Italian seasoning

⅓ cup olive oil

1. Allow the fire to burn down to hot coals.

2. Place the feta in the center of a square of aluminum foil. Add the garlic and Italian seasoning, and top with a second square of foil. Seal the packet on three sides. Drizzle the feta with the olive oil and seal the fourth side.

3. Place the foil packet in the coals and allow it to smolder for 3 to 5 minutes, just long enough to warm it through. Remove from the heat, unwrap, and serve with crackers and bread.

Kristen's Green Beans in Foil

When asked about her campfire cooking favorites, my friend Kristen immediately cited this childhood dish. It takes just two ingredients that are easily transportable and everyone loves it.

MAKES 4 SERVINGS

2 (14-ounce) cans green beans, drained

1 (14-ounce) can Italian-style diced tomatoes, drained

1. Allow the fire to burn down to hot coals.

2. Pour the green beans and tomatoes into the center of a large square of aluminum foil. Cover with a second square and seal around all four edges.

3. Place the packet in the coals and allow it to smolder for 5 to 6 minutes, or long enough to heat the vegetables through. Remove from the heat and carefully unwrap. Serve warm.

Bean Burritos in Foil

Plan on cooking the meat you bring on day one of your camping trip, finishing any leftovers on day two. Vegetarian meals like this one are a good choice for the third day, because the ingredients won't spoil.

MAKES 4 BURRITOS

1 (15-ounce) can refried beans

1 cup cooked Spanish rice (cooked at home)

¾ cup shredded Mexican cheese blend

¼ cup salsa

4 (10-inch) flour tortillas

1. Allow the fire to burn down to hot coals.

2. Divide the beans, rice, cheese, and salsa evenly among the four tortillas. Fold in the sides of each tortilla and roll up to seal. Wrap each tortilla in aluminum foil and tightly seal.

3. Place the burrito over the smoldering coals to the side of the main fire. Rotate four times over the course of 6 minutes to cook evenly. Allow to cool slightly before unwrapping and serving.

Vegetables in Foil

This simple packet of vegetables is always a hit. Depending on what you have available, you can always substitute whatever vegetable you like and season it with your dried herb blend of choice.

MAKES 4 TO 6 SERVINGS

Olive oil

1½ pounds fingerling potatoes, parboiled at home

1 small red onion, cut into wedges

2 green bell peppers, seeded and cut into strips

1 medium-size zucchini, cut into 1-inch pieces

1 yellow summer squash, cut into 1-inch pieces

8 garlic cloves, peeled

1 tablespoon Italian seasoning, divided

4 large pinches of kosher salt

1. Allow the fire to burn down to hot coals.

2. While the fire is burning, place four 12-inch squares of foil on a table and lightly oil each one. Evenly divide the vegetables among the squares. Sprinkle the vegetables with 1 teaspoon of Italian seasoning and a pinch of kosher salt each.

3. Place a second square of foil over each serving of vegetables and roll up the sides, sealing each packet well.

4. Place the packet on top of the coals and cook, turning occasionally with tongs, for 12 to 15 minutes. Remove the packets from the fire and allow them to cool for a minute. Carefully open the sides and serve.

Labor Day Potluck

STEAK *with* CHIMICHURRI   135

—

GARDEN PANZANELLA   136

—

ROSEMARY LEMON CHICKEN SKEWERS   137

—

HERBES DE PROVENCE
ROASTED VEGETABLE & ORZO SALAD   138

—

WATERMELON GOAT CHEESE SALAD   139

—

RHUBARB YOGURT CAKE   140

The beginning of September brings one last chance to celebrate summer. Even if school has already started, we always set aside the weekend to hang out at the beach and have a big bonfire with friends. For our potluck dishes I like to focus on serving whatever is left in our garden. There are usually plenty of vegetables and a few rhubarb stalks. Sometimes there is even some watermelon! No matter what we serve, fresh, refreshing food tastes like summer with each spoonful.

Steak *with* Chimichurri

A fresh grilled steak is perfect for a potluck party. Marinate it early in the day and grill it after everyone arrives. To take it on the go, grill and slice it earlier in the day and serve it at room temperature. Pack some fresh sauce in a container and drizzle it over the platter before serving.

MAKES 4 TO 6 SERVINGS

1½ pounds skirt steak

1 teaspoon kosher salt

2 tablespoons chopped fresh flat-leaf parsley

8 garlic cloves

1 teaspoon freshly squeezed lemon juice

2 tablespoons red wine vinegar

¼ teaspoon dried oregano

½ teaspoon freshly cracked black pepper

¼ teaspoon cayenne pepper

⅔ cup extra-virgin olive oil

1. Place the steak in a large, shallow bowl or plastic container and sprinkle with the kosher salt.

2. Place the remaining ingredients, except for the olive oil, in a food processor and pulse three times, or just until the garlic is minced. Pour in the olive oil and pulse until combined. Reserve half of the sauce and store in the refrigerator.

3. Drizzle the remaining sauce over the steak and turn it once or twice to coat. Place the steak in the refrigerator to marinate for at least 4 hours, or up to 12 hours.

4. To grill the steak, bring the grill to medium heat. Cut the steak into portion-size servings and discard the liquid it has been marinated in. Basting with the reserved sauce, grill each steak for 4 minutes on one side, flip, and grill for 3 to 4 minutes on the second side, or until it has reached the desired doneness. Allow it to rest for 5 minutes before slicing and serving.

Garden Panzanella

This salad is kind of like a deconstructed bruschetta and is perfect for August with the bounty of fresh tomatoes available. Try using pretty heirloom tomatoes in multiple colors for an attractive salad.

MAKES 4 TO 6 SERVINGS

6 ounces stale bread (we use ciabatta), cut into
  1-inch cubes

3 cups packed baby arugula, washed and dried

3 large tomatoes, seeded and chopped

¼ cup thinly sliced red onion

2 ounces feta cheese, crumbled

8 large basil leaves, cut in chiffonade

¼ cup extra-virgin olive oil

1 tablespoon balsamic vinegar

½ teaspoon kosher salt

¼ teaspoon freshly cracked black pepper

1. Preheat the oven to 350°F. Spread the bread evenly on a cookie sheet and bake it for about 10 minutes, turning as needed, until golden brown and crispy on the edges.

2. Meanwhile, in a large bowl toss the arugula, tomatoes, onion, feta, and basil. Set aside.

3. Whisk together the olive oil, vinegar, salt, and pepper.

4. Add the toasted bread to the vegetables, drizzle with the dressing, toss everything together, and serve.

Rosemary Lemon Chicken Skewers

Lemony grilled chicken seasoned with fresh herbs is always a hit. For summer parties, grill these in advance and wrap them in foil to take along. If you are grilling at the beach, bag them in the marinade so they can easily be grilled fresh.

MAKES 4 TO 6 SERVINGS

4 boneless skinless chicken breasts, cut into
  1-inch cubes

Grated zest and juice of 3 medium-size lemons
  (reserve the juiced lemons)

8 garlic cloves, minced

8 (4-inch) rosemary sprigs

1 cup olive oil

1 teaspoon kosher salt

1 teaspoon red pepper flakes

1. Divide the chicken cubes evenly among eight large skewers, leaving a little space between the pieces. Place them in a shallow baking dish or heavy-duty plastic bag.

2. In a large bowl, mix together the lemon zest and juice, garlic, olive oil, salt, and red pepper flakes. Mix well. Add the juiced lemon halves and rosemary. Pour this mixture over the chicken and turn it a few times to evenly coat. Allow the skewered chicken to sit, refrigerated, in the marinade for at least 4 hours, or up to overnight.

3. Bring the grill to medium heat and cook the skewers directly over the heat for 6 to 8 minutes, rotating the skewers as you go to ensure even cooking. Once the chicken is cooked through, transfer it to a platter and allow to cool before serving.

Herbes de Provence Roasted Vegetable & Orzo Salad

This salad is easy to make in advance and is perfect for the potluck table. It is mayonnaise-free and is full of fresh vegetables. Everyone always comments on the unique flavors from the herbes de Provence, one of my favorite spice blends, which I think is highly underappreciated.

MAKES 6 TO 8 SERVINGS

2 large zucchini, cut into a 1-inch pieces

2 red bell peppers, seeded and cut into 1-inch strips

1 small eggplant, cut into 1-inch pieces

3 shallots, peeled and cut into ½-inch slices

1 cup cherry tomatoes

2 teaspoons herbes de Provence

6 whole garlic cloves, peeled

⅔ cup good olive oil, divided

2 teaspoons kosher salt, divided

1 teaspoon freshly cracked black pepper, divided

½ pound orzo

¼ cup freshly squeezed lemon juice (from 1 large lemon)

2 teaspoons freshly grated lemon zest (from 1 large lemon)

10 large basil leaves, coarsely chopped

6 ounces feta, cut into ½-inch cubes

1. Preheat the oven to 425°F. Line a large baking sheet with parchment paper and set aside.

2. Toss the chopped vegetables with the herbes de Provence, garlic, ⅓ cup of the olive oil, 1 teaspoon of the salt, and ½ teaspoon of the pepper in a large bowl. Spread evenly on the prepared baking sheet and roast for 35 to 40 minutes, turning once with a spatula at the halfway point.

3. Meanwhile, cook the orzo according to package instructions and drain. Make the dressing by whisking together the lemon juice, lemon zest, remaining ⅓ cup of olive oil, remaining 1 teaspoon of salt, and remaining ½ teaspoon of pepper in a small bowl. Set aside.

4. When the vegetables have finished cooking, discard the garlic and scrape them into a large serving bowl along with any of the cooking juices. Fold in the cooked orzo and basil. Drizzle the dressing over the top and gently stir it into the salad. Once the vegetables have cooled completely, fold in the feta and serve.

Note This salad also tastes great served at room temperature. Store it in the refrigerator and bring to room temperature prior to serving.

Watermelon Goat Cheese Salad

This is the best fruit salad for summer salad for parties. The high water content of the watermelon makes it so refreshing. Plus, it is great for children. If you are able to find golden watermelon, use it for some of the watermelon portion of this recipe. It looks so pretty mixed in with the traditional red melon.

MAKES 6 TO 8 SERVINGS

- 8 cups cubed (1½-inch cubes) fresh seedless watermelon (from about a 2½ to 3 pound melon)
- 4 ounces plain goat cheese, crumbled
- 8 small basil leaves, cut in chiffonade
- 2 to 3 tablespoons balsamic syrup

1. Spread all the watermelon on a wide, shallow serving platter. Sprinkle the goat cheese and basil on top.

2. If you are preparing this salad in advance, at this point, cover it with plastic wrap and place it in the refrigerator to chill. Right before serving, remove the plastic wrap, drizzle it with the balsamic syrup, and serve.

Note If you can't find balsamic syrup at your local store, make it by combining 1 cup of balsamic vinegar with ½ cup of granulated sugar in a small saucepan. Bring it to a simmer over low heat, until the sugar dissolves and the vinegar reduces and gets syrupy, about 10 minutes. Allow to cool and store in the refrigerator until ready to serve.

Rhubarb Yogurt Cake

I first read about yogurt cake in Elizabeth Bard's food memoir, Lunch in Paris: A Love Story, with Recipes. *I loved her description of this simple, rustic cake that is commonplace in most French kitchens. It is light, yet moist, and the flavor improves and deepens with time. I make it for potlucks all summer long and add a variety of fresh fruit to it, depending on what is available. The size and density make it the perfect portable dessert. Plus, you never have to worry about frosting melting in the sun.*

MAKES 1 (10-INCH) CAKE

1 cup plain full-fat yogurt, well stirred

1 cup granulated sugar

1 teaspoon sea salt

½ teaspoon almond extract

½ cup vegetable oil

2 large eggs

1½ cups unbleached all-purpose flour, plus
   1 tablespoon for the rhubarb

1½ teaspoons baking powder

1 teaspoon baking soda

1½ cups rhubarb stalks, chopped into ½-inch
   pieces

1. Preheat the oven to 350°F. Lightly oil a 10-inch round springform pan and set aside.

2. In a large bowl, whisk together the yogurt, sugar, salt, and almond extract until smooth. Pour in the oil while whisking and continue to whisk until the batter is smooth and the oil is completely incorporated. Crack in the eggs and whisk them until the batter is smooth and thick.

3. Sift the flour, baking powder, and baking soda together in a small bowl. Use a spatula to gently fold the flour mixture into the wet ingredients, stopping just when the flour is no longer visible.

4. Pour the batter into the prepared pan and use the spatula to smooth it on top. Gently toss the rhubarb with the 1 tablespoon of flour and scatter it evenly on top of the cake.

5. Bake the cake for 42 to 45 minutes, or until a cake tester inserted in the center comes out clean and the top springs back lightly when touched. Allow the cake to cook for 10 minutes in the pan. Remove the sides of the springform and allow the cake to cool completely before slicing and serve.

Note This cake can be stored at room temperature, wrapped tightly in plastic wrap.

Fall

When fall arrives, finish your harvest, cut back the plants, and freeze the last of the produce. Dig out the Dutch ovens for stews and send the lobster pot downstairs to take its place. Stand back and admire your pantry full of fresh summer preserves. Stock the freezer with extra loaves of banana bread for lunchboxes and weeknight meals for busy school nights. Sharpened pencils and mugs of hot tea mark the start of a crisp, fresh new season.

GIVE YOUR TABLE CHARACTER Select flowers, produce, and decorative objects in shades of muted oranges, yellows, mossy greens, and browns. Arrange them in wooden bowls and use table linens in earth tones to evoke the subtler palate of fall. Candles in silvery votives or candlesticks with long, tapered candles illuminate the table.

Fall Crafts

How to Freeze Produce

In the fall, freeze as much fresh produce as possible so you can enjoy the flavor of summer all winter long. The process of freezing food takes a small amount of time and is well worth the effort. You can use frozen vegetables to flavor soups, stews, pasta sauces, and more. Fruit can be used for holiday pies, pastries, and breakfast smoothies. Not only is freezing home-grown produce economical, it makes winter meals taste so much better.

Decide whether you are going to freeze the item whole or sliced.

Produce to freeze whole: Strawberries, blueberries, raspberries, blackberries, bananas (peeled), hot peppers, green beans, asparagus, tomatoes, corn kernels cut from the cob.

Produce to freeze sliced, chopped, and pitted: Apples, peaches, plums, nectarines, cherries, bell peppers, melons, mango, winter squash, summer squash, rhubarb, broccoli, cauliflower, peas, leafy greens, carrots.

Produce of choice

Bowl of ice water

Colander

Paper towels

Rimmed baking sheets that can fit in the freezer

Parchment paper

Freezer bags and containers

Permanent markers

Masking tape

1. Wash all of your produce very thoroughly.

2. If you are freezing fruit, corn kernels, tomatoes, leafy greens, and squash, go directly to step 3. All other produce should be blanched before freezing: Bring a large pot of water to a boil and add the produce you are preparing to freeze. Boil for 30 seconds to 3 minutes, or until the vegetables have just barely softened. Plunge the produce into a bowl of ice water until has cooled down. Drain and pat the produce completely dry.

3. Line a rimmed baking sheet with parchment paper and lay out the vegetables in one even layer. Make sure they are completely dry. Place the tray in the freezer and chill until frozen solid, at least 6 hours.

4. Transfer the frozen produce to freezer bags or containers and label clearly, using a permanent marker to write the contents and date on masking tape. Use the heel of your hand squeeze out as much air as possible before sealing. Keep frozen until you are ready to use.

Tip　When freezing vegetables, make a medley of peas, cut carrots, and corn that is ready to be thawed and cooked into one dish at any time.

Tip　If you plan to use certain vegetables for soups, purée them before freezing. This way all you have to do is thaw the purée before cooking.

Note　When frozen produce is thawed, it is mushier than fresh, but it will still taste much better than the fresh out-of-season produce from the store.

How to Freeze Herbs

Toward the end of growing season, freeze as many fresh herbs as possible before the first frost hits. Freezing herbs isn't hard and takes very little time. When they are thawed midwinter, they still taste as bright and intense as the day they were picked. Use them to flavor soups, stew, and sauces whenever a recipe calls for them.

Fresh herbs
Fine-mesh sieve
Clean, dry kitchen towels
Thick resealable freezer bags
Permanent marker

1. Pick the herbs fresh right before you want to freeze them. Small leaves on thin stems, such as thyme, lemon thyme, rosemary, and dill, can be frozen in whole sprigs. Clip them from the bottom and line up the stalks of each kind of herb in one bunch. Larger-leafed herbs, such as basil, parsley, lemon verbena, oregano, mint, and sage, should be stripped from their stalks before freezing.

2. Prepare each herb separately: First, place them in a fine-mesh sieve and rinse them well under cool water. Brush around the leaves to remove any dirt or bugs, taking care not to bruise or tear any leaves. Place the herbs in a single layer between two kitchen towels and gently pat them dry. Line them up in a single layer on a fresh towel to dry completely.

3. Basil should be blanched before freezing. It will turn black in the freezer if it isn't. (Don't do it with other herbs because blanching leaches out the essential oils and flavor). Place the basil leaves in a strainer and pour boiling water over them. Then rinse them off with very cold tap water, place them between two kitchen towels, and pat them dry. Line them up in a single layer on a fresh towel to dry completely.

4. Mark the freezer bags with a permanent marker before packing the herbs. This will help you identify them later in the deep winter when you are pulling out the herbs to add to soup!

5. Line up the dry herbs in one layer in the freezer bag. Use the heel of your hand to press as much air out of the bag as possible before sealing it. Seal and stack the bags on your freezer shelf. As you use up the herbs you might find you'll be able to roll up the bags to save freezer space. To use the frozen herbs, open the freezer bag and remove the leaves or break off the sprigs as needed, press out the air, and reseal and freeze the bag.

Tea Tin Terrariums

When you are no longer able to decorate with fresh flowers, make tiny terrariums to add greenery to your home. These little environments can be made using any kind of small container, such as a miniature fish bowl, wide-mouth canning jar, or leftover tea or cookie tin. Whatever you use, it should be at least 3 inches deep to accommodate the layers of material. Buy succulents at your local grocery store: They are very inexpensive and will last indefinitely, with proper care.

MAKES 1 TERRARIUM

Tea tin or solid small container

Plastic bag

Finely crushed charcoal

Gravel

Cheesecloth

Potting soil

Small succulent plants

Moss (optional)

Rocks, shells, driftwood, or other small ornaments of choice

1. Thoroughly wash and dry the container (I used a tea tin that was about 4 inches wide by 5 inches tall). Cut a plastic bag so that it covers the bottom of the tin and goes 2 inches up the side all around. This will act as a liner so the bottom doesn't rust. Add the charcoal in one even layer about ¼ inch thick, followed by one layer of gravel about ¼ inch thick. Cut the cheesecloth into a square or rectangle that will perfectly cover the gravel and place it on top.

2. Fill the rest of the container with 2 inches of potting soil. Remove a succulent from the container it came in, keeping the root system intact. Dig a small hole in the soil and place the succulent into it, filling the soil back in so the plant stays upright. Pack as many succulents as you'd like into each container. Add moss if you have it, and decorate the container with rocks, shells, or small pieces of driftwood.

3. To care for your terrarium, water the plants enough to keep the soil moist to the touch for at least 2 weeks. After that, water lightly once a week. Succulents need very little water once their root systems are established, and your arrangement should last all winter.

4. Once your terrarium is up and running, you can also add fun decor to it. Last year Daphne dressed hers up with all kinds of plastic toys and a few Lego creations!

Sunflower Seed Butter Bird Feeders

Wildlife never ceases to amaze children. Daphne can spend hours looking at birds flitting about in the trees in our yard. To get the children involved in winterizing the yard, make these cool pinecone bird feeders. When making these with a school class, use nut-free sunflower seed butter. If you don't have allergy concerns, you can use peanut butter instead. Hang them in trees and bushes around your property to encourage winged visitors all winter long.

MAKES 6 LARGE BIRD FEEDERS

6 large pinecones, dried and open

String for hanging

2 (16-ounce) jars sunflower seed butter

3 cups birdseed mix

Shallow mixing bowl

1. Tie a string around each pine cone about 2 inches from the bottom. Be sure to leave enough string to tie it to a branch or porch railing.

2. Use a spoon to spread ½ to ¾ cup of the sunflower seed butter around each pinecone.

3. Pour the birdseed into the mixing bowl and roll the pinecone in it until all the butter is completely coated with seeds. Use your fingers to press them in if necessary.

4. Hang the bird feeder immediately and let the birds enjoy!

Glow-in-the-Dark Jars

We have what seems like hundreds of glass jars in my basement and they never, ever go to waste. They can be used for all sorts of things, including as packaging for dry cookie mixes, as glasses for iced tea, and for baking individual servings of cakes and rolls. In the fall, whip up some simple glow-in-the-dark paint and let children paint jars to serve as Halloween porch lamps and easy nightlights. When entertaining outside, line them up on picnic tables or use them to light pathways from the driveway into the backyard.

Small, disposable bowls

Glow-in-the-dark paints in various colors (usually found at your local hardware store)

White craft glue (such as Elmer's)

Paint stirrer

Long-handled paintbrushes

Clean glass jars

1. Prepare the paint: Place each color of paint in a different small bowl. Add 1 tablespoon of glue per 1 cup of paint. Mix well.

2. Dip a long-handled paintbrush into a mixture and brush it onto the inside and outside of a glass jar, carefully adding other colors with fresh paintbrushes, if desired. Repeat with additional jars. Place them on a clean surface to dry.

3. Once the jars are dry, hold them under a strong lamp or place them in the sun to charge up. At night they will glow brightly!

Baked Crayons

When you clean out your child's crayon bucket, set aside all the worn-out and broken ones to bake into funky marbled crayons. You can make any color you want and they make great gifts for classmates. Package them in tissue paper and decorate them with stickers to give out as holiday gifts.

MAKES 12 MINI MUFFIN-SIZE CRAYONS

12-cup mini muffin tin or similarly sized baking tin
   with fun shapes, such as hearts or stars
Mini muffin paper liners
3 cups crayon pieces in a variety of colors, paper
   labels completely removed
Cooling rack

1. Preheat the oven to 180°F. Line each muffin cup with a paper liner. Set aside.

2. Cut the crayons into pea-size pieces and let the children sort them into any color combination they would like.

3. Fill each muffin cup level to the top with the crayon pieces. Bake for 15 to 20 minutes, or just until the wax melts. Keep a close eye on them so they don't burn.

4. Remove the tin from the oven and allow it to cool completely before popping out the crayons and allowing them to cool on a cooling rack. They should cool for at least 6 hours, or until completely hardened, before using.

Back-to-School Breakfast Ideas

Feeding children hearty breakfasts is key for them to start the day off right. But getting a good meal on the table can be a challenge, especially on any given hectic school morning. It is fine to rely on healthy boxed cereals, but sometimes children need something more substantial. Come up with a game plan to make one or two bigger breakfasts each week. Once you get the routine, you'll see that it is easier than you think.

Eggy French Toast Squares

I came up with this method of making French toast as a way to get a protein-packed breakfast into Daphne before a long day at school. She is not a big fan of eggs but doesn't really notice them if they are used in French toast. This recipe doesn't require any soaking time: just a quick dip and they are in the skillet.

MAKES 4 SERVINGS

4 large eggs

3 tablespoons low-fat milk

Generous pinch of ground cinnamon

½ teaspoon pure vanilla extract

8 slices whole wheat bread

1 tablespoon unsalted butter, plus more as needed

Pure maple syrup, for serving

1. In a large, shallow bowl, whisk together the eggs, milk, and cinnamon until the mixture is completely incorporated and a little bit frothy.

2. Cut the bread slices into four squares or triangles (depending on your child's preference) and place them in the bowl with the egg mixture. Turn the bread slices once or twice until they are completely saturated.

3. Meanwhile, melt the butter over medium heat in a large, nonstick skillet. Add the bread pieces a few at a time without crowding the pan. Cook them for about 4 minutes on one side until golden brown, then flip and cook the other side for an additional 4 minutes. Repeat with the remaining squares, adding more butter as needed. Serve with warm maple syrup.

English Muffin Egg & Bacon Sandwich

When I need my family to start off the morning with extra energy, this is my recipe. It is filling and hits all the right notes with flavors. Hungry children have been known to eat two.

MAKES 4 SANDWICHES

4 English muffins
2 tablespoons unsalted butter, divided
4 large eggs
4 slices Cheddar cheese
8 slices cooked bacon

1. Slice the English muffins and toast until lightly browned. Immediately butter each side with about ½ teaspoon of butter per side.

2. Place the remaining 4 teaspoons of butter in a large skillet and warm it over medium heat. Crack the eggs into the skillet and let the whites set on the bottom. Use a knife to prick the egg yolks so they run out a little over the egg whites.

3. After 15 seconds, when the tops of the eggs start to look dry, top each egg with a slice of cheese and bacon. Scoop each egg onto an English muffin and sandwich shut with the other half. Slice and serve immediately.

Chocolate Chip Cookie Waffles

These waffles taste much like chocolate chip cookies because of the generous dose of vanilla and pinch of brown sugar. When they are hot off the press, sprinkle a few chocolate chips on them and watch them melt to become a sweet chocolate sauce.

MAKES 8 WAFFLES

Vegetable oil for waffle iron, if necessary

2 cups unbleached all-purpose flour

2 tablespoons light brown sugar

1½ teaspoons baking powder

½ teaspoon kosher salt

2 tablespoons butter, melted and cooled

2 large eggs, lightly beaten

1¾ cups whole milk

1 teaspoon pure vanilla extract

½ cup semisweet chocolate chips, for serving

Pure maple syrup, for serving

1. Preheat and grease the waffle iron according to the manufacturer's directions. In a small bowl, whisk together the flour, sugar, baking powder, and salt. Set aside.

2. In a large bowl, whisk together the butter, eggs, milk, and vanilla until completely smooth. Fold in the flour mixture, stirring until just combined. The batter should be fairly runny.

3. Cook the waffles according to the manufacturer's directions, using about ¼ cup of batter per waffle. The second a hot waffle comes off the iron, place it on a plate and sprinkle it with a few chocolate chips. Drizzle each waffle with a little maple syrup and serve!

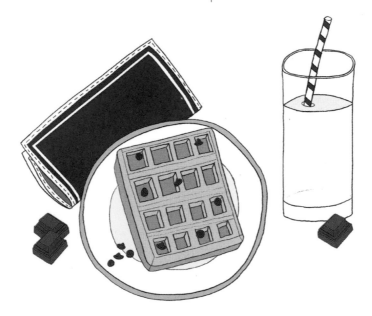

Salted Chocolate Nut Spread Pull-Apart Bread

It did not take long for our family to embrace the pull-apart bread fad. We love how easy it is to make, and how alarmingly easy it is to eat! It is so much fun to pick at over the course of a weekend morning or down a big slice right before it is time to leave for school. We like ours with Nutella, but you could use other chocolate nut spreads or peanut butter or nearly any filling you want.

MAKES 1 LOAF

⅓ cup whole milk, at room temperature

¼ cup lukewarm water

2¼ teaspoons (1 envelope) active dry yeast

3 cups unbleached all-purpose flour

¼ cup granulated sugar

½ teaspoon kosher salt

2 tablespoons unsalted butter, at room temperature

2 large eggs, at room temperature

Vegetable oil for dough bowl

½ cup chocolate nut spread (such as Nutella)

1 teaspoon fine sea salt

2 teaspoons coarse turbinado sugar

1. With an electric mixer fitted with the whisk attachment, mix together the milk, water, yeast, and a small pinch of granulated sugar on low speed in a large bowl until combined. Set aside until it is foamy, about 5 minutes. If foam doesn't form after this time it is likely that the yeast is dead. Toss the mixture and find some fresh yeast.

2. Fit the mixer with the dough hook and add the flour, sugar, salt, butter, and eggs. Knead the mix-ture until it is totally combined and a soft, sticky, and smooth dough forms.

3. Turn off the mixer and transfer the dough to a lightly oiled mixing bowl. Cover it with plastic wrap and let it sit in a warm place out of direct sunlight for 2 hours, or until it has doubled in size.

4. On a lightly floured surface, use a rolling pin to roll the dough into a 12 x 20-inch rectangle. Spread the chocolate nut spread thinly and evenly over the rectangle, leaving a 1-inch border all the way around. Sprinkle the sea salt evenly over the top.

5. Slice the dough vertically with a sharp knife into six equal 12-inch long strips and stack them on top of one another, folding in any long pieces of dough over the top so that the strips are the same size. Cut the stack into six squarish pieces and line up the stacks, cut edges up, in an 8 x 4-inch loaf pan. You may need to squeeze them together to fit. Sprinkle the top with the raw sugar. Cover the pan with a clean kitchen towel and let the dough rise for another hour.

6. Preheat the oven to 350°F and bake the loaf for 25 to 30 minutes, or until dark golden on top. Allow to cool for 15 minutes in the pan, then invert onto a platter and serve.

Pumpkin Pancakes

Daphne and I have a blast coming up with new pancake flavors and this one is a winner. Make these in the fall during pumpkin season. They can also be packed for lunch with a small container of maple syrup for dipping. Plus, they make great finger food for toddlers!

MAKES 10 TO 12 PANCAKES

1⅓ cups unbleached all-purpose flour

3 tablespoons granulated sugar

2 teaspoons baking powder

½ teaspoon ground cinnamon

¼ teaspoon ground ginger

¼ teaspoon kosher salt

1 cup buttermilk

½ cup canned pure pumpkin purée

1 large egg

2 tablespoons unsalted butter, melted and
    cooled, plus 3 more tablespoons for pan

1. In a large bowl, whisk together the flour, sugar, baking powder, cinnamon, ginger, and salt. Set aside.

2. In a smaller bowl, whisk together the buttermilk, pumpkin, egg, and melted butter. Pour this into the bowl with the flour mixture and mix with a wooden spoon until completely combined.

3. In a large skillet, melt a large pat of butter on medium heat and swirl the pan so it evenly coats the bottom. Add the batter in ¼-cup dollops so the pancakes can cook quickly without running into each other. Cook the pancakes on one side for 3 to 4 minutes, or until bubbles show on the top. Then flip them and cook for another 3 or so minutes on the other side. Transfer to a plate to serve and repeat with remaining batter until all the pancakes are made. Serve with maple syrup!

Note These are thicker pancakes. If you prefer thinner pancakes, add more buttermilk by the tablespoon until you reach the desired consistency.

Easy Cranberry Drop Scones

A warm scone straight from the oven is the best kind of breakfast treat. Make these on Sunday and warm them for breakfast early in the week. They can even be packed as a school snack.

MAKES 12 SCONES

2 cups unbleached all-purpose flour

⅓ cup packed light brown sugar

1 tablespoon baking powder

½ teaspoon kosher salt

4 ounces (1 stick) cold unsalted butter, diced

½ cup cold heavy whipping cream

1 large egg

1 cup dried cranberries

¼ cup whole milk

1 tablespoon coarse turbinado sugar

1. Preheat the oven to 400°F. Line a large, rimmed baking sheet with parchment paper and set aside.

2. In a large mixing bowl, whisk together the flour, brown sugar, baking powder, and salt. Use your fingers to pinch the butter into the flour mixture, working it with your hands until small pebbles form.

3. In a measuring cup, whisk together the cream and egg. Use a wooden spoon to stir this into the dry ingredients. The dough will look a little gluey and lumpy as it comes together. Stir in the dried cranberries.

4. Use your hands to form 2-inch loosely packed balls and place them at least 1 inch apart on the prepared baking sheet. Brush the top of each ball with a little milk and sprinkle with turbinado sugar. Bake them for 18 to 20 minutes, or until they are golden brown and set in the middle.

Baked Eggs in Muffin Tins

This easy method for preparing eggs is a great way to serve a substantial breakfast before the school day begins. Plus, in the time they bake, you can get the kids' bags packed and set for school!

MAKES 12 EGGS

Cooking spray

12 slices bacon, cooked but still pliable

12 large eggs

Kosher salt

Freshly cracked black pepper

2 tablespoons Parmesan cheese

1. Preheat the oven to 375°F. Lightly spray the cups of a regular-size 12-cup muffin tin with cooking spray.

2. Place one piece of cooked bacon in each tin, folding it in a circle around the inside of the tin so it will cup an egg. Crack an egg into each bacon cup. If you want to break the yolk, you may; it is dependent on your preference!

3. Sprinkle the top of each egg with a pinch of salt, a pinch of pepper, and a large pinch of Parmesan. Bake the eggs for 20 to 25 minutes, or just until they are set. Remove them from the oven and allow to cool for 2 minutes. Pop out the egg cups with a fork and serve. If you don't eat all of them, store in a closed container in the refrigerator. They can be reheated the next day and will stay good for up to 2 days.

Note Once you have this method down, you can make all kinds of variations. Try adding chopped vegetables or herbs to each cup to make different flavors!

Slow-Cooker Steel-Cut Oats

These oats are perfect for weekdays. I put my slow cooker to work and make a big batch on Sunday or Monday night. I then keep the cooked oats in a loaf pan and reheat slices of it for breakfast in a jiffy.

MAKES 6 TO 8 SERVINGS

1 cup steel-cut oats

2 tablespoons ground flaxseed meal

2 cups water

2 cups 2% milk

1 teaspoon ground cinnamon

1 tablespoon granulated sugar

½ teaspoon kosher salt

Pure maple syrup, honey, fresh berries, Greek yogurt, chopped toasted walnuts or pecans, sliced bananas, for topping

1. In a slow cooker that holds least 5 quarts, combine the oats, flaxseed meal, water, milk, cinnamon, sugar, and salt. Turn heat to the lowest setting and cook for 8 hours (it works perfectly to cook it overnight).

2. When the cooking has finished, stir the oats and ladle into bowls, sprinkle with your desired toppings, and serve. Scoop any unserved oatmeal into a 9 x 5-inch loaf pan and allow it to cool to room temperature. Cover the pan with plastic wrap and store in the refrigerator.

3. To serve, cut a 1-inch slice out of the loaf pan and place in a microwave-safe bowl. Heat at 50% power for about 1 minute, or until piping hot. The oatmeal will remain in the form of a slice. If you want to loosen it up, add ¼ cup of milk or water before heating and stir well. The heating time may vary depending on the power of your microwave. Top the oatmeal with your topping of choice and serve.

Back-to-School Weeknight Meals

No matter how well you plan, the school weeknight meal routine can drive you crazy. I rarely have any downtime between the time Daphne's school lets out and the dinner hour. We are constantly shuttling to different activities, doing homework, and trying to collect everything she needs for school the next day. I am also doing this solo since Duncan rarely arrives home before bedtime. To make it easier on myself, I have come up with a few tricks for keeping mealtime enjoyable and helping it, mostly, go off without a hitch.

Your Weeknight Meals Strategy

PREP AHEAD Make sure at least one menu item has been prepared in advance. This might mean reheating a casserole you put together that morning, thawing soup from the freezer, or marinating meats so they are ready for the oven. No matter what, having something prepared sets the stage for a smoother meal hour because it eliminates the need to cook everything from scratch all at once.

SERVE NO-COOK SIDES I frequently serve chopped vegetables, such as carrot sticks, cucumber slices, or zucchini rounds with ranch dip. For my husband and me, I'll serve a plate of sliced tomatoes and slivers of red onion drizzled with balsamic vinegar and olive oil in the summer. In the winter, I serve crackers with cheese and marinated olives alongside a bowl of soup. Any kind of healthy no-cook side saves valuable time.

COLD DINNERS ROCK I am a big fan of the dinner sandwich, especially on the nights when there is simply no time to turn on the stove. A healthy sandwich of vegetables, cold cuts, cheeses, or even leftovers can make a wonderful meal in a pinch.

BREAKFAST FOR DINNER Vegetable omelets or breakfast wraps are high in protein and make very filling meals. Or if your children need cheering up, serve a stack of fresh multigrain pancakes topped with fruity maple syrup. That always manages to put a smile on Daphne's face if she's had a bad day.

STICK TO A SIMPLE THEME Getting the children in on planning dinners can be a double-edged sword. Inviting their input can be an effective way to engage them in healthy eating habits without bogging them down with the tedium of meal planning. Sometimes I ask Daphne if she wants a theme night, such as "Paris Night" when we eat crêpes for dinner or "Green Night" when all our food has the color green in it. My son likes "Hungry Caterpillar" night where we eat all the foods found in our favorite book. Sometimes a new perspective is all it takes to shake things up!

EAT TOGETHER Do this whenever you can, but don't sweat it if it doesn't happen every night. I am a big proponent of the family dinner idea, but we are rarely able to sit down as a family during the school week. Instead, we make a point of enjoying our weekend meals together. Sometimes during the school week, the children will wait to eat their dessert until Duncan comes home. That way, at least we are all at the same table together for a few minutes despite our hectic schedules.

SALAD DRESSINGS FOR THE WEEK

To make your weeknight dinner routine easier, make a week's worth of one homemade salad dressing on Monday. All it takes is a few ingredients, a small whisk, and a glass jar, and you are all set with a versatile dressing/marinade/dip to use all week long.

Buttermilk Ranch Dressing

This easy ranch dressing is a staple in our house. Drizzle it over hearty salads or let the children use it to dip vegetables. If you have fresh herbs on hand, try adding fresh chopped basil, tarragon, or oregano, to play with the flavors.

MAKES 3 CUPS DRESSING

2 cups cultured buttermilk

¾ cup mayonnaise

2 teaspoons freshly squeezed lemon juice

¼ teaspoon paprika

1 teaspoon kosher salt

¼ teaspoon freshly cracked black pepper

1 teaspoon chopped fresh dill

2 tablespoons minced fresh parsley

1 tablespoon minced fresh chives

1. Whisk together the buttermilk, mayonnaise, and lemon juice together in a bowl until completely combined. Whisk in the paprika, salt, pepper, dill, parsley, and chives until everything is completely combined.

Parmesan Garlic Dressing

This tangy dressing is a winter favorite. The garlic and Parmesan aggressively season all kinds of leafy greens, even kale, and taste great with winter vegetables.

MAKES 2 CUPS DRESSING

1¼ cups extra-virgin olive oil

1½ tablespoons Dijon mustard

½ cup coarsely shredded Parmesan cheese

2 garlic cloves, finely chopped

½ teaspoon kosher salt

½ teaspoon freshly cracked black pepper

1. Place all the ingredients in a mason jar and shake vigorously to emulsify.

Easy Italian Dressing

This classic dressing is in heavy rotation year-round. In addition to mixing it with everyday tossed salads, use it as marinade for chicken and to season fresh vegetables, such as steamed green beans or broccoli.

MAKES 2 CUPS DRESSING

¼ cup white wine vinegar

¼ cup red wine vinegar

½ cup packed chopped fresh parsley

¼ cup freshly squeezed lemon juice

1 tablespoon dried basil

¾ teaspoon dried oregano

4 garlic cloves, finely chopped

½ teaspoon kosher salt

¼ teaspoon freshly cracked black pepper

1¼ cups extra-virgin olive oil

1. In a large bowl, whisk together the vinegar, parsley, lemon juice, basil, oregano, garlic, salt, and pepper. Then pour in the olive oil in a steady stream, whisking continuously until it is completely emulsified.

Lemony Vinaigrette

This dressing is very light and lemony and is perfect for summer. It is lovely for tossing in orzo or couscous salads or drizzling over platters of freshly grilled vegetables.

MAKES 1½ CUPS DRESSING

Grated zest and juice of 2 large lemons

½ cup red wine vinegar

1 teaspoon kosher salt

½ teaspoon freshly cracked black pepper

2 teaspoons Dijon mustard

1 cup extra-virgin olive oil

1. In a large bowl, whisk together the lemon zest and juice, vinegar, salt, pepper, and mustard until just combined. Then pour in the olive oil in a steady stream, whisking continuously until the dressing is fully emulsified.

Classic Balsamic Dressing

This go-to dressing is my favorite for serving in salads filled with strong cheeses, such as blue or Camembert. The acidity of the balsamic balances the fatty cheeses. This also works well in salads with eggs, such as a classic Cobb or frisée topped with a poached egg and crumbled bacon.

MAKES 2¾ CUPS DRESSING

6 garlic cloves, finely chopped

⅓ cup mayonnaise

¼ cup freshly squeezed lemon juice (from 2 large lemons)

2 tablespoons Dijon mustard

4 teaspoons light honey

1 tablespoon kosher salt

½ teaspoon freshly cracked black pepper

1 cup balsamic vinegar

1½ cups extra-virgin olive oil

1. In a food processor fitted with a blade, place the garlic cloves, mayonnaise, lemon juice, mustard, honey, salt, pepper, and vinegar. Pulse five or six times, or until the garlic is finely chopped and the ingredients are completely combined and smooth.

2. With the food processor running, pour the olive oil down the chute until the dressing is completely emulsified. Serve.

Avocado-Basil Dressing

This thick, creamy dressing is perfect for light greens, peppery arugula, or just drizzling over fresh cut vegetables. Without the olive oil, it is thick enough to use as a straight-up dip; leave it out if you prefer.

MAKES 2½ CUPS DRESSING

1 ripe Haas avocado, peeled and pitted

1 cup packed fresh basil leaves

1 cup low-fat plain Greek yogurt

4 scallions (white and green parts)

2 garlic cloves, peeled and halved

2 tablespoons freshly squeezed lemon juice

1 teaspoon granulated sugar

1 teaspoon kosher salt

¼ teaspoon freshly cracked black pepper

½ cup extra-virgin olive oil

1. Place the avocado, basil, yogurt, scallions, garlic, lemon juice, sugar, salt, and pepper in a blender and purée until smooth.

2. With the food processor running, pour the olive oil down the chute until the dressing is completely emulsified. Serve.

BLAT Dinner Salad

A hefty dinner salad is always welcome at the end of a long day. This one is crunchy and salty and dressed in creamy lemon dressing. If you want to add extra protein, top each portion with a freshly poached egg.

MAKES 4 SERVINGS

3 ounces slab bacon, cubed

Grated zest and juice of ½ lemon

1 teaspoon Dijon mustard

3 tablespoons extra-virgin olive oil

1 teaspoon light mayonnaise

½ teaspoon kosher salt

¼ teaspoon freshly cracked black pepper

1 head romaine lettuce, trimmed and coarsely chopped

1 cup cherry tomatoes, halved

1 Haas avocado, pitted, peeled, and cubed

1 cup seasoned croutons (optional)

1. In a medium skillet, sauté the cubed bacon until browned and crispy, about 10 minutes. Transfer the bacon with a slotted spoon to a paper towel–lined plate, reserving 2 tablespoons of bacon drippings.

2. In a small bowl, whisk together the bacon drippings, lemon zest and juice, mustard, olive oil, mayonnaise, salt, and pepper.

3. In a large salad bowl, toss the lettuce, tomatoes, avocado, croutons (if using) and cooked bacon. Drizzle well with the dressing and toss to mix. Divide among four salad bowls and serve.

French Onion Soup *with* Apple Cider

This soup is the perfect combination of fancy and comforting. It is ideal for serving from a big pot on a cold winter school night. You can even send the leftovers to school in a thermos the next day.

MAKES 6 CUPS SOUP

6 tablespoons unsalted butter

4 medium-size yellow onions, halved and thinly sliced

4 cups low-sodium beef stock

2 cups apple cider

2 teaspoons fresh thyme leaves

1 teaspoon kosher salt

4 (1½-inch-thick) slices country bread, toasted

5 ounces coarsely shredded Gruyère cheese (about ⅔ cup)

1. Melt the butter in a large, ovenproof, deep-bottomed pot (a Dutch oven works well) and heat over medium-low heat. Add the onions and sauté gently. Stir the onions every few minutes for about 20 minutes or so to keep them from sticking as they soften and caramelize and turn a dark brown color.

2. Once they have completely browned but not burned, pour in the beef stock, 3 cups of water, and the cider, thyme, and salt, scraping up the browned bits from the bottom of the pan with a wooden spoon. Raise the heat to high to bring it to a boil for 1 minute. Then return the heat to medium-low and allow the soup to simmer for about an hour, skimming the top of foam as necessary.

3. Turn the broiler to high and set a rack below it, as close as you can get to the broiler while still leaving room for the pot. Layer the slices of bread on the surface of the soup and sprinkle with the cheese. Carefully place the pot under the broiler and cook for about 5 minutes, watching very carefully, or until the cheese is lightly browned and bubbly. Serve one slice of cheesy bread per bowl.

Easy Peasy Chicken Pot Pie

The buttery crust and silky filling make this one of the best comfort meals on a cold fall evening. To make it weeknight-friendly, prepare the filling up to a day in advance and store it in the refrigerator. Right before baking, roll out the crust, place it over the dish, and throw the whole thing into the oven.

MAKES 4 TO 6 SERVINGS

FOR THE CRUST

8 ounces (2 sticks) unsalted butter, chilled and
   cut into small pieces, plus more for baking dish

2¼ cups unbleached all-purpose flour

1 teaspoon kosher salt

½ cup ice water

FOR THE FILLING

4 tablespoons (½ stick) unsalted butter, divided

1 pound cooked boneless skinless chicken
   breasts, cut into 1-inch cubes

1 medium-size yellow onion, finely chopped

2 large carrots, peeled and finely chopped

2 celery stalks, diced

1 teaspoon dried thyme

½ cup unbleached all-purpose flour

2 cups low-sodium chicken stock

1½ cups whole milk

1 cup fresh or frozen peas

½ cup fresh or frozen corn kernels (thawed if
   frozen)

1 tablespoon finely chopped fresh parsley

2 teaspoons kosher salt

½ teaspoon freshly cracked black pepper

1 large egg

1. Preheat the oven to 375°F. Generously butter the bottom and sides of a 13 x 9 x 2-inch baking dish and set aside.

2. To make the crust: Place the flour, salt, and butter in the bowl of a food processor fitted with a blade and pulse three or four times, or until the mixture becomes crumbly and small pebbles form. Working slowly, add the cold water through the tube of the food processor 1 tablespoon at a time, pulsing once or twice after each addition. Stop adding the water when the dough just begins to form a ball. Remove the dough from the food processor, form it into a disk, wrap it in plastic wrap, and chill while you make the filling.

3. To make the filling: In a large, heavy-bottomed pan or Dutch oven, melt 3 tablespoons of the butter over medium heat. Add the chicken, onion, carrots, celery, thyme, and a pinch of salt and cook for about 5 minutes, or until the onion is softened and translucent.

4. Add the remaining tablespoon of butter to the pan and allow it to melt. Add the flour and stir into the vegetables for 2 minutes until it no longer looks white and raw. Then pour in chicken stock and milk and allow the mixture to simmer, stirring occasionally, for 8 to 10 minutes, until it has thickened just enough to coat the back of a spoon.

5. Stir the peas, corn, parsley, salt, and pepper into the pan and cook just to warm through. Spoon the filling into the prepared baking dish.

6. Beat the egg with 1 tablespoon of water and whisk together in a small bowl. Remove the crust from the refrigerator and place it on a lightly floured surface. Roll it out to be 1 inch wider on all sides than the baking dish. Drape it over the pan and crimp the edges decoratively around the top to seal in the filling. Trim any raggedy edges with a sharp knife and make two or three decorative slits in the top of the crust to allow for ventilation. Brush the top of the pie with the egg wash and set the baking dish on top of a foil-lined baking sheet, in case the filling bubbles over.

7. Bake the pot pie for 25 to 30 minutes, or until the crust is golden brown and the filling is bubbly. Remove it from the oven and allow it to cool for about 5 minutes before serving hot.

Note To prepare this in advance, proceed through step 5. Cover the filled baking dish with plastic wrap and place it in the refrigerator. Bring it to room temperature before baking. It may need a couple of extra minutes in the oven.

Turkey Meatloaf

Meatloaf is an easy weeknight meal to prep ahead. Packed with protein and flavor, it can be served any number of ways. I prefer it on a bun, sandwich style, but my husband eats it sliced as is, and the children like it mashed with tomato sauce.

MAKES 1 LOAF

Cooking spray

1 tablespoon olive oil

1 medium-size yellow onion, finely chopped

1 pound ground turkey

1 large egg

2 teaspoons Worcestershire sauce

1 teaspoon dried basil

½ teaspoon dried sage

½ teaspoon dried oregano

½ teaspoon crushed red pepper flakes

⅓ cup good-quality tomato ketchup

3 tablespoons plain breadcrumbs

½ teaspoon kosher salt

½ teaspoon freshly cracked black pepper

1. Preheat the oven to 350°F. Spray the inside of a 9 x 5-inch loaf pan with cooking spray and set aside.

2. In a small sauté pan, heat the olive oil over medium heat. Add the onion and sauté for about 5 minutes, or until translucent. Remove from the heat.

3. Place the turkey in a large bowl and make a well in the middle. To the well add the cooked onion, egg, Worcestershire, herbs, red pepper flakes, ketchup, breadcrumbs, salt, and pepper and mix the ingredients together with clean hands or a wooden spoon until well combined.

4. Use your hands to form the meat into a loaf shape and stuff it inside the prepared loaf pan. Pat the top of the meat so that it is level and smooth in the pan but is not too firmly packed.

5. Bake the loaf for about 1 hour 5 minutes, or until the top is dark brown and a meat thermometer inserted into the center reaches 160°F. Allow to cool slightly, then slice and serve.

Note To make this in advance, prepare the meat through step 3. Then cover it with plastic wrap and keep in the refrigerator. Bring to room temperature before baking.

Roasted Tomato Mac & Cheese

Every parent needs a go-to mac & cheese recipe. This is mine and now it can be yours. The roasted tomatoes lend terrific sweet flavor to this classic pasta dish.

MAKES 6 TO 8 SERVINGS

6 tablespoons unsalted butter, plus more for baking dish

3 cups cherry tomatoes

1 tablespoon olive oil

1 pound elbow pasta

3 tablespoons unbleached all-purpose flour

2 tablespoons dry mustard

3 cups whole milk

½ teaspoon kosher salt

¼ teaspoon freshly cracked black pepper

24 ounces shredded Cheddar cheese (about 6 cups)

1. Preheat the oven to 400°F. Lightly butter the inside of a 4-quart baking dish and set aside. Line a large baking sheet with parchment paper.

2. Toss the tomatoes with the olive oil and place them on the prepared baking sheet. Roast the tomatoes in the oven for 20 to 25 minutes, or until they have shriveled and collapsed just a little bit. Remove from the oven and allow to cool. Lower the oven temperature to 350°F.

3. While the tomatoes are roasting, bring a large pot of salted water to a boil and prepare the pasta until al dente, about 2 minutes less than the recommended cooking time on the package. Drain and set aside.

4. Prepare the sauce by melting the butter in a large, heavy-bottomed saucepan over medium heat. Then whisk in the flour and dry mustard until smooth. Working carefully, slowly pour in the milk, whisking continuously, until the mixture is completely smooth and there are no lumps. Sprinkle the salt and pepper. Continue to whisk the sauce for 8 to 10 minutes, or until it thickens and coats the back of a spoon. Remove the sauce from the heat and stir in the cheese until completely melted.

5. Assemble the casserole by pouring the prepared pasta into the sauce and stir until mixed well. Fold in the roasted tomatoes and any juices.

6. Pour the pasta into the prepared baking dish and smooth the top with a spatula. Bake for 30 minutes, or until the cheese is bubbling and the casserole is browned on top.

Note To make this ahead of time, cover the prepared pasta and store it in the refrigerator. Then bring it to room temperature before baking.

Ricotta Gnocchi *with* Sage Brown Butter Sauce

For years I ordered gnocchi every time I saw it on menu. I was hesitant to make it until I found this super simple recipe in one of my favorite cookbooks, Tessa Kiros's Apples for Jam. *It comes together in a heartbeat and is fun to make with children. Serve this with a simple browned butter sauce made with fresh sage from the herb pot. It also is wonderful with a meaty ragout or simple marinara.*

MAKES 60 GNOCCHI

2 cups ricotta cheese

3 tablespoons finely grated Parmesan cheese, plus more for serving

1 cup unbleached all-purpose flour, plus more for dusting

1 teaspoon kosher salt, divided

6 tablespoons unsalted butter

1 tablespoon finely chopped fresh sage

1. Bring a large pot of salted water to a boil.

2. While the water is heating, combine the ricotta, Parmesan, flour, and ½ teaspoon of the salt in large mixing bowl, using a wooden spoon. If the dough feels tough and isn't absorbing the flour, lightly knead the dough with your fingertips until combined.

3. Flour a surface on your counter and rub some flour on your hands. Form the dough into one large ball, then divide it into four equal-size smaller balls. Use your fingertips to roll each ball into a long cylinder ¼ inch wide. Don't compress the dough so much that it is packed and hard; it should still feel soft under your fingers.

4. Use as sharp knife to cut the dough into pieces ½ to ¾ inch long. Drop the pieces into the boiling water and cook for 45 seconds to 1 minute, or until they are floating on the surface. Use a spider or a slotted spoon to transfer the gnocchi to a strainer to drain completely. Place the gnocchi in a large serving bowl.

5. Melt the butter over medium heat in a small skillet, then add the remaining ½ teaspoon of salt and the sage. Heat the butter until the milk solids turn toasty brown and fall to the bottom. The rest of the butter will turn a nutty golden hue. Immediately remove it from the heat and drizzle the sauce evenly over the bowl of gnocchi. Gently toss the gnocchi so it gets completely coated with the sauce. Serve in individual bowls, topped with Parmesan cheese.

Roast Chicken *with* Rosemary Potatoes

This is a great recipe to feed a hungry family because it makes so much food in one fell swoop. It also produces amazing leftovers for the next meal.

MAKES 4 TO 6 SERVINGS

Olive oil

1 pound fingerling potatoes, scrubbed and patted dry and cut into 1-inch pieces

1 large yellow onion, peeled and cut into 1-inch pieces

3 large carrots, peeled and chopped into 1-inch pieces

12 (6-inch) stalks fresh rosemary, divided

1 (5-pound) roaster chicken

6 tablespoons unsalted butter, at room temperature, cut into pieces

12 garlic cloves, peeled and smashed flat

Kosher salt and freshly cracked black pepper

1. Preheat the oven to 400°F.

2. Lightly oil the bottom of the roasting pan with olive oil. Place the potatoes, onion, and carrots in the pan in one even layer and nestle four of the rosemary stalks among them.

3. Working carefully, gently use your fingers to lift the skin of the chicken from the meat on both sides. Evenly slide half of the pieces of butter and six of the smashed garlic cloves under the chicken skin evenly around the body on both sides. Then rub the remaining butter all over the chicken skin and inside the cavity and season the chicken with salt and pepper. Place the remaining six garlic cloves and the remaining eight rosemary stalks in the cavity. Gently place the seasoned chicken directly on top of the potatoes.

4. Roast the chicken for 30 minutes, then lower the oven temperature to 375°F and roast for another 1 hour to 1 hour 10 minutes, or until the juices run clear when the thigh is pricked or a meat thermometer inserted into the thickest pieces of the thigh and breast registers 165°F. Carve the chicken into serving-size pieces and serve with the roasted vegetables.

Note As my friends at the Charleston Academy of Domestic Pursuits advise, if you have the room, you may as well roast a second chicken to have expressly for the rest of the week. With your main ingredient cooked and ready, you can plan out a whole week of chicken-based meals: chicken soup, chicken pot pie, chicken salad, and such. Much easier for you; and your whole family will be happy and well fed.

Portobello Mushroom Steaks

I had a hard time viewing mushrooms as a main course until I discovered how to marinate them for extra flavor. These hearty filling steaks are perfect for a weeknight meal and are great to prepare for Meatless Mondays.

MAKES 4 TO 6 SERVINGS

¼ cup olive oil

3 tablespoons freshly squeezed lemon juice

1 teaspoon kosher salt

½ teaspoon freshly cracked black pepper

10 portobello mushroom caps, cleaned, gills and
   stems removed

Leaves from 8 sprigs fresh thyme, divided

1. Whisk together the olive oil, lemon juice, salt, and pepper and pour it into a shallow baking dish.

Place the mushroom caps in the marinade in one even layer, turning once or twice to coat. Sprinkle half of the thyme leaves around the mushrooms. Allow the mushrooms to sit for 45 minutes at room temperature to marinate.

2. Preheat the oven to 400°F.

3. After the mushrooms have finished marinating, bake them for 25 to 30 minutes, or until dark on top and tender when pierced with a knife. Once they are finished, sprinkle the remaining thyme leaves on top and slice and serve drizzled with the pan juices.

French Onion Grilled Cheese

Elevate everyday grilled cheese in a hearty dinner sandwich by adding loads sweet caramelized onions. It instantly transforms a child's meal into something the adults will love, too.

MAKES 4 SANDWICHES

6 tablespoons unsalted butter, divided

2 medium-size yellow onions, peeled and thinly
   sliced

1 tablespoon dry sherry

8 slices Cheddar cheese

8 thick slices country bread

1. Melt 2 tablespoons of the butter in a large saucepan over medium heat and add the onions.

Cook for 25 to 30 minutes, stirring the onions every so often so they caramelize evenly and are a deep, rich brown; don't let them burn. Add the sherry to deglaze the pan, scraping the bottom to incorporate any browned bits. Remove the pan from the heat.

2. Assemble the sandwiches by setting out four slices of bread and topping each with a slice of cheese. Divide the caramelized onions evenly among the pieces of bread. Close the sandwiches with the remaining slices of bread.

3. Butter both sides of the sandwiches with the remaining 4 tablespoons of butter and place them in a large skillet over medium heat, in batches if needed. Cook the sandwiches for about 4 minutes per side, or until the bread turns a golden brown. Flip the sandwiches and toast the other side for about 3 more minutes. Remove from the skillet, slice, and serve.

Eggplant Parmesan Pasta

Eggplant Parmesan is one of my favorite dishes but it is so hard to pull together on a busy weeknight. Instead, make this sauce, which tastes exactly like the classic casserole but is so much simpler to prepare.

MAKES 4 TO 6 SERVINGS

1 pound spaghetti or similar long-stranded pasta

1 large egg

3 tablespoons olive oil

1 large eggplant, peeled and cut into ½-inch pieces

1 large shallot, peeled and finely chopped

2 garlic cloves, finely chopped

3 cups tomato sauce

¼ cup finely grated Parmesan cheese

¼ cup breadcrumbs

1. Cook the pasta in salted water according to the package directions. Drain and set aside. Beat the egg in a small bowl and set aside.

2. Heat the olive oil in a large skillet over medium heat. Add the eggplant and the shallot and sauté for 5 minutes, or until the eggplant begins to brown and the shallot turns translucent. Stir in the garlic and cook for 1 more minute.

3. Next, stir in the tomato sauce, Parmesan cheese, and breadcrumbs and mix well. Add a little bit of the sauce to the beaten egg to temper it, then stir it into the tomato sauce and incorporate well. Lower the heat to medium-low and simmer for 20 minutes, or until the sauce is thick and creamy. Stir the cooked pasta into the sauce to reheat the pasta, and serve immediately.

Crispy Skillet Lemon Pork Chops

These crispy buttery pork chops are ideal for a busy weeknight when you have to prepare far in advance. Bread the pork in the morning and store it covered in the fridge. Then you can cook it quickly at night.

MAKES 4 SERVINGS

2 tablespoons Dijon mustard

2 tablespoons mayonnaise

2 cups panko breadcrumbs

Grated zest of 1 medium-size lemon

2 tablespoons finely chopped fresh sage

1 teaspoon kosher salt

½ teaspoon freshly cracked black pepper

2 tablespoons olive oil

1 tablespoon unsalted butter

4 (1-inch-thick) slices boneless pork chop, pounded thin

1. In a shallow bowl, whisk together the mustard and mayonnaise. In another shallow bowl, combine the breadcrumbs, lemon, sage, salt, and pepper. Set the bowls next to each other.

2. In a large skillet, heat the olive oil and butter over medium-low heat.

3. While the butter is melting, place the pork between two sheets of waxed paper and tenderize with a meat pounder. It should be half as thick as when you started, but don't smash it so much that it tears.

4. One by one, dip the pork slices in the mustard mixture so that they are evenly coated, then dip them in the panko mixture, turning them so they are completely coated on both sides. Place the pork in the skillet and cook for 10 minutes per side, or until cooked through and no longer pink inside. Serve hot.

Ravioli Lasagna

This is one of the easiest dishes to make on a busy weeknight and is a real crowd-pleaser. It is essentially inside-out lasagna. Instead of noodles with cheese layers between them, the cheese layer is inside the noodles! You can use nearly any kind of fresh ravioli you can find to make this.

MAKES 6 TO 8 SERVINGS

Vegetable oil for the pan

1 (24-ounce) jar tomato sauce, divided

36 ounces fresh ravioli, or thawed frozen ravioli, with the filling of your choice, divided

5 ounces packed chopped frozen baby spinach, thawed and squeezed dry, divided

¼ cup packed fresh basil leaves, coarsely chopped, divided

1 cup coarsely shredded mozzarella cheese, divided

½ cup finely grated Parmesan cheese, divided

1. Preheat the oven to 350°F.

2. Lightly oil the bottom and sides of a 13 x 9 x 2-inch pan. Pour in about one-third of the tomato sauce and spread it around so that it coats the bottom of the dish.

3. Layer half of the ravioli in a single layer over the tomato sauce. Cover it with half the spinach, half of the basil, half of the mozzarella, and half the Parmesan. Pour another third of the sauce over the ravioli and repeat the layering one more time, ending with the remaining third of tomato sauce.

4. Cover the dish with foil and bake it for 20 minutes. Remove the foil and bake it for another 10 minutes, until the cheese is browned and bubbly. Remove the pan from the oven and allow it to cool slightly before slicing and serving.

Mushroom & Spinach Baked Risotto

I love risotto, but the endless stirring over the stovetop is nearly impossible on any given school night. Instead, I make this easy baked version. It can be prepped in advance easily and slipped in the oven before you are ready to eat.

MAKES 6 TO 8 SERVINGS

2½ tablespoons extra-virgin olive oil

2 medium-size yellow onions, finely chopped (about 4 cups)

2 cups sliced cremini mushrooms

4 garlic cloves, minced

2¼ cups arborio rice

1½ cups dry white wine

4½ cups low-sodium chicken stock

10 ounces baby spinach, rinsed, stems removed, and coarsely chopped

1 cup grated Parmesan cheese, divided

1 teaspoon kosher salt

1. Preheat the oven to 375°F.

2. In a Dutch oven over medium-high heat, heat the olive oil. Add the onions and mushrooms and cook until softened, about 5 minutes. Then stir in the garlic and cook for another minute, until it becomes fragrant but not burned.

3. Add the rice to the pan and stir until it is lightly toasted, about 2 minutes. Pour in the wine to deglaze the bottom of the pan, scraping the bottom to incorporate any browned bits, and allow the mixture to simmer until the wine is almost completely evaporated, 3 to 5 minutes. Finally, pour in the chicken stock and bring the mixture to a boil for 1 minute, lower the heat to a simmer, and cook for about 10 minutes, until the rice has started to plump up. Then stir in the spinach, ½ cup of the Parmesan, and the salt.

4. Top the risotto with the remaining ½ cup of Parmesan, place the lid on top, and bake for 30 minutes, or until the rice is tender and the cheese is melted.

Make-Ahead Turkey Meatballs

These lightened-up meatballs are perfect for making ahead and keeping in the freezer. They are one of my go-to meals when time is of the essence! Most of the time I serve them with fresh spaghetti and marinara sauce. Sometimes we eat them on rolls as meatball subs or chopped up on top of homemade pizza.

MAKES 34 (1½-INCH) MEATBALLS

2 slices white bread

½ cup whole milk

1 pound ground light meat turkey

½ cup freshly grated Parmesan cheese

2 large eggs, lightly beaten

1 garlic clove, minced

2 teaspoons finely chopped fresh parsley

1 teaspoon kosher salt

¼ teaspoon freshly cracked black pepper.

1. Place the bread in a small bowl and pour the milk over it. Allow the bread to soak for 2 minutes. Tear the bread into very small pieces and leave it in the bowl.

2. Preheat the oven to 400°F. Line a large, rimmed baking sheet with parchment paper and set aside.

3. Place the turkey in a large bowl and form a well in the middle. Add the cheese, egg, garlic, parsley, salt, pepper, and bread and mix the ingredients together with clean hands. Once everything is evenly distributed, stop working the meat.

4. Use your hands to pinch off part of the turkey mixture and form 1½-inch balls. Place them 1 inch apart on the lined baking sheet.

5. Bake for 15 to 20 minutes, or until they are browned all around and cooked through. If you are eating them right away, immediately toss them with sauce and serve over pasta. If you plan to freeze them, allow the meatballs to cool to room temperature on the baking sheet.

6. To freeze the meatballs, line up the meatballs on the baking tray without letting them touch. Cover it with plastic wrap and chill it in the freezer until they are frozen through. You can then pile them into a freezer bag and seal the bag tightly. They can be frozen for 3 months before using.

7. To reheat the frozen meatballs, place them in a pot of marinara sauce so they are just covered. Simmer the meatballs and sauce on medium-low heat until they are heated through, about 20 minutes.

Citrus Baked Chicken Thighs

This flavorful dish is easy to prepare during the day. Do it first thing in the morning and leave them in the fridge until you are ready to cook. The citrus flavors play off the dark chicken thigh meat. Serve them on a bed of couscous or rice for an easy school night dinner.

MAKES 4 TO 6 SERVINGS

2 garlic cloves, finely chopped

Grated zest and juice of 1 navel orange

Grated zest and juice of 1 large lemon

1 small bunch scallions (white and green parts only), finely chopped

¼ cup store-bought teriyaki marinade (such as Trader Joe's Soyaki)

2 tablespoons vegetable oil

1 teaspoon kosher salt

2 pounds chicken thighs (4 or 5 thighs)

Cooked rice or couscous, for serving

1. In a large bowl, whisk together the garlic cloves, orange juice and zest, lemon juice and zest, green onions, teriyaki marinade, vegetable oil, and salt.

2. Place the chicken thighs in a baking dish that is large enough for them to fit in one even layer. Pour the citrus marinade over the thighs and turn them a few times so they are evenly coated. Cover the dish with plastic wrap and refrigerate for at least 2 hours or up to overnight.

3. Preheat the oven to 350°F. Bake for 40 to 45 minutes, or until the chicken is cooked through and the sauce is bubbly and fragrant. Serve over rice.

Lunchbox Ideas

It wasn't until Daphne started kindergarten that I truly understood the struggle of packing the lunchbox. Each day I had to pack her a healthy lunch, along with two healthy snacks! For the first six weeks I found it no problem to come up with new, interesting foods. But then I hit a wall. All of a sudden I was fresh out of ideas and I fell into the trap of packing the same thing every day. Eventually, Daph complained and I snapped out of my complacency and made a list of everything she likes. Now, I refer to it every week as I plan out my shopping and lunch packing. It is a lifesaver!

Your Lunchbox Strategy

Make a list of everything your child loves. Then make a list of ideas for new things to try. Focus on fruity items for morning snacks, a protein-heavy lunch, and a savory, plus a small sweet treat in the afternoon.

Fruity Snacks

- Sliced fruit, including strawberries, blueberries, watermelon, mango, banana, apple, pear, and clementines
- Mini fruit smoothies
- Mini fruit-flavored yogurt cups
- Frozen fruit yogurt tubes
- Single skewer with a variety of fruit chunks
- Fruit-filled breakfast granola bars
- Freeze-dried or chewy dried fruits

Savory Snacks

- Baked vegetable chips
- Cheese crackers, or butter crackers with slices of cheese
- Chopped raw vegetables, such as carrots, cucumbers, or cherry tomatoes, with hummus or ranch dip
- Edamame
- Roasted Chickpea Crunchies (page 208)
- Salty trail mix

Main Course

- Homemade vegetable or chicken quesadilla wrapped in foil
- Heated soup in a thermal container
- Heated mini ravioli in tomato sauce in a thermal container
- Nut butter & jam sandwich
- Cheese sandwich
- Bagel with cream cheese and fruit jam
- Banana or zucchini bread with cream cheese
- Cold cut sandwiches
- Turkey and cheese roll-ups
- Waffle grilled cheese sandwich

Beverages (packed in a reusable water bottle)
- Water
- Fruit juice diluted half and half with water
- Homemade cherry lemonade
- Sparkling water with splash of cranberry juice

Small Sweet Treats
- All-natural fruit strips
- Homemade cookie
- Homemade gelatin fruit cups with real fruit
- Animal crackers
- Granola bars
- Mini corn or banana muffins
- Graham crackers
- Zucchini Applesauce Bread (page 88)

Rosh Hashanah

GREEN BEANS *with* SHALLOTS & ALMONDS   185

—

BAKED ROSEMARY CHICKEN *with* APPLES   185

—

SWEET POTATO KUGEL   186

—

SWEET NOODLE KUGEL   186

—

BROWN SUGAR APPLE CAKE   187

Celebrate the Jewish New Year with a feast of traditional Jewish foods. These easy recipes are a joy to make and share with friends.

Green Beans *with* Shallots & Almonds

This classic green vegetable dish is ideal for serving to friends and family. The crispy beans get a nice crunch from the addition of almonds.

MAKES 6 TO 8 SERVINGS

Kosher salt

3 pounds haricots verts, trimmed

2 tablespoons extra-virgin olive oil

3 large shallots, thinly sliced

½ cup slivered almonds

1. Bring a large pot of salted water to boil. Add the beans and cook until they are vibrant green and al dente, about 4 minutes. Drain and shake out any excess water.

2. Meanwhile, heat the oil in a large, nonstick skillet. Sauté the shallots over medium-high heat until soft and beginning to brown, about 4 minutes. Add the almonds and cook until golden, 4 minutes more.

3. Transfer the shallot mixture to a mixing bowl and toss together with the beans and 1 teaspoon of salt. Serve warm or at room temperature.

Baked Rosemary Chicken *with* Apples

This warm chicken is the best kind of comfort food to serve at your party. Prepare it in advance and slip it in the oven right before guests arrive.

MAKES 4 SERVINGS

¼ cup cider vinegar

2 tablespoons honey mustard

2 tablespoons olive oil

4 cloves garlic, minced

1 teaspoon kosher salt

1 tablespoon finely chopped fresh rosemary

2½ pounds boneless skinless chicken thighs

1 large Honeycrisp, Fuji, or Gala apple, cored and
    cut into ½-inch-thick wedges

2 large shallots, quartered

¼ cup white wine

1. In a gallon-size resealable plastic bag, combine the vinegar, mustard, olive oil, garlic, salt, and rosemary. Add the chicken to the bag, seal tightly, and swish the chicken around until coated in the mixture. Refrigerate for at least 2 hours or overnight.

2. Preheat the oven to 375°F.

3. Transfer the chicken and as much of the marinade as you can squeeze out of the bag into a

13 x 9-inch baking dish. Tuck the apple and shallot slices between the chicken and arrange in an even layer. Pour the white wine over the top. Bake in the oven for 1½ hours, until the chicken is very tender and the top is golden brown. Transfer the chicken to a serving platter and ladle the pan juices over the top.

Sweet Potato Kugel

Give your kugel a welcome twist by swapping out the egg noodles for sweet potato. The warm flavor and smooth texture is ideal for a festive meal. This will also be a favorite with the kids.

MAKES 6 TO 8 SERVINGS

2 pounds sweet potatoes (about 2 large), peeled and grated

1 pound Yukon Gold potatoes (1 large), peeled and grated

3 large shallots, thinly sliced

½ cup unbleached all-purpose flour

2 large eggs, lightly beaten

2 tablespoons melted butter, cooled

1 teaspoon kosher salt

1. Preheat the oven to 375°F.

2. In a large bowl, stir together both kinds of potatoes and the shallots, flour, eggs, butter, and salt until combined. Transfer the potato mixture to a 3-quart casserole dish and smooth into an even layer.

3. Bake the kugel for 45 to 50 minutes, until tender and golden brown. Cut into squares and serve.

Sweet Noodle Kugel

This classic noodle kugel is from my friend Melissa's aunt. My whole family loves it and our personal preference is to make it with raisins, but you can eat it plain if you want a more classic version.

MAKES 4 TO 6 SERVINGS

Butter for the pan

1 pound egg noodles

3 large eggs

½ cup granulated sugar

1 teaspoon ground cinnamon

1 teaspoon pure vanilla extract

⅛ teaspoon kosher salt

1 cup golden raisins

1. Preheat the oven to 350°F. Butter the bottom and sides of a 11 x 7-inch baking dish and set aside.
2. Cook the noodles to al dente according to the package instructions, drain, and set aside.
3. In a large bowl, beat the eggs until foamy. Slowly add the sugar and continue beating the eggs until thick and light in color, about 3 minutes. Beat in the cinnamon, vanilla, and salt.

Carefully fold in the cooked noodles, taking care not to break them. Fold in the raisins. Pour the batter into the prepared baking pan.
4. Bake the kugel for 45 minutes, or until the top is set and golden brown. The top layer will be a little bit crunchy. Allow it to cool for about 10 minutes. Slice and serve.

Brown Sugar Apple Cake

This sweet cake is the best kind of apple dessert. It is easy to make and begs to be served with a scoop of vanilla ice cream.

MAKES 6 TO 8 SERVINGS

3 tablespoons unsalted butter, plus more for pan

1 cup unbleached all-purpose flour, plus more for dusting pan

½ cup dark brown sugar

1 large egg

1 teaspoon almond extract

¾ teaspoon baking soda

¼ teaspoon kosher salt

1 teaspoon ground cinnamon

¼ cup whole milk

1 large apple (I used Cortland), peeled, cored, and thinly sliced

2 teaspoons freshly squeezed lemon juice

1 tablespoon turbinado sugar

1. Preheat the oven to 350°F. Butter and flour an 8-inch square baking dish and set aside.
2. With an electric mixer fitted with the paddle attachment, beat the butter and brown sugar on high speed in a large bowl until fluffy, about 2 minutes. Then add the egg and almond extract and beat well.
3. Sift together the flour, baking soda, salt, and cinnamon. With the mixer on low speed, slowly add the dry ingredients in two parts, alternating with the milk, until just incorporated.
4. Spread the batter in the prepared pan. Toss the apple slices with the lemon juice and arrange them in rows on top of the batter, allowing them to overlap as needed. Sprinkle with the turbinado sugar. Bake the cake for 25 minutes, or until the top springs back when touched and a cake tester comes out clean.

Apple-Picking Weekend

CHEDDAR SCALLOPED APPLES   189
—
NICOLE'S BUTTERMILK FRIED CHICKEN   190
—
WHOLE WHEAT APPLE CRUMBLE MUFFINS   191
—
SKILLET APPLE PIE   192

Every fall our friends Keith and Nicole host Applemania at their home in upstate New York. They invite friends from all over to go apple-picking at their local orchard followed by a feast in their backyard. Nicole goes all-out with apple-themed treats. Over time she has streamlined her menu and relies on old favorites again and again. Each year it gets easier to produce and everyone has come to look forward to her signature menu.

Your Apple-Picking Weekend Strategy

PLAN YOUR MENU Plan your apple-themed menu and make as many dishes in advance as possible.

PICKING Invite your friends to meet you at the orchard. Have everyone come prepared to pick their own apples to take home. You don't need them to bring the apples to your house and give them to you!

PRESENTATION Outdoor fall weekends beg for rustic themes. Set the meal buffet style on a long table in the backyard or on the porch. Keep the centerpiece apple-themed, using apples with tea lights fitted into the top.

CHILDREN'S ACTIVITIES To keep the children occupied while the adults socialize, set up a few games in the yard. Apple bobbing, corn hole, and apple-eating contests are all fun!

Cheddar Scalloped Apples

This is recipe has been passed around Cooperstown for years and years. It reminds me of my favorite snack: apples and cheese slice stacks. Your friends will love the unique take on a savory and sweet side dish featuring fall fruit.

MAKES 4 TO 6 SERVINGS

Butter for casserole dish
4 large tart apples, cored and sliced (about 4 cups)
1 teaspoon ground cinnamon
1½ tablespoons unbleached all-purpose flour
3 tablespoons granulated sugar
1 tablespoon lemon juice
2 tablespoons unsalted butter
1 cup coarsely grated sharp Cheddar cheese

1. Preheat the oven to 350°F. Lightly butter a 1½-quart casserole dish and set aside.

2. Place the apples in a large bowl and sprinkle with the cinnamon, flour, and sugar. Then carefully toss everything together with your hands so the slices are evenly coated.

3. Arrange the apple slices in a slightly overlapping pattern in the prepared baking dish. Mix ¼ cup of water and the lemon juice together and pour evenly over the apples. Then top the apples with dots of butter.

4. Cover the baking dish with foil and bake for 30 to 35 minutes, or until the apples are softened.

Carefully take the dish out of the oven, remove the foil, and sprinkle the apples with the cheese. Return the dish uncovered to the oven and bake for an additional 6 to 8 minutes, or until the cheese has melted. Remove from the oven and allow to cool. Serve warm.

Nicole's Buttermilk Fried Chicken

Nicole's fried chicken is the most delicious I've ever tasted. She makes huge batches of it for Applemania each year and we eat it in her backyard with our fingers and a huge stack of napkins. Double the recipe so you can have a second batch to serve over salads or eat in sandwiches the next day.

MAKES 6 TO 8 SERVINGS

2 cups cultured buttermilk
2 large eggs
2 teaspoons baking powder
1 teaspoon baking soda
6 boneless skinless chicken breasts (about 2 pounds), cut into 1-inch strips
2 cups unbleached all-purpose flour
1 teaspoon kosher salt
½ teaspoon freshly cracked black pepper
1½ tablespoons paprika
1 teaspoon garlic powder
1 teaspoon onion powder
Vegetable oil for deep frying

1. In a large, shallow bowl, whisk together the buttermilk, eggs, baking powder, and baking soda. The mixture will foam and bubble; this is normal.
2. Place the chicken breasts in the buttermilk mixture and turn it twice to coat. Cover the bowl with plastic wrap and refrigerate for at least 6 hours or overnight.

3. In a shallow baking pan, whisk together the flour, salt, pepper, paprika, garlic powder, and onion powder. Take the chicken out of the buttermilk mixture, allowing the excess liquid to drain off, and transfer it straight to the baking pan with the flour. Turn it two or three times to coat it well.
4. Fill a large, deep stockpot (a Dutch oven is ideal) with vegetable oil to a depth of 3 inches, and place it over medium-high heat. Heat the oil until it reaches 350°F on a thermometer. You'll know it is hot enough when a pinch of flour sizzles when it is dropped in the oil.
5. Shake off the excess flour from each piece of chicken and carefully add a few of them to the oil, without splashing or crowding. Fry for 3 minutes on each side, turning once halfway through, until the crust is golden brown and the internal temperature reaches 165°F. Transfer the chicken to a wire rack set over paper towels and let chicken drain. Allow the oil to come back to 350°F before adding the second batch of chicken pieces. Let the chicken drain and cool just slightly before serving hot.

Whole Wheat Apple Crumble Muffins

These taste like little bites of apple cake but are still healthy enough for breakfast or a late afternoon snack. Serve them for your apple buffet as a sweet option!

MAKES 12 MUFFINS

FOR THE TOPPING

½ cup white whole wheat flour

¼ cup old-fashioned rolled oats (not quick-cooking)

¼ cup packed dark brown sugar

2 teaspoons ground cinnamon

Pinch of fine sea salt

2 tablespoons vegetable oil

1 tablespoon whole milk

FOR THE MUFFINS

1 tablespoon cornstarch

2 large apples, peeled, cored, and chopped (about 1 cup)

½ cup granulated sugar

2 cups white whole wheat flour

2¼ teaspoons baking powder

½ teaspoon baking soda

½ teaspoon fine sea salt

2 teaspoons ground cinnamon

½ cup vegetable oil

½ cup whole milk

1. Preheat the oven to 350°F. Line a 12-cup muffin tin with paper liners and set aside.

2. To make the topping: Pinch the dry ingredients together in a large bowl. Then add the vegetable oil and milk and mix well. Set aside.

3. To make the muffins: In a large bowl, toss the cornstarch with the apples and set aside. Then sift together the granulated sugar, flour, powder, soda, salt, and cinnamon.

4. In a smaller bowl, whisk together the oil and milk. Then fold the wet ingredients into the dry ingredients and stir until smooth. Carefully fold in the chopped apples.

5. Fill each muffin tin about three-quarters full and top each muffin with equal amounts of the crumb topping. Bake for 25 to 30 minutes, or until the muffins are golden brown and a cake tester comes out clean. Allow to cool slightly, then serve warm.

Skillet Apple Pie

This supereasy apple pie recipe takes the guesswork out of crust baking. The apples bake beautifully and serving them in the skillet complements the rustic outdoor theme.

MAKES 1 PIE

FOR THE CRUST

1¼ cups unbleached all-purpose flour

2 tablespoons granulated sugar

½ teaspoon kosher salt

4 ounces (1 stick) cold unsalted butter, cut into small pieces

¼ cup ice water

FOR THE PIE

¼ cup granulated sugar

2 tablespoons cornstarch

¼ teaspoon ground cinnamon

¼ teaspoon ground ginger

2 tablespoons unsalted butter

7 large apples peeled, cored, and thinly sliced (about 7 cups) (we use Gala, Granny Smith, or Honeycrisp)

1 tablespoon freshly squeezed lemon juice

1 tablespoon milk

1 teaspoon coarse turbinado sugar

1. To make the crust: Place the flour, sugar, and salt in the bowl of a food processor fitted with a blade. Pulse for 5 seconds to combine. Add the butter and pulse about five times, or until the butter becomes pea-size balls. While pulsing the dough, pour the water 1 tablespoon at a time down the food processor chute, pulsing in between, until the dough forms in one large ball. Turn out the dough onto a lightly floured surface. Form it into a disk ½ inch thick, wrap it in plastic wrap, and chill for an hour.

2. To make the pie: Preheat the oven to 350°F. In a small bowl, combine the granulated sugar, cornstarch, cinnamon, and ginger. Set aside.

3. In a 10-inch cast-iron skillet, melt the butter. Add the apple slices and lemon juice and gently stir for 1 minute, to coat them in butter. Remove the skillet from the heat. Stir in the sugar mixture until the apple slices are evenly coated. Pat the apples evenly into the skillet.

4. Remove the dough from the refrigerator and roll it into a 12-inch circle on a lightly floured surface. Fit the dough over the skillet and tuck the overhanging dough into the skillet. Brush the top with the milk and sprinkle with the turbinado sugar. Cut a few small decorative holes in the top to allow for ventilation while baking.

5. Bake the pie for 40 to 45 minutes, or until golden brown and bubbly. Remove from the oven and allow to cool slightly before serving.

Harvest Dinner

CORN CHOWDER   195

—

MUSHROOMS *with* PINE NUTS & SPINACH   196

—

BUTTERNUT SQUASH & SAGE FARRO RISOTTO   197

—

APPLE-BRAISED PORK SHOULDER   198

—

WHOLE WHEAT PUMPKIN YOGURT LOAF   199

Harvest dinner was invented as our way to celebrate fall when Duncan's parents visit, and it's too early to celebrate Thanksgiving. Celebrate your harvest with your family and friends using this all-purpose fall menu. The food is full of fall flavor and is painless to execute. This way, you can spend more of your time raking leaves and hanging out instead of being in the kitchen.

Corn Chowder

This simple chowder is perfect for serving at the end of the corn harvest. It is warm and filling and tastes like the last breath of summer.

MAKES 6 TO 8 SERVINGS

4 slices apple wood–smoked bacon, cut into 1-inch pieces

1 teaspoon olive oil

1 cup finely chopped shallots (about 3 large shallots)

2 finely minced garlic cloves

2 teaspoons fresh thyme leaves

⅛ teaspoon smoked paprika

2 tablespoons unsalted butter

4½ cups fresh sweet corn kernels (from about 5 ears)

3 cups low-sodium chicken stock

1 cup whole milk

½ teaspoon kosher salt

½ teaspoon freshly cracked black pepper

1. In a heavy-bottomed pot, cook the bacon over medium-high heat until crisp, 7 to 10 minutes, turning as needed to ensure it cooks evenly. Transfer the cooked bacon pieces to a paper towel–lined plate to drain. Pour off and discard all but 1 tablespoon of the bacon drippings from the pan.

2. Add the olive oil and the shallots to the pot and cook them in the bacon drippings for about 6 minutes over medium heat, until they are golden brown and softened. Then add the garlic, thyme, and paprika and cook for 1 minute, or until the garlic is softened, but not burned.

3. Add the butter and corn to the pot and stir a few times to coat the corn in the shallot mixture. Return the bacon to the pot along with the chicken stock, milk, salt, and pepper and lower the heat to low. Simmer the chowder for about 30 minutes. Taste for seasoning. Ladle into bowls and serve warm.

Mushrooms *with* Pine Nuts & Spinach

This easy mushroom dish is a favorite of ours each fall. We love the earthy, rich flavors. It pairs beautifully with soups and stews and makes a nice appetizer when served on top of toasted baguette slices.

MAKES 4 SERVINGS

2 tablespoons pine nuts

2 tablespoons olive oil

1 pound cremini mushrooms, cleaned and sliced

Kosher salt

2 large handfuls baby spinach, stems removed

¼ cup white wine

1 teaspoon unsalted butter

1 tablespoon freshly grated Parmesan cheese

1. Place a large skillet over medium-low heat and toast the pine nuts very carefully, gently shaking the skillet, for a minute or two until they are lightly browned on all sides. Brush them out of the skillet into a small bowl to cool.

2. Return the skillet to the burner and add the oil. Add the mushrooms and a small pinch of salt and sauté the mushrooms for about 3 minutes, or until they are just cooked. Add the spinach and stir it into the mushrooms until it is completely softened and wilted, about 2 minutes. Add the wine and allow it to simmer until it has completely evaporated, about a minute. Then stir in the butter until melted.

3. Slide the mushrooms and spinach onto a platter and sprinkle the toasted pine nuts and Parmesan on top. Serve warm.

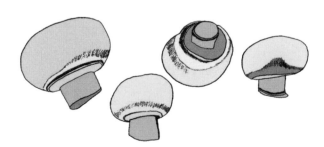

Butternut Squash & Sage Farro Risotto

I was turned on to using farro as a base for risotto after ordering it as the vegetarian option at a local restaurant. The farro has the same toothsome feel as arborio rice but is a little healthier because it is a whole, unprocessed grain. This is a great dish for highlighting fall flavors. You can use sweet potatoes in lieu of squash, if desired.

MAKES 6 TO 8 SERVINGS

1 tablespoon olive oil

1 medium-size yellow onion, peeled and finely chopped

2 garlic cloves, minced

¼ cup white wine

12 ounces (2½ cups) uncooked farro

4 cups vegetable stock

1 pound butternut squash, peeled and diced into 1-inch cubes

3 tablespoons unsalted butter

¼ cup finely grated Parmesan cheese

1 tablespoon finely chopped fresh sage

1 teaspoon kosher salt

½ teaspoon freshly cracked black pepper

1. In a large, heavy-bottomed pot, heat the oil over medium-high heat. Add the onion and cook until it is translucent and tender, 5 to 7 minutes. Then stir in the garlic and cook for 1 more minute. Pour in the wine and simmer until it has almost completely evaporated.

2. Add the farro and stir it for 1 minute so that it lightly toasts in the oil. Then stir in 1 cup of the stock and the butternut squash. Lower the heat to medium-low, add a second cup of the stock, and continue to stir well until the liquid is nearly all absorbed, 8 to 10 minutes. Continue to add the stock in ½-cup increments, stirring well until the liquid is absorbed after each addition. This should take 20 to 25 minutes; the farro and squash should be tender when the last of the stock has been absorbed.

3. Stir in the butter, cheese, sage, salt, and pepper once the farro is cooked. Taste for seasonings and add more salt if necessary. Allow to cool slightly and serve warm.

Apple-Braised Pork Shoulder

This is the time of year to cook heavier meats in long, slow braises that are so fragrant the aroma fills up the whole house. This dish is deceptively simple, which makes it perfect for serving a crowd. Assemble the ingredients, pop it in the oven, and leave it be until everyone is ready to eat!

MAKES 4 TO 6 SERVINGS

1 tablespoon vegetable oil

4 ounces pancetta, finely diced

3 pounds boneless pork shoulder, cut into
   1-pound pieces

1 large Vidalia onion, peeled and sliced thinly

Kosher salt

Freshly cracked black pepper

3 garlic cloves, minced

⅓ cup red wine

1½ cups apple cider

1½ cups low-sodium chicken stock

2 large apples (such as Gala or Honeycrisp),
   peeled, cored, and sliced into 8 wedges each

1. Preheat the oven to 325°F.

2. In a heavy-bottomed pot or Dutch oven, heat the oil and add the pancetta. Cook until crisp and lightly browned, about 5 minutes. Use a slotted spoon to transfer it to a plate lined with a paper towel.

3. Add the pork to the pot in batches and cook until it is browned on all sides. It will take 6 to 8 minutes per batch. Transfer the browned pork to the paper towel–lined plate.

4. Add the onion to the pot with a liberal pinch of salt and pepper and cook for about 5 minutes, or until it softens and becomes translucent. Add the garlic and stir for an additional minute so it is just fragrant but not burned. Pour in the wine and scrape up and browned bits on the bottom of the pan with a wooden spoon.

5. Pour the apple cider and chicken stock into the pot and bring it to a simmer. Add the pork back to the pot so that is in an even layer as possible. Cover the pot and place it in the oven to cook for 2 to 2½ hours, stirring once at the halfway point. The pork should be fork-tender when it is done.

6. Remove the pot from the oven and transfer the pork to a platter, using a slotted spoon. Add the apple slices and pancetta to the pan and place it on a burner over medium-low heat. Simmer the liquid until it has reduced by half and the apples are tender, about 10 minutes. Serve the pork on plates drizzled with the apple-pancetta pan sauce.

Whole Wheat Pumpkin Yogurt Loaf

I am a devoted pumpkin bread eater and make an alarming number of batches each fall. I usually end up doubling this recipe and freezing two loaves to save time. We go through them so quickly! To lighten up my favorite recipe a little, I use white whole wheat flour and swap out some oil for yogurt.

MAKES 2 LOAVES

Butter for loaf pans

1 cups white whole wheat flour

2 cups unbleached all-purpose flour

1 teaspoon baking soda

1½ teaspoons baking powder

1 teaspoon kosher salt

2 teaspoons pumpkin pie spice

3 large eggs

1 (15-ounce) can pure pumpkin purée

½ cup vegetable oil

1 teaspoon pure vanilla extract

½ cup packed light brown sugar

1½ cups granulated sugar

¾ cup plain Greek yogurt

1. Preheat the oven to 350°F. Lightly butter the bottom and sides of two 9 x 5-inch loaf pans and set aside.

2. In a large bowl, combine the flour, baking soda, baking powder, salt, and spice. Set aside. In a smaller bowl, beat the eggs, then add the pumpkin, vegetable oil, vanilla, sugars, and yogurt. Fold this wet mixture into the flour mixture and stir until smooth.

3. Divide the batter evenly between the loaf pans and smooth the tops with a spatula. Bake them for 55 to 60 minutes, or until a cake tester inserted comes out clean and the top springs back when touched.

4. Remove the loaves from the oven and allow them to cool for about 10 minutes in the pan. Then invert onto a cooling rack and allow to cool completely.

Grade School Birthday Party

CHICKEN DRUMSTICKS   201

—

HUMMUS   202

—

MINI ICE-CREAM SODAS   203

—

THREE-LAYER VANILLA CAKE
with CHOCOLATE BUTTERCREAM   204

Throwing a child's birthday party doesn't have to be stressful. I've found there is a certain art to making the celebration special enough to live up to a child's expectations, while keeping it simple enough to execute. Children don't care about fancy party favors and intricate decorations; they want one or two superfun activities, a little free-for-all playtime, and great kid food. Follow this game plan of a few surefire recipes plus a great cake, and the kids will have a good time, no matter what!

Your Grade School Birthday Party Strategy

ACTIVITY IDEAS The collective energy of children at a birthday party can be overwhelming if it's not constructively channeled. Have the first activity ready to go the minute they arrive. Food-related party activities kids enjoy include: decorating cookies, decorating graham cracker "gingerbread" houses, decorating the cake, and making ice-cream sundaes.

SNACKS To keep the children going until the main meal, keep some simple snacks around. A few bowls of goldfish, pretzels, and cheese crackers are plenty for them to nosh on between games.

GOODIE BAGS Start with brown paper bags or plain treat bags and embellish them with stickers, stamps, and all sorts of decorations. Fill them with three items: a sweet, such as a lollipop or mint; a craft item, such as stickers or a rubber stamp; and a cool writing implement, such as a fun marker or crayon.

Chicken Drumsticks

These supereasy drumsticks are a total hit with children. You can prepare them in one big batch in advance. Kids don't need any utensils to eat them and the drumsticks can be gobbled down while the guests chat with each other.

MAKES 8 SERVINGS

6 tablespoons honey
Grated zest and juice of 2 large lemons
½ cup light soy sauce
16 chicken drumsticks (about 4 pounds)
¼ cup sesame seeds

1. In a small bowl, whisk together the honey, lemon juice and zest, and soy sauce. Set aside.
2. Make three slashes about ¼ inch wide on the top of each drumstick so they can absorb the marinade. Nestle them snugly into two large baking dishes. Reserving ½ cup of the marinade for baking, pour the rest into the dish, turning each drumstick in full rotation so it is evenly coated. Cover and refrigerate for at least 3 hours, or up to 1 day.
3. Preheat the oven to 350°F. Line two large baking sheets with aluminum foil.
4. Place the drumsticks on the baking sheet, skin-side up, and sprinkle the sesame seeds over the drumsticks. Bake them for 45 minutes, brushing them with the reserved marinade halfway through. Remove from the oven and allow to cool for 10 minutes. Serve warm.

Hummus

Hummus is a universally loved dip among Daphne and her friends. Second only to ketchup, hummus is used for dipping a wide variety of foods from vegetables to crackers, chips, pita bread, and sandwiches. You can make it all kinds of different ways, depending on your preferences. Here are some of our favorite varieties.

MAKES 2 CUPS HUMMUS

1 (15-ounce) can chickpeas (garbanzo beans), drained

2 garlic cloves, finely chopped

3 tablespoons freshly squeezed lemon juice

2 tablespoons tahini (sesame paste)

½ teaspoon kosher salt

2 to 3 tablespoons olive oil, plus more for drizzling

2 to 3 tablespoons water

½ teaspoon paprika (optional)

1. Place the chickpeas, garlic, lemon juice, tahini, salt, 2 tablespoons of the olive oil, 2 tablespoons of water, and the paprika in a blender and purée until very smooth.

2. Take a small taste and add a touch more olive oil and water if you want the paste to be thinner.

3. Scoop the hummus into a bowl and drizzle with a little more olive oil. Serve!

VARIATIONS

SUN-DRIED TOMATO HUMMUS Prepare the basic hummus recipe. Add ½ cup of sun-dried tomatoes and pulse until very smooth. Scoop the hummus into a bowl and drizzle with a little more olive oil.

AVO-HUMMUS Prepare the basic hummus recipe. Add ½ fresh avocado to the blender and purée until very smooth. Scoop the hummus into a bowl and drizzle with a little more olive oil.

PUMPKIN HUMMUS Prepare the basic hummus recipe. Add ½ cup of pure pumpkin purée to the blender and blend until smooth. Scoop the hummus into a bowl, drizzle with olive oil, and top with toasted pepitas!

Mini Ice-Cream Sodas

Ice cream is always a must when there is birthday cake being served. To give ours a little twist, I make mini ice-cream sodas to drink alongside the cake. You can make this with any kind of ice cream you want.

MAKES 8 (4-OUNCE) SERVINGS

Chocolate syrup, as needed

Vanilla syrup, as needed

Strawberry syrup, as needed

32 ounces plain seltzer

2 cups ice cream of choice

1. Set out small cups and add 1 tablespoon of flavored syrup to the bottom of each. Pour equal amounts of seltzer into each glass and use a fork or small whisk to whisk the syrup up from the bottom. Top the cup with one small scoop of ice cream. Serve it with a straw!

Three-Layer Vanilla Cake *with* Chocolate Buttercream

The most important part of a child's birthday party is the cake. This simple recipe is our family's favorite cake that is just like the best bakery cake you've ever had: only better. It is soft and spongy with a rich vanilla flavor. Frost it with a smooth and creamy chocolate frosting that is also spread between each layer. The best part, however, is not in the recipe; it is the decoration. Let your child and the guests decorate the cake. While it may be a bit of a messy endeavor, I guarantee they will always end up with some very interesting creations that they adore!

MAKES 1 THREE-LAYER CAKE

FOR THE CAKE

1 cup plus 2 tablespoons (2¼ sticks) unsalted
   butter, at room temperature, plus more for pan
3½ cups unbleached all-purpose flour, plus more
   for dusting pans
2 teaspoons baking powder
1 teaspoon baking soda
1 teaspoon kosher salt
2 cups granulated sugar
6 large eggs
1 cup sour cream
1 tablespoon pure vanilla extract

FOR THE FROSTING

6 ounces (1½ sticks) unsalted butter, at room
   temperature
5½ cups confectioners' sugar
2 teaspoons pure vanilla extract
½ cup whole milk, plus more if needed
4 ounces milk chocolate, melted and cooled
M&M's, gummy bears, sprinkles, edible gold
   stars, mini marshmallows, mini pretzels,
   mini candy canes, chopped candy bars, and
   lollipops, for decorating

1. To make the cake: Preheat the oven to 350°F. Butter and flour three 8-inch round cake pans and set aside. In a large bowl, mix together the flour, baking powder, baking soda, and salt and set aside.
2. With an electric mixer fitted with the paddle attachment, beat the butter and granulated sugar on high speed in a large bowl until light and fluffy, about 5 minutes. Add the eggs, sour cream, and vanilla and mix on medium speed until the batter is smooth. With the mixer on low speed, slowly add the dry ingredients, mixing until it is just combined and no longer visible.
3. Divide the cake batter evenly among the three prepared pans and bake for 24 to 26 minutes. The tops of the cakes should spring back when touched and the sides should just be starting to pull away from the sides of the pan. Remove the cakes from the oven and allow them to cool for 5 minutes in their pans. Turn them out onto a cooling rack and allow them to cool completely before frosting.
4. To make the frosting: With an electric mixer fitted with the paddle attachment, cream the butter and confectioners' sugar on high speed in a large bowl until light and fluffy, about 3 minutes. With the mixer on medium speed, slowly add the vanilla, followed by the milk a little bit at a time.

The frosting should become glossy and volumi-nous. Add the melted chocolate and beat until it is completely incorporated. It should be thick, yet spreadable, and not at all runny. If it seems too thick, add more milk 1 teaspoon at a time, beating well after each addition, until desired consistency is reached.

5. Use an offset spatula to frost the cake. Place the first layer on a cake stand or serving platter and spread a thin layer of chocolate frosting over the top of the cake. Place the second layer on top of this and repeat. Finally, spread a layer of chocolate frosting on top of the third layer. Use the remaining frosting the spread along the sides of the cake, smoothing it as you go, with the offset spatula. Once the whole cake is evenly frosted, place the cake in the refrigerator to let the frost-ing harden a bit. Use whatever frosting remains to spread a second layer on top of the cake, covering any patchy places as necessary. Alternatively, let the children use the remaining frosting to stick some of their decorations on the cake!

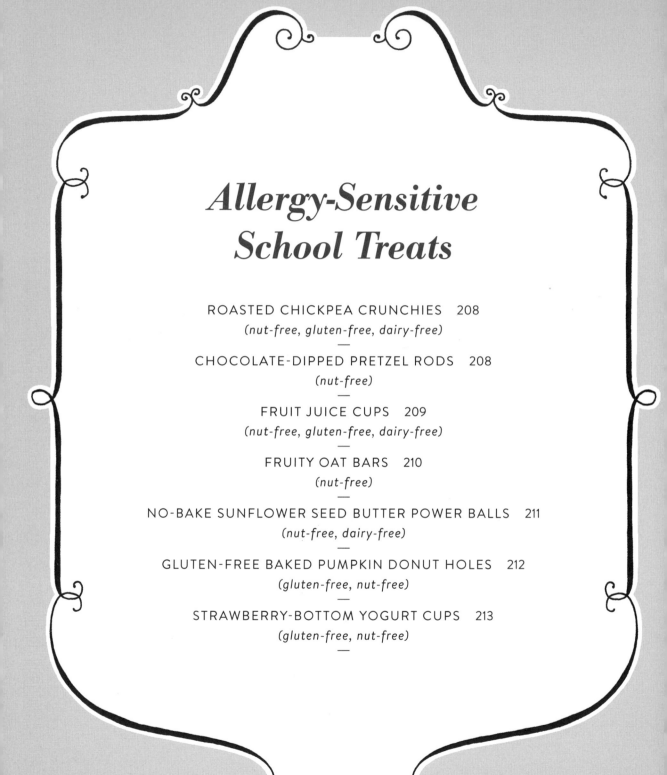

Allergy-Sensitive School Treats

ROASTED CHICKPEA CRUNCHIES   208
(nut-free, gluten-free, dairy-free)

—

CHOCOLATE-DIPPED PRETZEL RODS   208
(nut-free)

—

FRUIT JUICE CUPS   209
(nut-free, gluten-free, dairy-free)

—

FRUITY OAT BARS   210
(nut-free)

—

NO-BAKE SUNFLOWER SEED BUTTER POWER BALLS   211
(nut-free, dairy-free)

—

GLUTEN-FREE BAKED PUMPKIN DONUT HOLES   212
(gluten-free, nut-free)

—

STRAWBERRY-BOTTOM YOGURT CUPS   213
(gluten-free, nut-free)

Cooking for school can be a challenge because of the number of food allergies you must consider. It is so important to be hyperaware of what children can and can't eat before you plan what to bring in. Based on feedback from Daphne and her friends, I have curated a small but popular group of allergy-sensitive recipes that work for almost every situation. These have become the recipes that I revisit time and time again. If you have concerns about specific children in your classroom, speak with the teacher or call their parents directly.

Roasted Chickpea Crunchies *(nut-free, gluten-free, dairy-free)*

These little nibbles are healthy and can be flavored any number of different ways. A lot of children ask me whether these are round crackers because they are crunchy and salty. They are amazed when they learn they are actually eating beans!

MAKES 4 CUPS CRUNCHIES

2 (15-ounce) cans chickpeas, drained, rinsed, and
    patted dry
2 tablespoons olive oil
1 teaspoon fine sea salt
Grated zest and juice of 1 lemon

1. Preheat the oven to 425°F.

2. Line a large, rimmed baking sheet with parchment paper and pour the chickpeas on them in one even layer. Bake the chickpeas for 20 minutes, turning them once with a wooden spoon at the 10-minute point.

3. Meanwhile, in a large bowl, whisk together the olive oil, sea salt, and lemon zest and juice.

4. Remove the chickpeas from the oven, but leave the oven turned on. Carefully pour the hot chickpeas into the olive oil mixture and stir well so they are evenly coated.

5. Return the chickpeas to the lined baking sheet and roast them in the oven for 5 to 8 more minutes, until they are browned and fragrant. Allow them to cool before serving.

Note To add a little flavor to the chickpeas, use dried herbs and spices. For spicy chickpea mix, add ½ teaspoon off cayenne pepper. For herbed chickpeas, add ½ teaspoon of dried rosemary, thyme, or basil.

Chocolate-Dipped Pretzel Rods *(nut-free)*

I've taken these to Daphne's class before and they've been called everything from Magic Pretzel Wands to Light Sabers to Pretzel Pirate Swords. No matter what you call them, they are easy to make and fun to eat!

MAKES 24 PRETZEL RODS

Sprinkles, as needed
12 ounces semisweet chocolate chips
24 large pretzel rods

1. Line a baking sheet or large flat platter with waxed paper. Pour the sprinkles into a bowl. Set aside.

2. Place the chocolate to a microwave-safe bowl and heat in the microwave at 50% power in 10-second bursts, or until just melted. Stir the chips until smooth.

3. Working quickly, dip half the length of a pretzel rod into the melted chocolate and turn it to coat. Then dip the coated pretzel into the sprinkles. Place the finished rod on the prepared baking sheet to harden. Once all the rods have been dipped, place the baking sheet in the refrigerator to harden for 1 hour.

Note To further decorate the rods, drizzle the hardened chocolate decoratively with melted white chocolate. At Christmas, dip them in crushed candy canes instead of sprinkles.

Fruit Juice Cups *(nut-free, gluten-free, dairy-free)*

The homemade version of the classic Jell-O Jiggler uses real fruit juice and lots of fresh fruit. The children adore it and I feel good knowing that is safe for all of them.

MAKES 8 (½-CUP) SERVINGS

2 (0.25-ounce) envelopes unflavored gelatin
4 cups pure pineapple juice, divided
2 cups fresh pineapple, cut into ½-inch pieces

1. In a small bowl, sprinkle the gelatin over 1 cup of the pineapple juice and set aside.
2. Bring the remaining 3 cups of pineapple juice to a boil over medium heat, then remove it from the heat and whisk in the gelatin mixture until it is completely dissolved.
3. Once the mixture has cooled for about 15 minutes, pour it into your serving cups. Make sure they are heat-resistant so they don't melt.

4. Place the cups on a plate or tray and chill them in the refrigerator for 1 hour. At the 1-hour mark, drop a single pineapple piece into one of the cups. If it immediately sinks to the bottom, it needs to continue chilling. If it settles near the top, you can distribute the pineapple among the cups. Return the cups to the refrigerator and chill for another 3 hours, or until firm.

Note This also works well with the same proportions of white grape juice and sliced seedless white grapes.

Fruity Oat Bars *(nut-free)*

Once I started making these, Daphne stopped asking for granola bars from the grocery store. Now we make big pans of them and I send them to school for snack all week long. I also bring them in for school activities, as they are nut-free. To make them gluten-free, use gluten-free rolled oats. I like the Bob's Red Mill brand.

MAKES 16 SQUARES

2½ cups rolled oats

⅓ cup sweetened shredded coconut

¼ cup pepitas (pumpkin seeds)

Cooking spray

4 tablespoons (½ stick) unsalted butter, cut into pieces

3 tablespoons light brown sugar

1 teaspoon pure vanilla extract

½ teaspoon fine sea salt

⅓ cup wildflower honey

½ cup dried apricots, finely chopped

1. Preheat the oven to 350°F. Line a baking sheet with parchment paper and spread the oats, coconut, and pepitas evenly on it. Toast the oats for 8 to 10 minutes, turning them a few times with a spoon, until they are lightly golden brown. Transfer them to a large mixing bowl and allow to cool.

2. Line an 8-inch square baking pan with parchment paper, allowing a 1-inch overhang of parchment paper around the pan. Spray with cooking spray and set aside.

3. In small saucepan, combine the butter, sugar, vanilla, and salt over medium-low heat. Stir just until the butter is melted and everything is

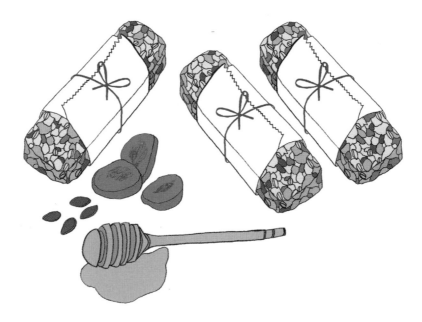

completely combined. Remove the pan from the heat and allow the mixture to cool for 5 minutes. Then pour the mixture into the bowl with the toasted oats, add the honey, and mix well until everything is combined. Use a spatula to fold in the apricots and the oat mixture.

4. Spoon into the prepared baking dish and press evenly into the pan, using damped fingertips or a wet spatula. Be sure the mixture is pressed down very hard so that it is as compact as possible. Freeze the bars for 2 hours. Then transfer to the refrigerator until ready to cut. Before cutting, allow the bars to thaw for 10 minutes at room temperature. Store in a sealable container in the refrigerator until ready to serve.

Note If you don't have pepitas, use sunflower seeds.

No-Bake Sunflower Seed Butter Power Balls
(nut-free, dairy-free)

These no-bake balls are naturally sweet treats that give the children energy and protein. Because they don't require any complicated technique to make, I often have Daphne join me in the kitchen to assemble them. She loves telling her classmates that she made them! To make these gluten-free, use gluten-free quick-cooking oats.

MAKES ABOUT 34 BALLS

2 cups quick-cooking oats
1 cup dairy-free semisweet chocolate chips
1 cup ground flaxseed meal
1 teaspoon fine sea salt
1 cup sunflower seed butter
⅔ cups wildflower honey
1 teaspoon pure vanilla extract

1. Line a rimmed baking sheet with parchment paper and set aside.
2. In a large bowl, mix together the oats, chocolate chips, flaxseed meal, and sea salt. Set aside.

3. In a small bowl, mix together the sunflower seed butter, honey, and vanilla until very smooth. Then stir it into the oat mixture until it is evenly distributed and the oats get very sticky.
4. Pinch of pieces of the mixture and roll them into 1½-inch balls, occasionally wetting your hands with water to keep the mixture from sticking, and place on the prepared baking sheet. Chill the balls in the refrigerator for 2 hours to set. Serve!

Note If you are not concerned about nut allergies, you can substitute your favorite nut butter for sunflower seed butter.

Gluten-Free Baked Pumpkin Donut Holes
(gluten-free, nut-free)

Once I discovered the King Arthur Gluten-Free Multi-Purpose Flour, making any treat gluten-free became a breeze. These spiced pumpkin bites are mini muffins masquerading as donut holes. They taste like fall and are perfect for little hands. For birthday celebrations, pile them on a platter, pyramid style, and put a candle on top! If you aren't worried about being gluten-free, regular unbleached all-purpose flour can be used.

MAKES 24 DONUT HOLES

Cooking spray

¾ cup gluten-free all-purpose flour blend (I like King Arthur)

2 teaspoons baking powder

¼ teaspoon kosher salt

1 teaspoon pumpkin pie spice

⅓ cup vegetable oil

½ cup packed light brown sugar

1 large egg

1 teaspoon pure vanilla extract

¾ cup pure pumpkin purée (not pumpkin pie filling)

½ cup whole milk

4 tablespoons (½ stick) unsalted butter, melted

½ cup granulated sugar

3 tablespoons ground cinnamon

1. Preheat the oven to 350°F. Spray the inside of a 24-cup mini muffin tin with cooking spray and set aside.

2. In a small bowl, whisk together the flour, baking powder, salt, and pumpkin pie spice.

3. In a large bowl, whisk together the oil, brown sugar, egg, vanilla, pumpkin, and milk until smooth and completely incorporated.

4. Carefully stir the flour mixture into the wet ingredients. Stir just until the flour is combined and no longer visible. Then divide the batter evenly among the muffin cups, filling each about three-quarters full. Bake for 18 to 20 minutes, or until the tops spring back when touched and a toothpick comes out clean.

5. Allow the muffins to cool for about 5 minutes in the pan. While they are cooling, place the melted butter in a large, shallow bowl. In a second bowl, stir together the granulated sugar and cinnamon.

6. Once the muffins are just cool enough to handle comfortably, pop them out of the pan and roll them all over in the butter, followed immediately by rolling in the cinnamon-sugar. Place them on a cooling rack situated over a rimmed baking sheet or paper towel, to catch any drips. Allow to cool for about 10 more minutes, then serve.

Strawberry-Bottom Yogurt Cups *(gluten-free, nut-free)*

Once you get the hang of this recipe, you can dream up almost any flavor you want. It is really fun to add to the list of berry treats to make after a day of strawberry picking!

MAKES 10 SERVINGS

1 pound strawberries, hulled and chopped

3 to 4 tablespoons agave nectar, or to taste

¼ teaspoon kosher salt

2 tablespoons cornstarch

2 tablespoons orange juice

3½ cups vanilla yogurt, plain yogurt, or plain
    Greek-style yogurt

1. In a medium saucepan over medium heat, combine the strawberries, agave, and salt. Simmer for about 2 minutes. Meanwhile, whisk together the cornstarch and the orange juice until the cornstarch is dissolved. Add this to the fruit and continue to simmer, stirring occasionally, for 5 to 6 minutes, or until the mixture has thickened. Remove from the heat and allow to cool.

2. Once the strawberry mixture is cool, layer 2 to 3 tablespoons in the bottom of a lidded glass jar, cup, or plastic container. Then top with about ½ cup of yogurt. Repeat with additional containers to make a total of ten single servings. Store covered in the refrigerator.

Note To play with the flavors, try stirring some fresh orange or lemon zest into the yogurt. A drizzle of honey or maple syrup on top would be delicious. If nuts or gluten are not a concern, you can garnish the top of the yogurt with a tablespoon of crunchy granola or your favorite cereal. For tropical fruit, skip the cooking step and just serve fresh finely chopped fruit at the bottom of the yogurt.

For School When taking this to school, it's best to use a container with a lid that can be sealed. Give children spoons and let them dig in!

Cran-Apple Sauce *(nut-free, dairy-free, gluten-free)*

This applesauce will remind of you of the beloved cranberry-apple juice from your childhood. Package it for school parties in little glass jars with lids and a ribbon tied around it.

MAKES 4 SERVINGS

2 pounds apples, peeled, cored, and roughly
chopped (I like juicy varieties, such as
Honeycrisp, Gala, or Macintosh)

1 cup fresh cranberries

⅓ cup pure maple syrup

¼ cup apple cider or juice

2 teaspoons ground cinnamon

2 teaspoons fresh grated lemon zest (from
1 medium-size lemon)

2 tablespoons vegan butter (I use Earth Balance)

1. In a large, heavy-bottomed pot, combine the apples, cranberries, maple syrup, cider, cinnamon, and lemon zest. Bring the mixture to a low simmer over medium-low heat and cook covered, stirring occasionally, for 15 to 20 minutes, or until the apples and cranberries are very soft.

2. Remove the mixture from the heat and allow it to cool slightly. Pour it into a food processor fitted with the blade attachment and pulse until you reach the desired consistency: It should be a chunky rose-colored applesauce. Stir in the vegan butter until it is completely melted. Allow the mixture to cool to room temperature before serving. It can be served at room temperature or chilled. Store in a covered container in the refrigerator.

Mini Banana Bread Muffins *(nut-free)*

This is one of the most popular recipes of all time on my blog, The Naptime Chef. They are perfect for school, can made in large batches, and can be easily frozen. For a sweet twist, stir a cup of mini chocolate chips into the batter.

MAKES 24 MINI MUFFINS

Cooking spray (optional)

1½ cups unbleached all-purpose flour

½ teaspoon ground nutmeg

¼ teaspoon kosher salt

8 ounces (1 stick) unsalted butter, at room temperature

½ cup granulated sugar

1 large egg, at room temperature

3 small bananas, mashed with a fork

1 teaspoon baking soda dissolved in 1 tablespoon hot water

1. Preheat the oven to 350°F. Line a mini muffin tin with paper liners or spray each cup with cooking spray and set aside. In a small bowl, mix together the flour, nutmeg, and salt, then set aside.

2. With an electric mixer fitted with the paddle attachment, beat the butter and sugar at high speed in a large bowl until light and fluffy, about 2 minutes. Then beat in the egg and bananas and mix well. Beat in the baking soda mixture.

3. With the mixer on low speed, beat in the flour mixture until just combined, with no visible streaks of flour.

4. Fill each muffin cup half-full and bake for 12 to 15 minutes, or until the muffins are golden brown and the tops spring back when touched. Allow to cool before serving.

Mini Corn Muffins *with* Jam *(nut-free)*

Make these for classroom Thanksgiving celebrations and again in the spring to eat with your first batch of strawberry jam. If you want to make these gluten-free, simply use a gluten-free all-purpose baking blend instead of the flour.

MAKES 24 MINI MUFFINS

Cooking spray

1 cup unbleached all-purpose flour

1 cup cornmeal

1½ teaspoons baking powder

¼ teaspoon baking soda

1 cup buttermilk

½ teaspoon kosher salt

1 large egg

¼ cup vegetable oil

½ cup fresh sweet corn kernels, cooked (about ½ ear of corn) (optional)

1. Preheat the oven to 375°F. Spray the inside of a 24-cup mini muffin tin with cooking spray and set aside.

2. In a small bowl, combine the flour, cornmeal, sugar, baking powder, and baking soda. Set aside.

3. In a large bowl, whisk together the buttermilk, salt, egg, and oil until smooth and completely combined. Add the flour mixture and stir until smooth with no visible streaks of flour. Stir in the corn kernels, if using.

4. Fill each prepared muffin cup about three-quarters full and bake for 12 to 15 minutes, or until the muffin tops are golden brown and spring back when touched.

5. Allow the muffins to cool for 5 minutes in the pan. Then pop them out onto a cooling rack to cool completely. Serve with fresh jam!

Thanksgiving

The point of Thanksgiving is to be together and enjoy great food, not to get overwhelmed by your to-do list. Your guest list might vary slightly from year to year, but this is the occasion to stick with dishes you know and love. All it takes are a few foolproof recipes with some personal touches to make your holiday meal a complete success. Then you can turn your focus to making memories with friends and family.

Rosemary Parmesan Dinner Rolls

Even if you don't normally bake your dinner rolls from scratch year-round, homemade rolls are a must at Thanksgiving—and they're much easier than you'd think. These soft white rolls are a family classic that everyone loves. Prep the dough the day before and bake fresh while the turkey is resting.

MAKES 12 ROLLS

¼ cup extra-virgin olive oil

2 tablespoons chopped fresh rosemary

3¼ cups unbleached all-purpose flour

1 cup finely grated Parmesan cheese

2 teaspoons kosher salt

1 cup warm water

2¼ teaspoon (1 packet) active dry yeast

1. Infuse the olive oil with the rosemary by combining the two in a small saucepan and heating over medium-low heat for 10 minutes: The oil should just steam but not bubble. Remove the saucepan from the heat and let cool for 20 minutes. In a large bowl, combine the flour, cheese, and salt. Set aside.

2. Meanwhile, pour the water into a small bowl and sprinkle the yeast on top. Let it stand for about 5 minutes, long enough for the yeast to start to foam. If nothing happens, discard the yeast and start over with fresh yeast.

3. With an electric mixer fitted with the blade attachment, combine the cooled oil, the yeast mixture, and ¾ cup of the flour mixture on low speed in a large bowl for about 1 minute, then slowly add the rest of the flour mixture 1 cup at a time, beating well after each addition.

4. Once all the flour mixture is added, switch out the paddle for a dough hook attachment and knead the dough for 5 minutes, or until a smooth ball has formed that pulls away from the sides.

5. Turn the dough out onto a lightly floured surface and knead once or twice. Then place it back in its bowl and cover it with a clean kitchen towel. Let it rise for 1 hour, or until it has doubled in size.

6. Punch down the dough and let it rest for 15 minutes. Then line a baking sheet with parchment paper and divide the dough into twelve equal-size pieces. Roll each piece into a smooth, round ball. Place the balls 2 inches apart on the baking sheet. Cover the pan with plastic wrap and let it rise for another hour.

7. Preheat the oven to 375°F. Remove the plastic wrap from the rolls and bake them for 18 to 20 minutes, or until golden brown on top. Transfer the rolls to a cooling rack to cool.

Tip Don't overbake these rolls; when they are just golden brown and firm, they're done. If overbaked, they will quickly turn hard.

Classic Roast Turkey

Once I mastered cooking a moist, buttery turkey, I never looked back. I swear by this classic approach because it always gets rave reviews, plus the leftovers make the best turkey sandwiches the next day! The rule of thumb is about one pound turkey per serving; plan accordingly if you want leftovers.

MAKES 1 (12-POUND) TURKEY, ABOUT 12 SERVINGS

2 medium-size lemons, divided

4 ounces (1 stick) unsalted butter

1 (12-pound) turkey

Kosher salt

Freshly cracked black pepper

10 sprigs rosemary

1 Vidalia onion, quartered

8 garlic cloves, halved

1. Preheat the oven to 350°F.

2. Juice and zest one of the lemons, and combine the zest and juice with the butter in a microwave-safe bowl. Heat the butter at 50% power in 10-second bursts until it is just melted. Quarter the second lemon, and set aside.

3. Remove the giblets from the turkey and place the bird in a large roasting pan. Sprinkle a liberal amount of salt and pepper inside the turkey cavity, spreading it all around the inside. Stuff the bird with the rosemary, onion, garlic, and the quartered lemon. Tie the legs together with kitchen string.

4. Generously brush the outside of the turkey with the lemon butter, making sure to get both under and over the skin. Lightly sprinkle the top of the bird with more salt and pepper.

5. Roast the turkey breast-up for 2½ to 3 hours, or about 13 minutes per pound. It is done when a meat thermometer inserted into the thickest part of the thigh reads 165°F and the juices run clear when the bird is pricked with a knife. Place the turkey on a platter or cutting board and cover it with aluminum foil (reserve the pan drippings for the gravy). Allow it to rest for 20 minutes. Carve and serve!

Classic Turkey Gravy

It is important to have a foolproof turkey gravy recipe in your repertoire. With this one you'll get perfect creamy gravy every time.

MAKES 4 TO 6 SERVINGS

2 tablespoons unsalted butter

4 tablespoons unbleached all-purpose flour

2 cups pan drippings from the turkey, fat skimmed off the top

¾ cup low-sodium chicken stock

1. In a shallow, wide skillet over medium heat, melt the butter. Whisk in the flour and cook it for about 2 minutes, or until it becomes a smooth paste. Carefully whisk in the pan drippings and chicken stock ½ cup at a time, whisking until smooth after each addition. Once everything is added, simmer the gravy for about 2 minutes, whisking continuously.

Tip If you have less than 2 cups of pan drippings, add chicken stock until you reach the 2-cup mark. Or, for a thicker gravy, reduce the pan drippings to 1½ cups.

Tip Once you are comfortable with this gravy recipe, you can add more flavor to it by stirring in 1 teaspoon of fresh thyme leaves.

Quick Cranberry Sauce

Condiments shouldn't take a lot of time to make when you are preparing so much food. This sauce is perfect for the big feast. The warm spices complement the meat and it comes together easily.

MAKES 4 CUPS SAUCE

¾ cup granulated sugar

1½ cups water

4 cups fresh cranberries, rinsed and picked over

⅛ teaspoon ground cloves

⅛ teaspoon ground nutmeg

¼ teaspoon ground cinnamon

1 teaspoon freshly grated orange zest

1 tablespoon freshly squeezed orange juice

1. Combine the sugar and water in a large saucepan and heat them over medium-low heat until the sugar is completely dissolved.

2. Carefully add the cranberries, spices, and orange zest and juice and continue to stir everything over medium-low heat until the cranberries collapse and the mixture turns a brilliant red, about 20 minutes. Lower the heat to low and allow the sauce to thicken for 10 more minutes, stirring occasionally.

3. Remove the pan from the heat and allow it to cool to room temperature before serving. It will continue thickening as it cools. Store in a sealed container in the refrigerator until serving.

Bacon & Walnut Ciabatta Stuffing

Stuffing is just as important on Thanksgiving Day as it is on turkey sandwiches the following day. This easy stuffing is perfect for both. The chewy bread absorbs all the delicious flavors and the toasted walnuts add a wonderful nutty crunch.

MAKES 6 TO 8 SERVINGS

4 tablespoons (½ stick) unsalted butter, divided, plus more for baking dish

6 ounces bacon

2 medium-size yellow onions, peeled and finely chopped

2 carrots, peeled and finely chopped

2 large celery stalks, finely chopped

1 cup chopped walnuts

2 tablespoons finely chopped fresh sage

1 pound day-old ciabatta, cut into 1-inch cubes

¾ cup coarsely grated Parmesan cheese

1¼ cups low-sodium chicken stock

1 teaspoon kosher salt

¼ teaspoon freshly cracked black pepper

2 large eggs, lightly beaten

1. Preheat the oven to 350°F. Butter the bottom and sides of a 13 x 9 x 2-inch baking dish.

2. Melt 2 tablespoons of the butter in a large skillet and add the bacon. Cook the bacon in the butter over medium-high heat, turning, until cooked and crisp, about 8 minutes. Transfer the bacon to a paper towel–lined plate to drain. When the bacon is cool enough to touch, break it into small pieces.

3. Drain all but 1 tablespoon of bacon fat off the skillet and add the remaining 2 tablespoons of butter. Once the butter has melted, add the onions, carrots, and celery. Cook the mixture over medium heat until the vegetables are softened and translucent, 8 to 10 minutes. Stir in the walnuts and sage, then turn off the heat and scrape the mixture into a large mixing bowl.

4. Add the bacon pieces, bread, and cheese to the bowl and toss everything well to coat. Then slowly pour in the chicken stock, adding just enough to moisten all of the bread. Stir in the salt, pepper, and eggs.

5. Transfer the mixture to the prepared baking sheet and covered it with foil. Bake it for 35 to 40 minutes, or until heated through. Remove the foil and bake for an additional 10 minutes, or until the top is golden brown. Remove from the oven and allow to cool before serving.

Green Beans *with* Tarragon Mustard

Make your green beans with this sweet mustard dressing. It pairs wonderfully with turkey and there is no canned soup in sight! For an easy dinner at home, this recipe halves easily.

MAKES 6 TO 8 SERVINGS

2 pounds green beans, washed and trimmed

¼ cup red wine vinegar

¼ cup Dijon mustard

1 teaspoon honey

½ teaspoon kosher salt

¼ teaspoon freshly cracked black pepper

1 tablespoon finely chopped fresh tarragon

¼ cup extra-virgin olive oil

1. Bring a large saucepan of water to a boil over medium-high heat. Add the green beans and cook them for 3 to 5 minutes, or until they can be easily speared with a fork. While the beans cook, prepare a large bowl with ice water and place it in the sink.

2. When the beans are finished cooking, immediately drain them and plunge the beans into the ice water. Swish them around to cool them down. Then remove them from the water and pat them completely dry.

3. Make the mustard dressing by combining the vinegar, mustard, honey, salt, pepper, and tarragon in a large bowl. Pour the olive oil into the mixture in one continuous stream and whisk well until the dressing becomes completely emulsified.

4. Place the green beans in a large serving bowl and pour the mustard dressing over them. Cover the bowl with plastic wrap and chill for at least 3 hours, or up to overnight.

5. Before serving, bring the beans to room temperature and scoop them into a fresh serving bowl or directly onto plates.

Twice-Baked Sweet Potatoes

These sweet potatoes will be an instant hit at your table. They are sweet and creamy without being too heavy. They are also terrific for little children!

MAKES 4 TO 6 SERVINGS

4 large sweet potatoes, scrubbed

1 tablespoon olive oil

4 ounces cream cheese, at room temperature

¼ cup whole milk

3 tablespoons dark brown sugar

½ teaspoon ground cinnamon

½ teaspoon ground ginger

2 tablespoons light brown sugar

½ cup chopped pecans

1. Preheat the oven to 350°F.

2. Cut off the hard, pointy ends of each potato and lightly rub the outsides with olive oil. Place them on the oven rack and bake for 45 minutes to 1 hour, or until the potatoes are baked through and can easily be speared with a fork. Transfer the potatoes to a cooling rack to cool completely.

3. When comfortable to touch, cut each potato in half and carefully scoop out the flesh into a large mixing bowl, being careful to leave the skins intact with a little bit of sweet potato flesh for extra sturdiness, about ¼ inch. Use a wooden spoon to mix in the cream cheese, milk, dark brown sugar, and spices until thoroughly combined and lump-free. Refill each potato half with the mixture, mounding it slightly, and place them on an ungreased baking sheet. In a small bowl, mix together the light brown sugar and chopped pecans and top each potato with the mixture.

4. Bake the potatoes for an additional 20 minutes, or until hot all the way through.

Notes

To make these ahead of time, proceed through step 3. Then place the stuffed potatoes on a baking sheet and cover completely with plastic wrap. Store in the refrigerator for up to 2 days. Bring to room temperature before baking.

Sweet potatoes are more delicate than potatoes. When handling them, use a light touch and use as sharp a knife as possible to cut them, so they don't tear or collapse.

Caramelized Shallot Mashed Potatoes

Take a break from plain mashed potatoes and flavor yours with lots of caramelized shallots and cheese. It gives them a whole new taste that pairs so well with turkey.

MAKES 6 TO 8 SERVINGS

1 tablespoon olive oil

1 tablespoon unsalted butter

4 large shallots, peeled and thinly sliced

1 teaspoon kosher salt

2½ pounds large Yukon Gold potatoes, peeled and quartered

1 cup half-and-half

¼ cup finely grated Parmesan cheese

1. In a small skillet, melt the olive oil and butter over medium heat. Add the shallot slices and salt, turn the heat to medium-low, and allow them to simmer for 25 to 30 minutes, stirring occasionally, until they are dark golden brown and caramelized.

2. Meanwhile, bring a large pot of water to a boil and add the potato pieces. Boil them for 15 to 20 minutes, or until they can easily be speared through with a fork.

3. Drain the potatoes and use a potato ricer or masher to mash the potatoes to a desired consistency. Stir in the cream and Parmesan until the potatoes are light and fluffy. Then stir in the caramelized shallots and season with salt as needed. Serve warm.

Pumpkin Maple Tart *with* Gingersnap Crust

Here is your new Thanksgiving dessert tradition: pumpkin pie with a twist. There's maple syrup for a natural sweetness and a spicy crust made out of gingersnaps. This beautiful tart always pleases a crowd and transports well.

MAKES 1 (10-INCH) TART

2 cups gingersnap cookie crumbs, divided (about 40 small gingersnap cookies)

6 tablespoons unsalted butter, melted

1 (15-ounce) can pure pumpkin purée

3 large eggs, at room temperature

¾ cup granulated sugar

3 tablespoons pure maple syrup

2 tablespoons unbleached all-purpose flour

1 teaspoon pumpkin pie spice

1 teaspoon kosher salt

½ cup heavy whipping cream

1. Preheat the oven to 350°F.

2. In a large bowl, mix together the cookie crumbs and melted butter with a wooden spoon. Press the mixture evenly on the bottom and up the sides of a 10-inch tart pan. Place the pan on a large baking sheet and bake it for 15 minutes. Allow the pan to cool on the baking sheet while you make the filling.

3. With an electric mixer fitted with the whisk attachment, beat the pumpkin and one of the eggs on medium in a large bowl until smooth. Add the remaining eggs one at a time, beating well after each addition. Then whisk in the sugar, maple syrup, flour, spice, salt, and cream until completely smooth.

4. Pour the filling into the prepared tart crust and bake it for 45 to 50 minutes, or until the top is completely smooth and no longer wet looking. Transfer the pan to a cooling rack and allow to cool completely before serving.

Pecan Pie Bars

Instead of making two pies, make a big pan of pecan pie bars. Everyone loves how much easier they are to handle and their portability makes them an ideal treat to eat with one hand while watching Thanksgiving Day football.

MAKES 16 SQUARES

- 4 ounces (1 stick) unsalted butter, at room temperature, plus more for pan
- ⅔ cup packed light brown sugar
- 2 cups plus 1 tablespoon unbleached all-purpose flour, divided
- 1 teaspoon kosher salt, divided
- 4 large eggs
- 1 cup packed dark brown sugar
- 1½ cups light corn syrup
- 2 teaspoons pure vanilla extract
- 2 cups pecan halves

1. Preheat the oven to 350°F. Generously butter the bottom and sides of an 8-inch square baking dish and set aside.

2. With an electric mixer fitted with a paddle attachment, beat the butter and light brown sugar on high speed in a large bowl until light and fluffy, about 3 minutes. Lower the speed to low and mix in 2 cups of the flour and ½ teaspoon of the salt until just combined. Transfer the soft dough to the prepared baking dish and press it evenly into the bottom of the pan with your fingertips. Bake the crust for 13 to 15 minutes, or until lightly golden around the edges. Remove from the oven and allow to cool.

3. Wipe out the mixing bowl with a paper towel. Place the eggs, dark brown sugar, corn syrup, and vanilla in the bowl and beat with the electric mixer on medium speed until smooth, scraping down the bowl so that all the ingredients are combined. Then beat in the remaining 1 tablespoon of flour and the remaining ½ teaspoon of salt until well blended.

4. Arrange the pecans evenly on top of the cooled crust. Pour the filling evenly over them, tilting the pan as necessary and smoothing the top with a spatula. Bake the bars for 35 to 40 minutes, or until the top is puffed and golden brown and the middle is set. Allow to cool completely before serving.

Winter

No month of the year is quite as exciting and overwhelming as December. It is full of parties, excited children, and endless to-do lists. It is always fun, but there is never enough time to accomplish all you set out to do. To make it easier in the kitchen during the holidays, stick with the tried and true. This is the time for traditions, both old and new, and making family memories with the perfect Christmas dinner. All it takes is a little advance planning and you can set yourself up for culinary success every time.

Once Christmas draws to a close, turn to your collection of easy comfort foods, such as Roasted Tomato Mac & Cheese (page 171) and Chicken Pot Pie (page 168) to keep you warm all winter long. Mine your freezer for frozen produce and herbs from the summer garden, and use them to flavor winter meals. Entertain indoors with bourbon-spiked cider and bowls of meaty chili sopped up with cornbread, and take a rest from outdoor routines.

GIVE YOUR TABLE CHARACTER Draw inspiration from the winter landscape by picking flowers, produce, and objects in shades of browns, greens, or reds. Arrange them in simple containers, such as glass jars, wide shallow bowls, and low platters, and set them in the center of the table. Surround the displays with soft evergreen branches, simple vines, or decorative strands of silver or gold thread. Set up tea lights in silver or gold votives to illuminate the table while you eat.

Holiday Crafts

Making holiday gifts with Daphne is one of my favorite activities of the season. Not only do these crafts give her a chance to get supercreative, it gives us something special to do together amid the commercial chaos of the season.

Your Holiday Crafting Strategy

Instead of attempting to tackle loads of new crafts each holiday season, mix a couple of traditional favorites with a few new ideas. Choose your craft based on the age and skill level of your children. Start with the simpler crafts for the younger kids and work your way up to more involved ones as they get older.

Peppermint Candy Wreath

Every December, Daphne and I look forward to making this wreath and hanging it on her bedroom door. It also makes a great gift for friends or a teacher.

MAKES 1 (8-INCH) WREATH

1 (8-inch) Styrofoam wreath form
Piece of cardboard larger than the wreath form
Water-based spray paint (your choice of colors)
White craft glue
2 pounds peppermint candies, unwrapped
Large decorative ribbon for hanging

1. Place the wreath form on the cardboard outside in a well-ventilated area. Use spray paint to color the wreath any color you want. Allow the wreath to dry completely before proceeding.
2. Working carefully, place a large dot of glue on the back of each candy and place them on the wreath so they are tightly packed together. Once all of your candies are on, place the wreath in a safe place to dry completely.
3. When the wreath has dried, wrap the ribbon around the top of it and tie a large bow to use as a hanger. Now it is ready to be hung up and enjoyed!

Note This wreath can also be made with any kind of hard candy that won't soften or melt at room temperature. Don't forget to remind your children that they shouldn't pick off and eat the candy. The glue and Styrofoam are not edible!

Pomanders

These simple holiday decorations are perfect for novice crafters. The ingredients are easy to find and there is no cooking or measuring involved. Package them as gifts for friends or teachers in clear cello bags (page 262) with a bright ribbon.

MAKES 4 POMANDERS

Toothpicks

4 navel oranges or large lemons

Rubber bands (optional)

1 cup whole cloves

4 (10-inch-long) ribbons (optional)

Large needle (optional)

1. Use a toothpick to poke a hole in the skin of an orange in any design you want. We like to make stripes or spell words, such as joy or noel. To make a perfect stripe, slip a rubber band around the orange and poke holes alongside it.

2. Push the cloves into the toothpick holes, making sure they fit snugly. Once you are finished, secure a bow around the pomander by threading a large needle with a 10-inch-long ribbon and pushing it through the orange. Make a knot at the bottom to ensure it will stay. Make a loop at the top of the orange and use it to hang the pomander. You could also arrange them in a large bowl as a centerpiece.

Tip For extra fragrance, once the pomanders are finished, but before you add the bow, roll them in a dry spice mixture of ground cinnamon, ginger, nutmeg, and cardamom.

Note Fresh pomanders will last for 4 to 5 days on display. To lengthen their display time, place the finished pomanders in a paper bag in the refrigerator for 3 days to dry before displaying. To preserve them for even longer, roll the finished pomanders in ¼ cup of orris root powder, a natural preservative that can be found in many spice stores.

Cinnamon Glue Ornaments

Of all our seasonal decorations, these are the most aromatic. They retain their fragrance year after year. The only hard part is remembering that they aren't edible.

MAKES ABOUT 3 DOZEN ORNAMENTS

Large baking sheets or cutting boards
Parchment paper
Large, disposable bowl
8 ounces ground cinnamon, plus more for dusting the surface
2 teaspoons ground ginger
1 teaspoon ground cloves
1 cup store-bought applesauce
⅓ cup white craft glue (such as Elmer's)
Rolling pin
Cookie cutters
Skewer
Ribbons
Paint pens
Glitter pens, or glue and glitter

1. Line two flat surfaces with parchment paper. I like to use baking sheets or large cutting boards because the ornaments will rest on the parchment for the next 4 days: It makes them easier to move.

2. In the bowl, mix together the spices, applesauce, and glue until a dough forms.

3. Lightly dust a surface with ground cinnamon. Use a rolling pin to roll out the dough to ¼-inch thickness. Use the cookie cutters to cut out the shapes of the ornaments. Use a skewer to make holes in them where you want the ribbon to be when they hang from the tree. Add the ribbons cut to the desired length.

4. Place the ornaments on the lined sheets and place them in cool, dry place away from sunlight. Allow them to dry for at least 4 days, or until they are solid and firm.

5. Decorate the ornaments as you desire, with paint pens, glitter pens, or anything else you want.

Idea Tie your homemade ornaments to the large gifts and personalize with people's names for an extra-special touch.

Salt Dough Ornaments

At Christmas Daphne and I pull out our big bag of holiday cookie cutters and go crazy making salt dough ornaments in all our favorite shapes. You can hang them around your house or give them away as gifts.

MAKES 24 (3-INCH) ORNAMENTS

Large, rimmed baking sheet

Parchment paper

Large mixing bowl

2 cups unbleached all-purpose flour, plus more for dusting

1 cup fine table salt

Water

Wooden spoon

Rolling pin

Cookie cutters

Skewer or plastic straw

Spray paint

Large sheet of cardboard (optional, if using spray paint)

Paint pens

Glitter pens, or glue and glitter

Ribbons or twine

1. Preheat the oven to 250°F. Line a large, rimmed baking sheet with parchment paper and set aside.

2. Combine the flour, salt, and 1 cup water in a large mixing bowl and stir with a wooden spoon until the dough comes together. Then use clean hands to knead the dough three or four times until it forms a smooth ball.

3. Lightly flour a surface and roll out the dough to ⅛-inch thickness. Use your cookie cutters to cut dough shapes and place them on the prepared pan. The dough does not expand while it bakes, so

the ornaments can be about ¼ inch apart. Reroll the dough as necessary to use it all up and make as many ornaments as possible.

4. Use a skewer or plastic straw to make holes in the tops of the ornaments. Make sure the holes are at least ⅛ inch from the edge of the ornaments, to ensure that it will hang well and won't crack around the hole. The holes need to go all the way through the ornaments and be wide enough to accommodate the ribbon or twine you plan to hang them with.

5. Bake the ornaments for 2 hours, or until they are completely dried out and flat in the pan. They will not change color as they bake. It is fine if the ornaments have small cracks in the surface, they will be covered up with paint. Transfer the ornaments to a cooling rack and allow them to cool at room temperature for at least 12 hours or up to 1 day.

6. To decorate the ornaments, choose your favorite method of painting. At Christmas we like to line up the ornaments on a piece of cardboard outside and spray paint them green, red, white, gold, and silver. Once they have dried we bring them inside and decorate them with paint pens, glitter pens, and all kinds of odds and ends from the craft drawer. Once all of the decorations have dried, thread the ribbon through the hole and hang them up to enjoy!

Note Once baked, the dough will not go bad, so the ornaments can be stored and enjoyed for many years to come.

Graham Cracker Gingerbread Houses

One of our favorite holiday crafts is making graham cracker gingerbread houses with Daphne's class. The night before, Duncan and I assemble the houses and take them to school to following day. In class, the children get to decorate the houses like crazy and take them home to their parents. Daph likes to begin slowly eating hers the moment she brings it home. Other children, I've been told, position them on the mantle and won't let anyone touch them for the entire season! Note: The first time you make these, you should be prepared to waste frosting while you get the hang of using it. It takes patience and is best done with two people.

MAKES 10 HOUSES

FOR THE HOUSES

2 tablespoons powdered egg whites

1 pound confectioners' sugar, plus more if needed

1 teaspoon pure vanilla extract

6 tablespoons lukewarm water

40 whole rectangular graham crackers, plus 10 more broken into squares

1 (10-ounce) container store-bought classic vanilla icing

FOR ASSEMBLY

Pastry bag or large resealable plastic bag

Stiff cardboard plates

Permanent marker

Assorted candies

Small paper cups

Popsicle sticks

Assorted candies, for decorating

1. To make the icing: Place the powdered egg whites and confectioners' sugar in a large bowl. With an electric mixer fitted with the whisk attachment, add the vanilla on medium speed, then add the water 1 tablespoon at a time. Add just enough water so that the icing comes together but is still stiff enough that it can be rolled into a ball between your fingers. It should be the consistency of a stiff toothpaste. If it seems too watery add confectioners' sugar 1 tablespoon at a time until it stiffens up.

2. Scoop the icing into a pastry bag fitted with a small tip or into a resealable plastic bag with a small piece of one corner snipped off so that it functions like a pastry bag.

3. To assemble each house: Place the cardboard plates on a stable countertop or table. Write the children's names on the rims or bottoms of each plate.

4. Place one rectangular graham cracker and one square graham cracker end to end in an L shape on a plate to form one long wall and one short wall of the house. Pipe the icing along the bottom edge of each graham cracker, on both the inside and outside. Press the graham crackers down firmly so that they stand up in an L shape on the plate. Then pipe the icing on the outside and inside of the corner where the graham crackers are touching. Repeat this process with the second rectangular and second square graham cracker, making the L shapes join together to form the base of the house. When it is completed, the graham crackers should form an open-topped house on the plate. The base and corners of the house should be iced on both the inside and outside. Let the structure dry while you assemble the base of the remaining houses.

5. To make the roof: Pipe a generous amount of icing on to the top of the long sides of each house and place two more rectangular graham crackers firmly in it to make a pitched roof. (You could also make flat-roofed houses, for variety!) Let the graham crackers lean toward the center of the house so they meet at the top. Prop up the top with your finger so the graham crackers are just touching and pipe the icing across the top to secure the peak of the roof. Look for any gaps or shakiness in the structure and add any additional icing as necessary to secure it. Allow the houses to dry for at least 12 hours before decorating.

6. To decorate the houses: Scoop the store-bought icing into the small paper cups. Let the children use Popsicle sticks to smear the icing on to the houses and affix their candies as desired.

Notes

These houses are often being assembled by children with food allergies. To avoid problems, I used powdered egg whites to make the royal icing. Before purchasing commercially prepared vanilla icing, check with the teachers about whether it needs to be dairy-free. Because the frosting is shelf-stabilized, it doesn't need to be refrigerated and there are no risky raw ingredients.

The royal icing should be used immediately after you make it. If you are using small bits at a time, cover the unused icing with a moist paper towel. When you are ready to use it, loosen it up with a whisk. Royal icing doesn't store well, so be sure to use it the day you make it!

For fewer houses, make the whole batch of frosting and use the leftover frosting to decorate the houses, rather than using the store-bought icing, making designs on the roof and little windows on the side.

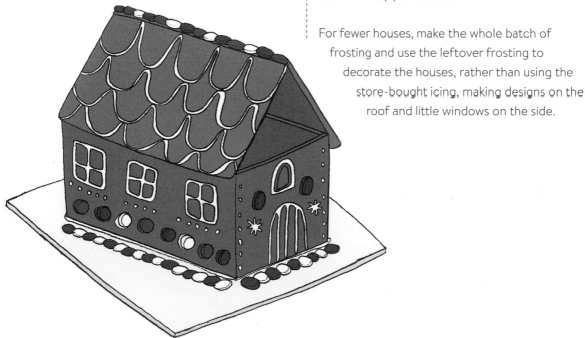

Christmas Dinner

CHERRY WALNUT BAKED BRIE   237

—

SWEET & SPICY PARTY MEATBALLS   237

—

BLUE CHEESE & BACON WRAPPED DATES   238

—

MULLED WINE   239

—

THE WRIGHT PARTY PUNCH   239

—

BOOZY EGGNOG   240

—

HOLIDAY POMEGRANATE GLAZED HAM   241

—

PARMESAN POPOVERS   241

—

CRUNCHY ROASTED POTATOES   242

—

ROAST BRUSSELS SPROUTS *with* BACON & CRANBERRIES   243

—

BAKED CINNAMON RICE PUDDING   244

—

DOUBLE-SOAKED BUTTER RUM CAKE   245

Make Christmas dinner easy on yourself and have a full menu up your sleeve. A glass of wine, sliced ham with all the trimmings, and a plate of sweet nibbles are all you need to enjoy your family day. This approach will allow you to get out of the kitchen and focus on enjoying food and making memories with your loved ones.

Cherry Walnut Baked Brie

A warm wheel of savory baked Brie surrounded by crackers and baguette slices is one of the most comforting, no-stress appetizers I know. It comes together in minutes and is perfect for a fancy celebration at home.

MAKES 1 (5- TO 6-INCH) WHEEL

½ cup walnut halves, lightly toasted and chopped

¼ cup cherry jam

2 tablespoons balsamic vinegar

1 sheet frozen puff pastry, thawed

1 (8-ounce) wheel Brie cheese

1 large egg

1. Preheat the oven to 375°F. In a small bowl, stir the walnuts, jam, and vinegar together and set aside.

2. Place the sheet of puff pastry on a lightly floured work surface. Arrange the walnut mixture in circle, a little smaller than the Brie, in the center of the dough.

3. Place the Brie on top of the walnuts and fold the pastry dough around the Brie wheel as if you are wrapping a present. Pinch the ends together to seal and pat around the side of the Brie so everything is snugly tucked in.

4. Place the wrapped Brie seam-side down in a small ovenproof baking dish. Whisk together the egg and 1 teaspoon of water and lightly brush the mixture over the top of the puff pastry. Bake for 30 minutes, or until the pastry is golden brown and crispy. Let stand for 15 minutes before serving with a platter of crispy crackers and baguette slices.

Sweet & Spicy Party Meatballs

This one is an oldie but a goodie from my grandmother's friend: We haul it out year after year. The sweet and spicy flavors make these insanely addictive. One batch will be feed a hungry family or serve a small party. The recipe also doubles well.

MAKES 50 TO 60 MEATBALLS

2 pounds ground beef (80% lean)

1 large egg

1 medium-size yellow onion, peeled and grated

1 teaspoon kosher salt

1 (12-ounce) jar chili sauce

1 (16-ounce) jar grape jelly

1 tablespoon freshly squeezed lemon juice

1. Place the meat in a large bowl and form a well in the center. Add the egg, onion, and salt to the well and mix the ingredients together with clean hands. Roll the meat into 1-inch round balls and set aside.

2. In a large saucepan over medium heat, stir together the chili sauce, grape jelly, and lemon juice. When the mixture comes to a low simmer, add the meatballs and simmer for about 20 minutes, or until they are browned and cooked all the way through. Pour the meatballs and sauce into a chafing dish to keep warm or serve in a shallow bowl, with the meatballs in one even layer. Set out toothpicks for people to serve themselves.

Blue Cheese & Bacon Wrapped Dates

Whenever I am asked to bring something savory to a holiday party, this is the recipe I turn to. These bite-size appetizers are the perfect flavor trifecta. In each bite, the salty bacon and sharp cheese contrast perfectly with the sweet dates. For serving a crowd, this recipe can easily be doubled or tripled.

MAKES 30 DATES

30 pitted dried dates
4 ounces soft blue cheese
10 ounces bacon, cut into thirds lengthwise

1. Preheat the oven to 375°F. Line a rimmed baking sheet with parchment paper and set aside.
2. Slice the dates in half and stuff 1 teaspoon of cheese into the center on each one. Close the date and wrap it in the bacon so that the bacon complete overlaps on the bottom. Use a toothpick to secure the two ends of the bacon.

3. Place the wrapped dates on a baking sheet and bake them for 10 to 15 minutes, or until the bacon is completely cooked and the cheese is lightly browned, turning once at the halfway mark. Remove from the oven and transfer to a paper towel–lined plate to drain and cool for about 5 minutes. Serve warm.

Note To fancy these up even more, arrange them on a platter and drizzle lightly with honey or balsamic vinegar before serving.

Mulled Wine

For non-eggnog drinkers, make mulled wine. This sweet spiced wine is easy to pull together and the warm spices instantly make the house smell like Christmas. While I like to serve wine year-round, this drink has become a classic among our family and friends. Every year I hand out the recipe and I've noticed it popping up on party menus around town.

MAKES 7 CUPS WINE

1 large navel orange

2 (750 ml) bottles Cabernet Sauvignon

⅓ cup granulated sugar

8 whole cloves

4 cinnamon sticks

1 star anise

¼ teaspoon ground nutmeg

½ cup Cointreau

1. Peel the orange (reserve the flesh for some other use), cut the rind into strips, and place the strips in a large saucepan. Add one of the bottles of wine and the sugar, cloves, cinnamon, star anise, nutmeg, and Cointreau. Bring the mixture to a simmer over medium-low heat and stir until the sugar is dissolved. Lower the heat to low and simmer for about 15 more minutes. Remove the pan from the heat and stir in the second bottle of wine. Serve warm.

The Wright Party Punch

Growing up, the Wright family was known for its epic Christmas Eve soirees. Because it was a family party, Cheryl and Peter always made sure there was just as much food for the children as for the adults. This punch was always, in my young eyes, the absolute best concoction out there. It is now my favorite nonalcoholic alternative to serve a crowd whenever we host a big gathering. Of course, if you want it to be expressly for the adults, you can always spike it with a little vodka!

MAKES 20 SERVINGS

1 (10-ounce) jar maraschino cherries

1 (12-ounce) can frozen lemonade concentrate

1 (46-ounce) can apricot nectar

1 (46-ounce) can pineapple juice

2 liters ginger ale

1. Make an ice ring by pouring the cherries and their juices into a small Bundt pan or any decorative ring-shaped dish. Pour in enough water to cover the cherries by ½ inch. Freeze the ring until it is solid ice.

2. In a large punch bowl, stir the lemonade concentrate, nectar, and pineapple juice until smooth. Carefully stir in the ginger ale. Remove the ice ring from the Bundt pan and float it on top of the punch. (If you have trouble removing the ice from the pan, fill a wide dish with hot water and dip the bottom of the pan in it just long enough to loosen the ice.) Serve.

Note I like to serve this in my grandmother's punch bowl to give it a particularly fancy look. If you don't have a punch bowl, make mini ice rings and divide the punch among several pretty glass pitchers at the bar.

Boozy Eggnog

Eggnog is a requirement during the holiday season. Although I've tried just about every store-bought brand out there, homemade is still the best. This recipe is simple enough that you don't need any mixing experience for it to always turn out perfectly.

MAKES 8 CUPS EGGNOG

8 large eggs, yolks and white separated

1½ cups granulated sugar, divided

1 quart 2% milk

2 cups half-and-half

2 teaspoons pure vanilla extract

1 teaspoon ground nutmeg

⅔ cup spiced rum

⅔ cup bourbon

1. With an electric mixer fitted with a whisk attachment, beat the egg yolks and ½ cup of the sugar on high speed in a large bowl until the sugar is completely dissolved. Set aside.

2. Place the milk, half-and-half, vanilla, and nutmeg in a medium saucepan and heat over high heat, whisking so that the ingredients are combined. Bring to a boil for 10 seconds, then remove the pan from the heat. Temper the egg yolks by whisking ¼ cup of the hot milk mixture into them. Slowly add an additional ¼ cup of the hot milk to the egg yolks, whisking until completely combined. Pour the tempered mixture back into the saucepan and heat the milk slowly over medium-high heat until it reaches 175°F on a meat thermometer, about 2 minutes. Remove the pan from the heat and stir in the rum and bourbon. Strain the mixture into a punch bowl or pitcher and place it in the refrigerator to chill completely.

3. Meanwhile, with an electric mixer fitted with a whisk attachment, beat the egg whites on high speed in a large bowl until they hold stiff peaks, about 4 minutes. When you raise the whisk attachment, the whites should stand straight up in the bowl. Then with the mixer going on high speed, slowly add the remaining 1 cup of sugar until stiff peaks form. If you think not all the guests will want to consume raw eggs, then dollop the whipped whites into a bowl on the side of the punch bowl for people to plop on top of their drink as desired. If there are no concerns, then use a spatula to gently fold the egg whites into the chilled eggnog and serve.

Holiday Pomegranate Glazed Ham

The trick to Christmas dinner is cooking large amounts of food in very little time. With all the presents to unwrap and general revelry, it is hard to carve out hours upon hours in the kitchen. For this reason, ham is a great main course. Brush it with a simple glaze, place it in the oven, and let the thermometer tell you when it is done. It is the simplest way to get a delicious meal on the table and still have time to enjoy the holiday!

MAKES 10 TO 12 SERVINGS

1 (5 to 6) pound boneless smoked ham
¾ cup pomegranate molasses
¼ cup Dijon mustard
2 tablespoons bourbon
1 teaspoon kosher salt
1 teaspoon freshly cracked black pepper

1. Preheat the oven to 325°F. Line a large roasting pan with aluminum foil and place the ham in it. Use a sharp knife to score the ham fat, making 2-inch-wide crosshatch marks that cut into only the skin, not the meat.

2. In a small bowl, mix together the pomegranate molasses, mustard, bourbon, salt, and pepper. Brush the meat with a thick coat of glaze so that it is completely covered. Reserve any leftover glaze for basting.

3. Bake the ham for 1 hour 45 minutes, basting occasionally with the reserved glaze, until it has an internal temperature of 140°F. Remove the ham from the oven and transfer to a cutting board. Allow it to rest for 15 minutes before slicing and serving.

Parmesan Popovers

Serve popovers with Christmas dinner because they are snap to make and never fail to taste great. They are like giant cheese puffs and pair beautifully with the salty, sweet ham.

MAKES 12 POPOVERS

Cooking spray
2 tablespoons unsalted butter, melted and
    cooled slightly
1½ cups unbleached all-purpose flour
1 teaspoon kosher salt
3 large eggs
1½ cups whole milk
¾ cup finely grated Parmesan cheese

1. Preheat the oven to 425°F. Spray the cups of a popover pan with cooking spray and place it in the oven to warm up while the oven is preheating.

2. In a large mixing bowl, whisk together the butter, flour, salt, eggs, milk, and cheese until completely smooth.

3. Remove the popover pan from the oven and fill each cup half-full with batter. Bake for 30 minutes without opening the oven, or until the popovers have risen and are a burnished golden brown. Remove from the oven, allow the popovers to cool in the pan slightly, then transfer them to a basket or platter lined with a clean cotton towel. Repeat the baking process with any remaining batter.

Crunchy Roasted Potatoes

Curiously, neither of my children liked mashed potatoes as toddlers but they loved crunchy roasted potatoes. As a result, this dish has become a mainstay at our holiday meals. You'll love how the edges of the potatoes get all raggedy and crunchy, almost like a crispy French fry. This recipe makes a lot of potatoes because it serves a crowd. For a smaller family dinner, it can easily be halved.

MAKES 8 TO 10 SERVINGS

8 large russet potatoes, scrubbed, peeled, and
    cut into 1½-inch cubes
⅓ cup vegetable oil, divided
2 tablespoons sea salt
1 tablespoon grated Parmesan cheese

1. Preheat the oven to 425°F. Line two large, rimmed baking sheet with aluminum foil and brush the bottom with half of the oil. It is fine if it pools a little bit, so be generous with the brushing and then set the pan aside.

2. Bring a large pot of salted water to a boil and add the potatoes. Return the water to a boil and cook the potatoes for about 10 minutes, or until a fork can be passed through them with a little bit of pressure applied.

3. Drain the potatoes and return them to the empty pot. Put a lid on it and shake the pot vigorously for 1 minute to help fluff up the edges.

4. Spread the potatoes in an even layer on the baking sheet. Drizzle the remaining oil over the potatoes and once cool enough to handle, toss them lightly with your hands, to ensure they are evenly coated. Sprinkle the tops with the sea salt.

5. Roast the potatoes for 35 to 40 minutes, turning the once with a spatula halfway through for even browning. Once the edges are golden brown and crispy, remove the potatoes from the oven and quickly sprinkle with the cheese. Return the potatoes to the oven for 5 more minutes to allow the cheese to melt. Serve hot.

Roast Brussels Sprouts *with* Bacon & Cranberries

It took me a long time to come up with a Brussels sprouts dish everyone likes. Turns out combining their vegetal flavor with sweet cranberries and salty bacon was just the ticket. There is a little something in the dish to please everyone. For hassle-free serving at the big meal, transfer the salty, sweet sprouts to a large serving bowl and tuck in a big spoon.

MAKES 6 TO 8 SERVINGS

4 ounces bacon, chopped into 1-inch pieces

30 ounces fresh Brussels sprouts, or three (10-ounce) packages frozen (thawed), trimmed and halved

1 teaspoon kosher salt

½ teaspoon freshly cracked black pepper

1 cup dried cranberries

1. Preheat the oven to 375°F.

2. Place the bacon to a large, ovenproof skillet and cook over medium heat until it is just beginning to crisp around the edges. Transfer to a paper towel–lined plate, leaving the grease in the pan.

3. Add the halved sprouts to the pan and toss to coat with the salt and pepper. Then place the pan in the oven and bake for about 30 minutes, turning the sprouts once or twice with a spoon. Add the bacon bits to the skillet and cook for 10 more minutes.

4. Remove from the oven and transfer the mixture to a large bowl. Toss in the dried cranberries and serve!

Baked Cinnamon Rice Pudding

In recent years, I adopted a tradition from my friend Barbara's family of serving this pudding with Christmas dinner. It adds another layer of deliciousness to the meal and is kind of like getting a sneaky taste of dessert while you're eating dinner.

MAKES 10 TO 12 SERVINGS

1 tablespoon unsalted butter, at room temperature, plus more for dish

¾ cup long-grain white rice

½ teaspoon kosher salt

2 cups whole milk

⅔ cups granulated sugar

½ cup heavy whipping cream

2 large eggs

1 teaspoon pure vanilla extract

1 teaspoon ground cinnamon, plus more for dusting

1. Preheat the oven to 350°F. Butter the bottom and sides of a 2-quart soufflé dish and place it in a large roasting pan. Set aside.

2. Bring 2 cups of water to a boil in a large saucepan. Pour in the rice and salt and continue to simmer until the water is absorbed and the rice is tender, about 20 minutes.

3. Slowly pour the milk and sugar into the rice, stirring continuously as you do. Continue to cook for an additional 5 minutes, stirring a few times. The rice will be softened and tender but should not flake apart. Remove the pan from the heat and stir in the cream.

4. In a large bowl beat the eggs, vanilla, and cinnamon until well blended. Fold the rice mixture into the eggs until completely incorporated. Pour the rice mixture into the soufflé dish and dust the top with one or two more pinches of cinnamon.

5. Pour boiling water into the roasting pan until it comes halfway up the side of the soufflé dish. Bake it for an hour, or until a knife inserted into the center comes out clean. Allow to cool for at least 20 minutes before serving warm.

Double-Soaked Butter Rum Cake

My favorite holiday dessert is this heavenly Christmas pound cake thick with holiday flavors. It is large enough to serve as the crowning end to a large festive meal or take to the office to share with co-workers at a holiday party. Serve it with vanilla ice cream.

MAKES 1 TUBE CAKE, 12 TO 16 SERVINGS

FOR THE CAKE

8 ounces (2 sticks) unsalted butter, at room temperature, plus more for pan

3 cups unbleached all-purpose flour, plus more for dusting pan

2 teaspoons ground cinnamon

¼ teaspoon ground nutmeg

1 teaspoon baking powder

1 teaspoon kosher salt

1 (8-ounce) package cream cheese, at room temperature

2¼ cups granulated sugar

6 large eggs

1 tablespoon pure vanilla extract

1 tablespoon dark rum

FOR THE GLAZE

⅓ cup dark rum

1 cup light brown sugar

3 tablespoons unsalted butter

Confectioners' sugar for dusting

1. To make the cake: Preheat the oven to 325°F. Butter and flour the inside of a 10-inch-diameter tube pan. Combine the flour, cinnamon, nutmeg, baking powder, and salt in a mixing bowl and set aside.

2. With an electric mixer fitted with the paddle attachment, cream the butter, cream cheese, and granulated sugar on high speed in a large bowl until light and fluffy, about 3 minutes. Add the eggs one at a time, beating well after each addition. Beat in the vanilla and the rum.

3. Working slowly, add the flour mixture until it is evenly incorporated, stopping once to scrape down the sides of the bowl.

4. Pour the batter into the prepared tube pan and spread the top flat with a spatula. Bake the cake for 1 hour 10 minutes to 1 hour 15 minutes, or until a cake tester comes out clean. Allow the cake to cool in the pan for 5 minutes. Then turn it out onto a cooling rack positioned over a sheet of parchment paper and liberally pierce the top and sides of the cake with a toothpick.

5. Make the glaze while the cake is cooling: Combine the rum, brown sugar, and ¼ cup of water in a small saucepan over medium heat. Heat the mixture just until the sugar is completely dissolved. Then stir in the butter until just melted. Remove the pan from the heat and carefully drizzle half the glaze over the cake. Allow the glaze to absorb into the cake for 1 minute, then drizzle it again with the remaining glaze. Allow the cake to cool completely. For a decorative touch, lightly dust the cake with confectioners' sugar, using a sieve or sifter before slicing and serving.

The Festive Christmas Cookie Plate

Everyone loves Christmas cookies; however, producing a wide variety during the season can be very difficult. The solution is to pick three of your favorite cookies each year. Rotate your recipes from year to year or stick with three cookies you love and let them become your signature. Prepare the dough ahead of time, doubling or tripling the recipe depending on how many you need, and freeze it. Bake the cookies fresh when you need them.

TIPS FOR MAKING CHRISTMAS COOKIES WITH CHILDREN

· ·

- Set out decorations in nonbreakable bowls with plastic spoons.
- Cover your table or decorating surface with something easy to clean, such as a plastic tablecloth, craft paper, or newspapers. Place the cookies on a rimmed plate to catch errant sprinkles and sugar balls.

- Scoop frosting into small plastic cups and give each child a Popsicle stick for spreading the frosting.
- Move the cookies to dry in a safe place out of reach after they've been decorated.
- To transport the cookies, place them on flat paper plate, then slide the plate into a large resealable bag.

Sparkling Spiced Shortbread

Shortbread is perfectly acceptable to eat with a morning cup of tea or an afternoon cup of cocoa. For Christmas, spice it up with a little cinnamon and nutmeg. The fragrant, sparkling cookies instantly add cheer to any cookie plate. To make this for your cookie platter, freeze the dough logs in advance, then slice and bake when you are ready.

MAKES ABOUT 4 DOZEN SHORTBREADS

1½ cups (3 sticks), unsalted butter, at room temperature

1 cup confectioners' sugar

2 teaspoons pure vanilla extract

3 cups unbleached all-purpose flour

1 teaspoon kosher salt

¼ teaspoon ground nutmeg

1 teaspoon ground cardamom

1 teaspoon ground cinnamon

½ cup sanding sugar (I use white, but red or green would be festive, too!)

1 large egg white

1. With an electric mixer fitted with the paddle attachment, beat the butter and confectioners'

sugar on high speed in a large bowl until light and fluffy, about 4 minutes. Turn off the mixer and scrape down the sides of the bowl with a spatula, then beat in the vanilla.

2. In a small bowl, whisk together the flour, salt, and spices. With the mixer on low speed, add the flour slowly, beating until just incorporated.

3. Turn the dough out of the mixing bowl onto a lightly floured surface and divide it into two balls. Roll each ball into a log 2 inches in diameter. Wrap the logs in plastic wrap and twist the ends closed. Refrigerate them for at least 6 hours or overnight. Alternatively, you can wrap the logs in plastic and then an outer layer of foil and freeze them for up to 3 months.

4. Preheat the oven to 350°F. Line two baking sheets with parchment paper or a silicone mat.

Pour the sanding sugar into a shallow bowl or plate. Lightly brush each log with the beaten egg white and roll it in the sanding sugar so that it is evenly coated. Slice the logs into rounds that are about ¼ inch thick.

5. Place the cookies 1 inch apart on the prepared cookie sheets. Bake for 12 to 14 minutes, rotating them halfway through to ensure even baking. Remove from the oven and allow the cookies to cool for 2 minutes on the baking sheet. Transfer them to a cooling rack to cool completely.

Almond Thumbprint Cookies

To give these cookies holiday flair, use thick red or golden jams, such as strawberry, raspberry, or apricot. Dust these with a light coating of confectioners' sugar before serving; it makes them look so pretty on the cookie plate.

MAKES ABOUT 3 DOZEN COOKIES

⅔ cup unsalted roasted whole almonds

3½ cups unbleached all-purpose flour

½ teaspoon kosher salt

1½ cups (3 sticks) unsalted butter, at room temperature

1 cup granulated sugar

1 teaspoon almond extract

Thick strawberry, raspberry, or apricot jam

Confectioners' sugar, for serving

1. Place the nuts in a large food processor bowl fitted with the blade attachment and pulse until finely ground. In a large mixing bowl, stir together the flour and salt and set aside.

2. With an electric mixer, cream the butter and sugar on high speed in a large bowl until light and fluffy, about 3 minutes. Beat in the almond extract. With the mixer on low speed, slowly add the flour mixture followed by the almonds, mixing until just incorporated. Form the dough

into a round ball and wrap well with plastic wrap. Refrigerate for 1 hour.

3. Preheat the oven to 350°F. Line two baking sheets with parchment paper or a silicone mat and set aside.

4. Pinch off balls of dough the size of your palm and roll into 1¼-inch balls. Place them on at least 1½ inches apart the prepared baking sheets. Use your thumb to make a small well in the top of each cookie and fill it with ¼ teaspoon of the jam of your choice.

5. Bake the cookies for 20 to 25 minutes, or until the bottoms are lightly browned. Allow them to cool on the baking sheet for 2 minutes, then transfer to a cooling rack to cool completely. Dust with confectioners' sugar before serving.

Note When filling the cookies, use a thick jam because thinner jams tend to run and spill out over the edges of the cookie. A thick marmalade works well, too.

Shortbread Chocolate Hazelnut Sandwich Cookies

While growing up I filled these buttery sandwich cookies with delicate swipes of jam in the middle. However, once I discovered Nutella, I abandoned tradition and began using it exclusively. These intensely rich cookies are ideal for a Christmas dessert or a sweet treat any time of year.

MAKES ABOUT 3 DOZEN SANDWICH COOKIES

2 cups unbleached all-purpose flour, plus more for dusting

½ teaspoon baking powder

1 teaspoon kosher salt

6 ounces (1½ sticks) unsalted butter, at room temperature

1 cup granulated sugar

1 large egg

1 teaspoon pure vanilla extract

Confectioners' sugar for dusting

1 cup chocolate hazelnut spread (such as Nutella)

1. In a small mixing bowl, whisk together the flour, baking powder, and salt and set aside.

2. With an electric mixer fitted with the paddle attachment, beat the butter and sugar on high speed in a large bowl until light and fluffy, about 3 minutes. Beat in the egg and vanilla. Lower the mixer speed to low and beat in the flour mixture until just combined.

3. Form the dough into two disks and wrap in plastic wrap. Chill for at least 2 hours or up to a day.

4. Preheat the oven to 375°F. Line two baking sheets with a silicone mat or parchment paper and set aside.

5. Unwrap one of the dough disks and place on a lightly floured surface. Roll it out to ¼-inch thickness and use an 1½-inch round cookie cutter to cut round cookies, placing the cut cookies 1 inch apart on the prepared cookie sheet. Reroll the dough as needed to use it all up. Bake the cookies for 8 to 10 minutes, or until the edges are golden brown. Allow the cookies to cool for 2 minutes on the baking sheet, then transfer them to a cooling rack to cool completely. Repeat with remaining disk of chilled dough.

6. Once the cookies have cooled, dust them lightly with confectioners' sugar. Turn half of them over and swipe the bottom of those with 1 teaspoon of chocolate hazelnut spread. Close with the remaining cookies.

Note These cookies also taste great with all sorts of spreads. In lieu of chocolate hazelnut, try Biscoff Spread, sweet jam, or nut butter. The possibilities are endless!

Peppermint Chocolate Crackles

These might just be the most popular cookies in our house. They are soft and chewy with a wonderful peppermint flavor that makes them taste like a chocolate candy cane. They are fun to make with children, especially when rolling them in confectioners' sugar.

MAKES ABOUT 4 DOZEN CRACKLES

8 ounces bittersweet chocolate, finely chopped (not chocolate chips)

1¼ cups unbleached all-purpose flour

1 cup unsweetened cocoa powder

1 teaspoon baking powder

1 teaspoon kosher salt

4 ounces (1 stick) unsalted butter, at room temperature

¾ cup packed light brown sugar

½ cup granulated sugar

2 large eggs

1 teaspoon peppermint extract

Confectioners' sugar for rolling

1. Preheat the oven to 350°F. Line two baking sheets with parchment paper or a silicone mat and set aside.

2. Place the chopped chocolate in a microwave-safe bowl and melt it in the microwave in at 50% power at 30-second intervals, stirring after each interval. Stop microwaving once the chocolate has melted enough to be stirred until completely smooth. Set aside and allow to cool.

3. In a small bowl, whisk together the flour, cocoa powder, baking powder, and salt and set aside.

4. With an electric mixer fitted with the paddle attachment, beat the butter and sugars on high speed in a large bowl until light and fluffy, about 5 minutes. Beat in the eggs one at a time until combined, then beat in the peppermint extract. With the mixer on low speed, beat in the cooled chocolate.

5. Scrape down the sides of the bowl with a spatula, beat in the dry ingredients on low speed until just combined.

6. Pinch the dough into 1 teaspoon-size pieces and roll them in the confectioners' sugar until fully coated. Place them 2 inches apart on the prepared baking sheets and bake for 15 to 18 minutes, or until the tops are set. Allow to cool for 2 minutes on the baking sheet, then transfer to a cooling rack to cool completely.

Caramel-Stuffed Snickerdoodles

Over the years I've experimented with different variations of this holiday classic and we've come to love stuffing them with caramel. If you prefer the classic cookies, you can simply omit the caramel in this recipe.

MAKES ABOUT 3 DOZEN SNICKERDOODLES

2¾ cup unbleached self-rising flour

½ teaspoon kosher salt

4 ounces (1 stick) unsalted butter, at room temperature

½ cup nonhydrogenated vegetable shortening

1¾ cups granulated sugar, divided

2 large eggs

2 teaspoons ground cinnamon

15 chewy caramels, unwrapped and halved

1. Preheat the oven to 400°F. Line two baking sheets with parchment paper or a silicone mat and set aside. In a small bowl, whisk together the flour and salt and set aside.

2. With an electric mixer fitted with the paddle attachment, beat the butter, shortening, and 1½ cups of the sugar on high speed in a large bowl until light and fluffy. Then add the eggs one at a time, beating well after each addition. With the mixer on low speed, slowly mix in the flour mixture until just incorporated.

3. In a small bowl, stir together the remaining ¼ cup of sugar and the cinnamon. Roll pieces of the dough into 1¼-inch balls. Tuck half a caramel into the center and pinch the dough tightly around it. Roll each cookie in the cinnamon-sugar mixture. Place the cookies 2 inches apart on the prepared cookie sheets.

4. Bake the cookies for 8 to 10 minutes, rotating the trays halfway through, or until the edges are golden brown and the tops are set. Allow them to cool for 2 minutes on the baking sheet, then transfer them to a cooling rack to cool completely.

Classic Gingerbread Made Two Ways

Daphne goes crazy for gingerbread. She loves to eat it just as much as she loves to decorate it. Over the years I've settled on one particular recipe for gingerbread. To make this into cookies, roll it thick so it stays moist and chewy. To make ornaments, roll it thin so it bakes up stiff and sturdy.

MAKES 20 TO 30 COOKIES OR ORNAMENTS, DEPENDING ON YOUR COOKIE CUTTERS

5¼ cups unbleached all-purpose flour, plus more for dusting

1½ teaspoons baking soda

½ teaspoon kosher salt

2 tablespoons ground ginger

1 tablespoon ground cinnamon

¼ teaspoon ground nutmeg

¼ teaspoon ground cloves

8 ounces (2 sticks) unsalted butter, at room temperature

¾ cup granulated sugar

½ cup packed dark brown sugar

1 large egg, at room temperature

1 cup molasses

Royal Icing (optional; recipe follows)

1. In a large bowl, whisk together the flour, baking soda, salt, and spices. Set aside.

2. With an electric mixer fitted with the paddle attachment, beat the butter and sugars on high speed in a large bowl until light and fluffy, about 3 minutes. Then add the egg and molasses and beat until they are incorporated. With the mixer on low speed, add the flour mixture slowly, beating just until the flour is no longer visible and scraping down the sides of the bowl as needed with a spatula.

3. Divide the dough into three small disks that are equal in size. Wrap the disks in plastic wrap and chill in the refrigerator for 1 hour.

4. Preheat the oven to 350°F. Line three large baking sheets with parchment paper or a silicone mat and set aside.

5. Prepare a rolling surface for the dough by generously dusting an area on the counter top with flour. Lightly dust the rolling pin. Remove one disk at a time from the refrigerator and roll out as follows.

6. To make cookies: Roll out the dough to ¼-inch thickness. Dip the bottom of each cookie cutter in flour before cutting the dough. Cut as many cookies as you can, placing them 1 inch apart on the prepared cookie sheets as you go. Reroll the dough scraps as needed to use up all of the dough. Dust the counter and rolling pin with flour as needed.

7. Bake the cookies for 9 to 11 minutes, or until they are lightly browned around the edges. Allow them to cool on the baking sheet for 2 minutes, then transfer them to a cooling rack to cool completely. Decorate with royal icing, if desired.

8. To make ornaments: Roll out the dough to ⅛-inch thickness. Cut the shapes with cookie cutters as directed above. Once the cookies are on the baking sheet, use a skewer to poke a hole in the top of the cookie at least ¼ inch from the edge. This is where you will string the ribbon through once they are baked.

9. Bake the ornaments for 8 to 10 minutes, or until the edges turn lightly brown. Allow them to cool on the baking sheet for 2 minutes, then transfer them to a cooling rack to cool completely.

Decorate with royal icing, if desired. Draw a ribbon through each hole once the ornaments have cooled completely.

Royal Icing

Both cookies and edible ornaments can be decorated with royal icing. If you want to get extra-fancy, try sprinkling the icing with colored sugars or use it as a base for candy decorations. This recipe makes a lot of icing, so use it liberally.

MAKES 3 CUPS ICING

¼ cup powdered egg whites
1 pound confectioners' sugar

1. With an electric mixer fitted with the whisk attachment, beat the egg whites and sugar with ¼ cup of water on high speed in a large bowl. Slowly add up to ¼ cup of water by the tablespoon just until the icing is pliable but not runny. It is supposed to be fairly stiff so that it can form a loose ball when it is rolled between your palms. It should be the consistency of a stiff toothpaste.

2. Scoop the icing into a large resealable plastic bag with a very small part of the corner clipped off, or use a pastry bag. Squeeze the icing toward the corner of the bag and twist the top of the bag shut. Use this bag to pipe the frosting along the cookies and ornaments as desired.

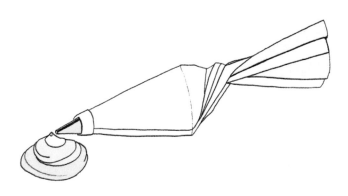

Brown Sugar Crisp Cut-Outs

These cookies are a true family favorite. I started making these with my mother when I was just five years old! Now I bake them with Daphne and Garner and they have just as much fun decorating them as I once did. On their own, the cookies are simple and plain. Sugar them up with gorgeous sprinkles, frostings, and any other sweet edible decoration you can dream up!

MAKES 3 DOZEN COOKIES

4 cups unbleached all-purpose flour

1 teaspoon baking powder

¼ teaspoon baking soda

1 teaspoon kosher salt

12 ounces (2½ sticks) unsalted butter, at room temperature

1½ cups packed dark brown sugar

2 large eggs, at room temperature

1 teaspoon pure vanilla extract

Sprinkles (optional)

Cinnamon dots (optional)

Sanding sugar (optional)

Vanilla frosting (optional)

1. Sift the flour, baking powder, baking soda, and salt into a large bowl and set aside.

2. With an electric mixer fitted with the paddle attachment, cream the butter and brown sugar on high speed in a separate large bowl for 2 minutes. Then beat in the eggs one a time, beating well after each addition. Beat in the vanilla.

3. With the mixer on low speed, slowly add the dry ingredients, scraping down the sides of the bowl with a spatula as needed. Mix just until the flour mixture is completely incorporated. Divide the dough into two pieces and press each into a disk about 2 inches thick. Wrap each disk tightly in plastic wrap and chill for about 1 hour or up to 12 hours. If not using within a day, freeze the dough for up to 1 month.

4. Preheat the oven to 350°F and line two baking sheets with parchment paper or a silicone mat. Use one disk from the refrigerator at a time, letting each sit at room temperature for 10 minutes before rolling.

5. Generously flour a surface and a rolling pin. Roll out the dough to ⅛ inch thick and use cookie cutters to cut desired shapes. Decorate them with sprinkles and edible decorations as desired, or leave plain for frosting after baking. Use a spatula to transfer the shapes to the prepared pan. Bake the cookies for 8 to 10 minutes, or until golden brown around the edges. Allow the cookies to cool for 2 minutes on the baking sheet, then transfer them to a cooling rack to cool completely. Once the cookies have cooled, frost and decorate.

Candy Cane Fudge

This fudge is the best option for the non–cookie lover and is a nice break from rich chocolate desserts. It is also gluten-free and nut-free, so it is perfect for taking to school.

**MAKES 1 (8-INCH SQUARE) PAN
(ABOUT 16 SQUARES)**

Cooking spray
20 ounces white chocolate, coarsely chopped
1 (14-ounce) can sweetened condensed milk
½ teaspoon peppermint extract
1½ cups crushed candy canes or peppermints,
    divided

1. Line an 8-inch square baking dish with parchment paper so that there is a 2-inch over-hang on each side. Lightly spray the paper with cooking spray.

2. In a large saucepan, melt the chocolate and condensed milk over medium-low heat. Stir just until everything and completely combined. Remove the pan from the heat and stir in the peppermint extract and 1 cup of the crushed candy canes.

3. Pour the mixture into the prepared baking dish and scatter the remaining candy cane pieces evenly on top. Chill the fudge for 2 hours in the refrigerator before cutting and serving.

Easy Salted Caramels

I can't tell you how many times I have burned caramel when trying to use recipes from fancy pastry chefs. Once I found this recipe, I never looked back. It is easy enough for even the most novice candy maker and the smooth, chewy caramels are incredible. Tie them up in waxed paper twists and set them out in candy dishes around your house.

MAKES ABOUT 80 CARAMELS

Cooking spray
2 cups granulated sugar
½ cup light corn syrup
1 (14-ounce) can sweetened condensed milk
2 teaspoons pure vanilla extract
¼ teaspoon kosher salt
2 teaspoons sea salt

1. Line an 8-inch square baking dish with parchment paper, allowing for overhang. Lightly spray the paper with cooking spray and set aside.

2. In a small saucepan, bring the sugar, corn syrup, and ¼ cup of water to a boil over medium-high heat, whisk continuously so that the sugar dissolves completely. Continue to whisk the mixture for 10 to 12 minutes, until it turns a medium amber brown.

3. Remove the mixture from the heat and immediately whisk in the condensed milk. The mixture will froth and bubble, but continue to whisk until it forms a smooth dark caramel mixture without any lumps.

4. Return the pan to the heat and clip a candy thermometer to the side. Whisk the caramel until it reaches 240°F. Remove it from the heat and stir in the vanilla and kosher salt.

5. Pour the caramel into the prepared pan and allow it to cool for 10 minutes, then sprinkle the sea salt evenly over the top. Allow the caramel to cool completely at room temperature.

6. To cut the caramel, chill the dish in the freezer for an hour. Then lift the caramel slab from the pan by holding on to the parchment paper, and place it on a hard cutting board. Run a sharp chef's knife under hot water and cut the hardened caramel into desired sizes. Wrap each piece of caramel in a twist of waxed paper. Store in a cool, dry place.

HOW TO HOST A COOKIE SWAP

Everyone I know assembles slightly different Christmas cookie platters and has a unique take on classic recipes. The best way to sample everyone's delicious baked goods and increase the selection of your own stash is with a cookie swap.

This easygoing, festive event is a great way to socialize with friends and help one another out. The concept is that all the guests bring a huge batch of their favorite cookie and exchange them. This saves time and money because it is so much easier to make one large batch of a single recipe than several different recipes. It is also the perfect way to discover cookies you've never tried before.

SIX WEEKS IN ADVANCE Set the date and send criteria for your cookie swap. Ask each guest to prepare enough cookies to provide one dozen cookies per attendee. For example, if ten guests attend, then each guest would bring 120 cookies. Add a note that each person can prepare more cookies for sampling, if desired. Try to provide your guests with an accurate head count about two weeks before the event so they can prepare accordingly. If you prefer guests to arrive with their cookies prepackaged in sets of one dozen, note that in the invitation.

COOKIE NOTES Communicate to your guests whether any cookies need to be prepared to accommodate food allergies. Let them know whether there is any size, shape, or portability restriction. If allergies are a concern for guests, ask attendees to provide an ingredients list for each type of cookie to make sure they are safe.

PREPARE REFRESHMENTS The purpose of the swap is to send most of the cookies home, unless extra cookies for sampling have been prepared. To draw guests away from eating the swap cookies, prepare a small table of treats for nibbling. Eggnog, mulled wine, spiced nuts, dips, and sliced rum cake are some easy, festive snacks.

PREPARE THE TABLE Set out trays and cake stands on a large table that are easy to browse. Set out labels and a marker for the trays. When the guests arrive, they should arrange their respective cookies on a tray and label it. Alternatively, if guests arrive with their cookies prepackaged, these can be grouped and displayed in large baskets.

START THE SWAP Direct everyone around the table to select a dozen of each cookie variety and place them in the container they brought. Continue to send people around the table until all the cookies are gone.

PACKING In case people need extra packing materials for the cookies they are taking home, have resealable plastic bags, paper plates, parchment paper, and aluminum foil on hand. This way, people can wrap up an extra plate or two, if need be.

Homemade Gifts

Growing up, my parents made homemade gifts for their friends in Cooperstown every Christmas. My father would spend August canning his famous bread & butter pickles to give out and my mother would make all kinds of breads, jams, and sweets to distribute in pretty, cloth-lined baskets. I've inherited their love of making gifts and continue the tradition in my community. A jar of homemade vanilla extract with a special wooden spoon or marinated olives with a vintage silver olive fork are fun gifts to give and are far more sentimental than anything I could ever buy in the store. Sometimes I even get Daphne involved and we select one of our favorite easier recipes to make so she can make gifts for her friends, too.

Your Homemade Gift Strategy

Making edible gifts shouldn't add to the stress of an already busy holiday season. Each year select one or two recipes to make and double or triple the volume. The gifts can then be wrapped identically and distributed. You'll be happier concentrating on a large batch of one recipe than small batches of several different items.

GIFT PACKAGING

A simple but elegant wrapping job is the right approach. There is no need to spend lots of money on expensive materials to transform an ordinary container into a pretty holiday package.

Gift Tags

Buy pretty gift tags in stationary stores, or make your own with kraft paper or plain manila tags.

Kraft paper or plain manila paper tags
Scissors or pinking shears
Hole punch
Decorative markers
Rubber stamps and ink pads
Ribbons or baker's twine

1. If using kraft paper, cut out the gift tag with scissors or pinking shears and punch a hole for hanging.
2. Adorn with decorative markers or rubber stamps.
3. Fasten the tag to the package with ribbon or bakers' twine.

Note When presenting a gift with baking or cooking directions, be sure to cut your gift tag large enough to include the directions on the back.

Jars

When packaging jars, decorate the lid. Whatever is in the jar itself is pretty and doesn't need to be gussied up with paper or ribbons.

Jars with lids

Thin, decorative cloth

Scissors

Baker's twine or thin ribbons

Gift tag (page 260)

1. To make the fabric lid cover, start with a 6-inch square of pretty cotton fabric. Place the lid of the jar in the center and cut an even circle from the fabric that is 2 inches wider than the jar lid. It may help to use a compass, or find an object that

is 2 inches wider than the jar lid and trace it onto the cloth to make the cut even. Screw the lid onto the jar and center the circle of cloth on top of the lid.

2. To finalize the decoration, tie baker's twine three or four times around the outside of the rim, to hold the cloth in place. If using a gift tag, tie it onto the bakers twine.

Boxes & Tins

Package large items, such as shards of chocolate bark, piles of cut-out cookies, or heavy shortbread bars, in a box or tin.

Box or tin

White or tan parchment paper

Scissors

Transparent tape

Thick, festive grosgrain ribbons

Gift tag (page 260)

1. Before packing the food, line the bottom and sides of the container with white or tan parchment paper: Cut two pieces of paper to fit the bottom and sides with 2 inches of overhang. Arrange

the paper so that it overlaps on the bottom and there is an equal overhang on all four sides of the container.

2. Place the food in the container on top of the paper and fold the overhang on top of it. Then close the container.

3. Place a tiny bit of tape on each of the four sides of the container to keep it closed. Then use the ribbon to wrap the container and tie a bow on top. Make a gift tag as desired and affix it to the base of the bow before presenting your gift.

Cookie Bags

Package cookies or brownies stacked up in a clear cello bag.

Cello bag

Scissors

Cardboard

Parchment paper

Twist ties

Grosgrain ribbons

Gift tag (page 260)

1. Cut out a square of cardboard that will hold the bottom of the bag flat. Then cut out a square of parchment paper the same size to go over it.

2. Stack the cookies on top of the parchment paper. If they seem as though they might stick together, cut a little square of parchment paper to fit between each one. Leave at least 2 inches at the top of the bag.

3. Twist the bag shut and seal it tightly with a twist tie. Cover with a beautiful grosgrain ribbon and tie a big bow. Add a gift tag to the base of the bow before gifting.

Peppermint Swirl Marshmallows

These are so much fun to make with children. Watching the gelatin expand in the mixing bowl is nothing short of magic to them! To package them place the squares in large, waxed, food-safe bags and seal with decorative stickers. For a heftier gift basket include hot cocoa mix and two holiday mugs.

MAKES 20 MARSHMALLOWS

Cooking spray

3 (0.25-ounce) envelopes unflavored gelatin

½ cup cold water

1¾ cups granulated sugar

⅔ cup light corn syrup

1 teaspoon sea salt

¼ teaspoon peppermint extract

Confectioners' sugar for coating

1. Lightly spray a 9-inch square baking pan with cooking spray and line with plastic wrap, leaving a 2-inch overhang on each side.

2. In a large mixing bowl, sprinkle the gelatin over the cold water. Allow to rest undisturbed for 10 minutes.

3. Meanwhile, in a shallow saucepan over medium heat, combine the sugar, corn syrup, and ¼ cup of water and bring to a rapid boil for 1 minute. Dip a pastry brush in the water and brush down the crystals on the side of the pan as needed while it boils.

4. Remove the pan from the heat. Pour the boiling sugar syrup into the gelatin mixture, using a spatula to scrape out every last drop. With an electric mixer fitted with a whisk attachment, begin mixing the gelatin mixture at medium-high speed. With the motor running, carefully sprinkle the salt and peppermint extract into the bowl and continue to whisk on high speed for 10 minutes. The mixture will quadruple in volume and turn a light foamy white.

5. Once the marshmallow is white and holds stiff peaks (when you lift the whisk attachment the white will stand straight up), spray a spatula with cooking spray and scrape the marshmallow mixture into the prepared pan. Flatten it down with the spatula, respraying as necessary, and fold the overhang of plastic wrap over the top.

6. Let the mixture stand at room temperature for 3 hours to set. Use the plastic to remove the marshmallow slab from the pan and turn it out onto a surface dusted with sifted confectioners' sugar. Use a pizza cutter or sharp knife to cut the marshmallows into squares. Then roll them in the confectioners' sugar before packaging, to keep them from sticking.

Note   To make vanilla marshmallows, use 1 teaspoon of vanilla extract in lieu of the peppermint extract.

Decoration Ideas   The finished marshmallows can be decorated any number of ways. Try dipping them in melted chocolate and then dipping them in sprinkles before popping in the refrigerator to harden. For peppermint marshmallows, spread a thin layer of frosting on them and dust with crush candy canes.

Tip   To make these extra special, cut them into shapes with cookie cutters, dip them in confectioners' sugar, and stick them on lollipop sticks for a fun treat!

Chocolate Fudge in Cookie Cutters

These sweets are practically ready-made to be packaged as gifts and the recipient can keep the cookie cutters long after the fudge is gone. Daphne and I make these using a fudge recipe that is so simple even she can execute it.

MAKES 6 (3-INCH) CANDIES (YIELD MAY VARY DEPENDING ON THE CUTTER)

Cooking spray

1 pound semisweet baking chocolate, coarsely chopped (do not use chocolate chips)

1 (14-ounce) can sweetened condensed milk

2 tablespoons unsalted butter

1 teaspoon kosher salt

1 tablespoon pure vanilla extract

Peppermints, colored edible balls, holiday sprinkles, candy cane dust, for decorating

1. Wrap the bottoms of six 3-inch cookie cutters with aluminum foil to form a base for them and place them on a baking sheet. Lightly spray the inside of the cookie cutters with cooking spray.

2. In a large, microwave-safe bowl, melt the baking chocolate, condensed milk, butter, and salt at 50% power in 30-second intervals until the butter is totally melted. Stir the mixture until it is completely smooth. Stir in the vanilla.

3. Pour the mixture into the cookie cutters until each one is filled nearly to the top. Place the cookie sheet in the refrigerator and chill for 3 hours, or until firm. Remove and decorate as desired with candies and icing.

Note To give these cookie cutters as gifts, remove the aluminum foil backing and package them in cello bags (page 262) tied with a red ribbon and a holiday gift tag (page 260). Keep chilled in the refrigerator until gifting.

Tip To make chocolate mint fudge, use ½ teaspoon of peppermint extract in lieu of the vanilla extract.

Multigrain Pancake Mix

This is one of the first homemade gifts Daphne ever made for her friends. It doesn't require any cooking and it is a great way to introduce children to measuring and sifting. Package it in glass jars and attach a label with the instructions on how to cook the pancakes.

MAKES 5 CUPS MIX

FOR THE DRY MIX

3 cups unbleached all-purpose flour

3 cups white whole wheat flour

1 cup quick-cooking oats

⅓ cup ground flaxseed meal

2 teaspoons ground cinnamon

2½ tablespoons baking powder

1 tablespoon baking soda

½ cup granulated sugar

1 teaspoon kosher salt

FOR THE PANCAKES

1 cup multigrain pancake mix

1 cup buttermilk

1 large egg

2 teaspoons pure vanilla extract

2 tablespoons unsalted butter, melted, plus more for the pan

1. To make the mix: In a large bowl, combine the flours, oats, flaxseed meal, cinnamon, baking powder, sugar, and salt and whisk together. Then carefully scoop 1 cup of the mix into a lidded glass jar, leaving about a 1-inch headspace at the top, and close tightly with the lid. The mix will stay fresh stored in a cool, dry place, for up to 1 month.

2. To make the pancakes: In a large bowl, whisk together the pancake mix, buttermilk, egg, vanilla, and melted butter. Whisk until smooth. Melt an additional tablespoon of the butter over medium-low heat in a nonstick skillet, swirling it so it covers the entire bottom of the pan. Scoop ⅓ cup of the mix into the skillet for each pancake and cook until bubbles appear on the top, about 3 minutes. Flip the pancakes with a spatula and cook for 2 more minutes, or until the bottoms are golden brown. Repeat this with the remaining pancake mix, adding more butter to the skillet as necessary.

Hazelnut & Cherry Dark Chocolate Bark

This the best treat to make for the chocolate lover in your life. It is like a grown-up candy bar. It doesn't require any baking and you can play with flavor variations by changing up the dried fruit or types of nuts you use.

MAKES 4 TO 6 SERVINGS

⅔ cup hazelnuts, skins removed

⅔ cup coarsely chopped dried cherries

½ teaspoon ground cinnamon

1 teaspoon coarse sea salt

12 ounces dark chocolate bar (not chocolate chips)

1. Line a rimmed baking sheet with parchment paper and set aside.

2. Place the hazelnuts in a dry skillet over medium-low heat and lightly toast for 3 to 5 minutes, or until they turn a light golden brown. Transfer them to a cutting board and allow to cool slightly. Once they are comfortable to touch, coarsely chop them.

3. In a small bowl, mix together the chopped hazelnuts, cherries, cinnamon, and sea salt, and set aside.

4. Place the chocolate in a microwave-safe bowl and heat at 50% power in 30-second increments, or until completely melted. Stir the chocolate until smooth and spread it evenly on the prepared baking sheet in an 8 x 10-inch rectangle that is ⅛ inch thick. Sprinkle the hazelnut mixture evenly over the chocolate, pressing down lightly so it is in one even layer and sticks to the warm chocolate.

5. Place the baking sheet in the refrigerator and chill for at least 3 hours. Break into pieces and package in cello bags (page 262) or serve.

Holiday Spiced Butterscotch Sauce

Make this silky butterscotch sauce for friends who love ice cream and frozen treats. They can drizzle it over vanilla bean ice cream, cheesecake, or just eat it with a spoon. Package this in a small glass jar and tie with a ribbon.

MAKES 2 HALF-PINTS SAUCE

1½ cups packed light brown sugar

4 ounces (1 stick) unsalted butter

1 cup half-and-half

½ teaspoon kosher salt

2 teaspoons pure vanilla extract

1 teaspoon ground cinnamon

½ teaspoon ground ginger

¼ teaspoon ground nutmeg

1. In a saucepan over medium heat, melt the sugar, butter, half-and-half, and salt. Whisk everything together and continue cooking for about 6 minutes as it thickens. If the mixture begins to bubble and spurt, lower the heat until only small bubbles form.

2. Once it has thickened, stir in the vanilla, cinnamon, ginger, and nutmeg, and cook for another 5 minutes. Remove the sauce from the heat and allow it to cool for about 15 minutes. The sauce will continue to thicken as it cools. Then carefully ladle it into two half-pint glass jars and store in the refrigerator.

Note For sea salt butterscotch, omit the spices and add ½ teaspoon of fine sea salt instead.

Marinated Olives

Our holiday season is full of both formal and informal gatherings. When people stop over for a quick hello, I set out a plate of olives and a bowl of nuts for grazing while we catch up. These are great for giving as hostess gifts throughout the season. The hostess can set them out at her own party or eat them as a midnight snack with some cheese.

MAKES 4 PINTS OLIVES

Grated zest and juice of 2 lemons
8 garlic cloves, thinly sliced
1½ tablespoons red pepper flakes
2 cups extra-virgin olive oil
8 cups green olives

1. In a large saucepan over low heat, combine the lemon zest and juice, garlic, red pepper flakes, and olive oil. Heat the mixture for about 3 minutes to infuse the oil. Do not let the garlic brown. Remove it from the heat and stir in the olives. Allow the mixture to cool for about 10 minutes before proceeding.

2. Set eight sterilized 8-ounce glass jars on the counter (see page 92 for how to prepare the jars). These could be canning jars or decorative wide-mouth jars. Scoop 1 cup of the olives into each jar. Top off with the infused oil.

3. Seal the jars and place the olives in the refrigerator. Refrigerated, they will last for up to 3 months. Allow them to come to room temperature before serving.

Note Other herbs that would work well in lieu of tarragon are rosemary, basil, sage, or chives. Make sure all herbs are rinsed and patted dry before using.

Vanilla Extract

This is my go-to gift for bakers. Although I give it most often at Christmas, it is an excellent gift any time of year. The most important thing to remember is that it should be made eight weeks in advance of when you give it. This way, the recipient can use it the minute it is received.

MAKES 4 HALF-PINTS EXTRACT

1 liter plain vodka
4 large vanilla beans

1. Slit the vanilla beans down the middle and fold them into four clean half-pint jars. Fill the jars with vodka and allow them to rest in a cool, dry place for 6 to 8 weeks. Every few days, give them a gentle shake to agitate the mixture. Very gradually the vodka will turn a deep dark brown and become infused with the vanilla flavor. Once you have reached the 8-week mark, the vanilla will be a medium amber color and is ready to use. The color will continue to deepen with time and, as it deepens, the flavor will intensify.

Tip Tell the recipient that once there only a few tablespoons are left in the jar, simply remove the old vanilla bean, add a fresh slit bean, and refill the jar with fresh vodka, keeping the last of the original extract in it. The homemade vanilla extract supply will be endless!

Vanilla Sugar

This easy gift is always a favorite bakers. Friends of mine said they even use it for their Christmas cookies!

MAKES 4 HALF-PINTS VANILLA SUGAR

4 large vanilla beans
4 cups granulated sugar

1. Slit the vanilla beans down the middle, scrape out the seeds, and stir the seeds into the sugar, reserving the emptied beans.
2. Fold each bean into a clean, dry half-pint jar, pour 1 cup of the sugar mixture on top, then seal with a lid. Place the jars in a cool, dry place for 2 weeks. Every few days give it a gentle shake to agitate the sugar and infuse it with the vanilla flavor. After 2 weeks of storage, it is ready to use in any baking projects as you would use regular sugar.

Tip Compose a gift package with vanilla extract and vanilla sugar and a set of pretty measuring spoons alongside.

New Year's Day Brunch

Long gone are the days of our eating New Year's Day breakfast at a Manhattan diner around four a.m. Now Duncan and I usually spend the evening with friends and are home well before midnight so the babysitter can make it to her (much more exciting) party. To celebrate New Year's without losing too much valuable sleep, invite people over for brunch on New Year's morning and fill your dining room table with your ace-in-the-hole winter brunch menu of egg strata, crispy bacon, and Champagne. With a crackling fire in the fireplace, it is a warm way to start the year on a high note.

Pomegranate Mimosas

New Year's Day brunch can go either way when it comes to morning cocktails. Your guests may swear off them, or they may ask for a little hair of the dog. Either way, this slightly sweet sparkling treat always hits the spot. It is perfectly festive for a winter gathering and is the best way to start your year off right.

MAKES 4 MIMOSAS

8 ounces chilled pomegranate juice
1 (750 ml) bottle dry Champagne
2 ounces Triple Sec

1. Fill each champagne flute one-third full with the pomegranate juice. Then top with enough Champagne to fill the rest of the flute almost to the rim. Top each flute with a splash of Triple Sec and serve.

Ham & Artichoke Strata

When you get up craving something eggy and cheesy, this strata is the best thing to make. Then take an aspirin, clutch a coffee mug, and wait for your strata salvation to be ready.

MAKES 8 TO 10 SERVINGS

2½ cups 2% milk
8 large eggs
1 teaspoon kosher salt
½ teaspoon freshly cracked black pepper
4 ounces plain goat cheese, crumbled
2 cups coarsely grated fontina cheese
   (16 ounces cheese)
Butter for baking dish
1 loaf ciabatta, cut into ½-inch cubes
14 ounces artichoke heart quarters packed in
   water, drained
4 ounces smoked ham, cut into ¼-inch cubes

1. In a large bowl, whisk together the milk, eggs, salt, and pepper. Then add the goat cheese and fontina. Set aside.

2. Generously butter the bottom and sides of a 13 x 9 x 2-inch baking dish. Layer the strata ingredients as follows: one-third of the bread cubes, followed by one-third of the artichoke hearts and ham, followed by one-third of the egg mixture. Repeat this layering pattern two more times, finishing with the last of the egg mixture.

3. Cover the baking dish with plastic wrap and refrigerate it overnight or for at least 8 hours.

4. Preheat the oven to 350°F. Let the dish sit at room temperature for at least 30 minutes. Bake the strata for 45 to 50 minutes, or until the topping is golden brown and the casserole puffs up and begins to pull away from the sides. Allow to cool for about 10 minutes and serve hot.

Sweet & Spicy Baked Bacon

Once I figured out how to bake bacon, I never cooked it on the stovetop again. It cooks much more evenly in the oven and it is easier to flavor. We like our bacon with a thin, sweet glaze and just a hint of spice. Serve this up on a big platter for your friends on New Year's Day morning.

MAKES 4 TO 6 SERVINGS

12 ounces thick-cut bacon
2 tablespoons good-quality pure maple syrup
½ teaspoon cayenne pepper

1. Preheat the oven to 400°F.

2. Line the bottom and sides of a large, rimmed baking sheet with aluminum foil. Place the strips of bacon in one layer on the foil. Bake it for 15 to 20 minutes, or just until the ends begin to brown.

3. Remove the pan from the oven and carefully and gently brush the tops of each strip with maple syrup. Then sprinkle the strips with the cayenne.

4. Return the bacon to the oven and bake it for 4 to 5 more minutes, or until the strips are crispy. Remove from the oven and transfer the bacon to a paper towel–lined plate to cool.

Note This recipe is very flexible. The baking time will depend on the thickness of the bacon you use. You can omit the syrup and cayenne for regular baked bacon.

Winter Fruit Salad *with* Vanilla Syrup

To buoy your spirits on the first morning in January, make this lively salad. It is inspired by fresh citrus flavors and adds an instant ray of sunshine to your table.

MAKES 6 TO 8 SERVINGS

¼ cup granulated sugar

1 large vanilla bean, split lengthwise

5 blood oranges

2 ripe mangoes, peeled, pitted, and chopped

5 kiwis, peeled and diced

1 pineapple, peeled, cored, and cut into chunks

1 cup pomegranate arils

1. In a small saucepan over medium heat, combine the sugar, 1 cup of water, and the vanilla bean. Bring the mixture to a simmer and cook just until the sugar is dissolved. Remove from the heat, strain out the bean, and allow to cool completely.

2. To prepare the salad, segment the blood oranges by removing the rind and white pith. Hold an orange over a large salad bowl and cut between each segment and membrane, scooping out the segments. They should come out in perfect wedges. Repeat with remaining oranges.

3. Toss the remaining fruit with the orange segments bowl and drizzle with the vanilla syrup. Serve.

Rustic Pear Crostatas

A sweet, buttery crostata is easy to prepare for your guests and is the perfect sweet treat to cap off your brunch. It can also be made with apples if those are all you have available.

MAKES 16 SERVINGS

FOR THE CRUST

2 unbleached all-purpose flour

¼ cup granulated sugar

½ teaspoon kosher salt

8 ounces (2 sticks) cold unsalted butter, cut into small pieces

¼ cup ice water

FOR THE FILLING

3 pounds Bosc pears, peeled and cut into 1½-inch pieces

½ cup unbleached all-purpose flour

½ cup granulated sugar

½ teaspoon kosher salt

½ teaspoon ground cinnamon

⅛ teaspoon ground nutmeg

4 ounces (½ stick) cold unsalted butter, cut into small pieces

½ cup sliced almonds

1 tablespoon coarse turbinado sugar

1. To make the crust: Combine the flour, granulated sugar, salt, and butter in the bowl of a food processor fitted with a blade. Pulse six or seven times, or until small crumbs form. Slowly pulse while adding the ice water 1 tablespoon at a time through the feed tube of the machine. Pulse just until a smooth ball of dough forms. Transfer the dough to a floured surface and divide it into two equal-size disks. Wrap them in plastic wrap and chill them in the refrigerator for at least 2 hours or up to 24 hours.

2. Preheat the oven to 350°F. Line two baking sheets with parchment paper. Roll each disk into a 10-inch circle and place them on the prepared baking sheets.

3. To make the filling: Arrange equal amounts of the pears in the middle of each crust, leaving a 2-inch border. Mix the flour, granulated sugar, salt, cinnamon, and nutmeg in a small bowl. Pinch in the butter with your fingers until small pebbles form. Sprinkle the mixture evenly on top of the pears. Fold up the border of each tart, folding the sides as needed so it fits. Sprinkle the almonds and coarse sugar evenly over the top of both tarts.

4. Bake the crostatas for 30 minutes, or until the crusts are lightly browned. Let them cool on the pans for 10 minutes, then transfer to serving platters. Cut into slices and serve.

New Year's Resolution

Your New Year's Resolution Strategy

To right the ship after a December filled with glorious Christmas sweets, focus on fresh, light dishes that make you feel good. It is not about juice cleanses or fancy diets; it is about eating smart to start the new year on a positive note.

Give your kitchen an insta-resolution makeover, rid the cabinets of any lingering holiday desserts, buy the ingredients for a few of your favorite healthy meals, and swap out soda and alcohol for a big pitcher of flavored water. A few simple changes and a roster of healthy recipes are all you need to make your healthy start.

Banana Peanut Butter Breakfast Smoothie

This simple smoothie is based on one of my favorite healthy snacks: bananas dipped in peanut butter. On winter mornings, fuel up on this and skip the heavily caffeinated coffee drinks. It has enough protein to hold you through until lunchtime and tastes like a dream.

MAKES 2 SMOOTHIES

3 ripe medium-size bananas

4 tablespoons wildflower honey

2 cups unsweetened rice milk, or other nondairy milk, such as almond, soy, or coconut

4 tablespoons smooth peanut butter

2 pinches of ground nutmeg

1. Put the bananas, wildflower honey, rice milk, and peanut butter into a blender and blitz until completely smooth. Pour into two glasses, sprinkle with a pinch of nutmeg, and serve.

Pineapple Coconut Milk Breakfast Smoothie

This fruity smoothie has a distinct tropical flavor to it. I love it because I am usually dreaming of tropical destinations come January! While it may not turn your kitchen into an island oasis, at least it tastes like one.

MAKES 4 SMOOTHIES

2 cups fresh pineapple cut into chunks, chilled
1 cup canned coconut milk, chilled
1 teaspoon finely minced fresh ginger

1. Place the pineapple, milk, and ginger in a blender and blitz until completely smooth. Pour into four glasses and serve.

Glazed Salmon

This salmon dinner only requires three ingredients and takes less than five minutes to pull together at the end of a long winter day. To round out this healthy main course, add a side of steamed green beans with almonds or serve it over a bed of wilted spinach.

MAKES 4 SERVINGS

2 pounds salmon fillet
⅓ cup teriyaki sauce (such as Trader Joe's Soyaki)
1 lemon, cut into wedges

1. Preheat the oven to 400°F.
2. Cut the salmon into four equal-size pieces and arrange it skin-side down in a baking dish. Drizzle with the sauce and turn the fish twice so that it is evenly coated.
3. Bake the salmon for 15 to 18 minutes, or until it flakes with a fork. Serve with lemon wedges.

Easy Shrimp & Vegetables

A quick healthy meal of shrimp and vegetables is the perfect easy dinner for a cold winter night. It is flavored with fresh herbs and lots of lemon. The bright flavors almost make you forget that you are working on resolutions.

MAKES 4 SERVINGS

1 teaspoon cornstarch

½ cup cold water

2 tablespoons soy sauce

2 tablespoons vegetable oil

1 medium-size yellow onion, halved and sliced into half-moons

1 red bell pepper, halved, seeded, and cut into strips

1 yellow bell pepper, halved, seeded, and cut into strips

1 medium-size zucchini, sliced

1 medium-size yellow summer squash, sliced

4 garlic cloves, finely chopped

1½ pounds peeled and deveined uncooked shrimp

1 teaspoon grated lemon zest

2 tablespoons chopped fresh parsley

¼ teaspoon crushed red pepper flakes

1. In a small bowl, whisk together the cornstarch, water, and soy sauce until smooth. Set aside.

2. In a large, nonstick skillet, heat the oil over medium-high heat. Add the onion, red pepper, yellow pepper, zucchini, and squash and stir-fry for 4 minutes, or until softened. Then add the garlic, shrimp, lemon zest, parsley, and red pepper flakes and stir for about 2 minutes. The shrimp will turn pink and the vegetables tender. Stir in the soy sauce mixture and cook for about 2 minutes, stirring until the sauce has reduced and thickened. Remove from the heat and serve.

Note For a light meal, serve the shrimp and vegetables on their own. To make the dish a little heartier, serve over brown rice or quinoa.

Spicy Roasted Cauliflower

When it comes to cleaning up my act in the new year, I rely heavily on vegetables. The more in my diet, the better. Roasting veggies makes them taste amazing without having to add heavily caloric butters or sauces. This is a snap to prepare on a weeknight and is also great for children.

MAKES 3 TO 4 SERVINGS

1 large head cauliflower, cut into florets

2 tablespoons olive oil

⅛ teaspoon kosher salt

¼ teaspoon freshly cracked black pepper

¼ teaspoon crushed red pepper flakes

1. Preheat the oven to 425°F. Line a rimmed sheet pan with parchment paper.

2. In a large bowl, toss the cauliflower florets with the olive oil until they are lightly coated. Then add the salt, pepper, and red pepper flakes and toss to coat.

3. Spread the cauliflower evenly on the prepared pan and bake for 30 to 35 minutes, or until the edges of the cauliflower are dark brown and it is easily speared through with a fork. Remove it from the oven and allow it to cool slightly before serving.

Avocado, Grapefruit & Arugula Salad

Light winter eats don't have to be devoid of flavor. This awesome salad is packed with bright citrus and smooth avocado. To make it into a healthy main course, serve some grilled shrimp on top.

MAKES 4 TO 6 SERVINGS

2 tablespoons Dijon mustard

⅔ cup freshly squeezed lemon juice

1 teaspoon kosher salt

¾ teaspoon freshly cracked black pepper

¾ cup extra-virgin olive oil

1 large bunch baby arugula, rinsed and dried

¼ small red onion, peeled and thinly sliced

1 large ruby red grapefruit

2 Haas avocados, peeled and pitted

1. In a small bowl, whisk together the mustard, lemon juice, salt, pepper, and olive oil until completely emulsified.

2. In a large bowl, combine the arugula and onion. Remove the rind and pith of the grapefruit. Using a sharp paring knife, cut between each membrane and grapefruit segment and carefully pull out the segments with the tip of the knife. Add the grapefruit to the arugula mixture.

3. Finally, dice each avocado, adding it to the salad right after cutting. Immediately drizzle the avocados with the dressing and toss the salad well. Serve.

Nutty Kale & Pear Salad

This salad was inspired by Amanda Hesser's on Food52.com. It is ideal for making when you want to eat your kale but don't want to tackle anything too involved. It comes together in a snap, perfect for when you are hungry for something healthy.

MAKES 4 TO 6 SERVINGS

5 cups baby kale, torn into small pieces

2 small scallions, peeled and thinly sliced

2 tablespoons extra-virgin olive oil

1 tablespoon brown rice vinegar

½ teaspoon coarse sea salt

¼ teaspoon freshly cracked black pepper

1 pear

¼ cup whole raw unsalted almonds, chopped and lightly toasted

¼ cup Parmesan cheese shaved with a vegetable peeler

1. In a large salad bowl, combine the kale, scallions, olive oil, vinegar, salt, and pepper. Set aside.

2. Peel the pear and core and slice it very thinly. Add the pear slices to the salad, tossing them gently so they don't break. Sprinkle the almonds and Parmesan on top and serve.

Fruit-Flavored Waters

After a holiday season full of indulgent drinks and sweets, you need to give your body a break. Eating well is only half the battle; it is important to drink well, too. To wean yourself off of alcohol and caffeine, stock up on herbal teas and always make sure there is a pitcher of naturally flavored fruit water in the fridge. It satisfies your cravings for something sweet and fruity without the unwanted calories. Drinking lots of it also helps you stay well hydrated and strips away all the bloating from the holidays.

All of the following are some of our favorite flavored water combinations: take your pick.

MAKES 8 CUPS FLAVORED WATER

LEMON-LIME WATER 1 large unwaxed lemon, cut into ⅛-inch-thick slices, and 2 small unwaxed limes, cut into ⅛-inch-thick slices.

CUCUMBER MINT WATER 2 large cucumbers, peeled, seeded, and sliced into ¼-inch-thick half-moon shapes, and ¼ cup of coarsely chopped fresh mint leaves.

PINEAPPLE BASIL WATER 2 cups (1-inch cubes) of cubed pineapple and 6 large, coarsely chopped fresh basil leaves.

ORANGE WATER 2 large unwaxed navel oranges, cut into ⅛-inch-thick slices.

MANGO MINT 2 cups (2-inch) strips of mango flesh and ¼ cup of coarsely chopped fresh mint leaves.

To make flavored water, place the sliced fruit, vegetables, and herbs in the bottom of a large pitcher. Pour 8 cups of room-temperature water over them and stir with a wooden spoon to make sure none of the fruit pieces are stuck together. Cover the pitcher with a lid and chill in the refrigerator for a minimum of 3 hours. Drink as needed!

Less Guilt Dark Chocolate & Orange Pudding Cups

Just because you reset your eating habits after the holidays doesn't mean you have to give up sweets entirely. These pudding cups are just the thing for satisfying chocolate cravings without overdoing it.

MAKES 4 SERVINGS

½ cup granulated sugar

¼ cup cornstarch

2 tablespoons unsweetened cocoa powder

⅛ teaspoon kosher salt

2 cups 2% milk

2 ounces dark chocolate, finely chopped

Zest of 1 large navel orange

1 teaspoon pure vanilla extract

1. In a large saucepan, whisk together the sugar, cornstarch, cocoa powder, and salt. Then pour in the milk and bring it to a boil over medium-high heat, whisking to make sure no lumps form.

2. Once the mixture is boiling, stir in the dark chocolate and orange zest and lower the heat to medium-low. Continue to whisk the mixture continuously until the pudding has thickened, 1 to 2 minutes. Remove the pan from the heat and stir in the vanilla. Divide the hot pudding evenly among four bowls. Allow it to cool for at least 10 minutes before serving warm.

3. Alternatively, cover each bowl with plastic wrap, pressing the plastic directly on the pudding, and refrigerate until ready to serve. Divide the pudding among four bowls and serve!

Book Club Food

ROASTED EGGPLANT DIP   284

—

QUICK SPICED ALMONDS   285

—

BAKED SPINACH & FETA DIP   285

—

MEYER LEMON CREAM TART   286

—

DARK CHOCOLATE BROWNIES
with CHOCOLATE CHUNKS   288

Book club is an occasion for meeting up with friends to discuss great writing and catch up on life. While food is not the focus, it certainly plays an important supporting role. Whoever is hosting often solicits someone to bring a sweet treat and then prepares the rest. This way you always end up with just the right amount of evening snacks to nibble on during your conversation. While most book clubs meet all year long, I confess that I like our meetings more in the winter. Getting into a good book seems more satisfying when I am cozy inside by the fire.

Your Book Club Food Strategy

FOOD The three most important points of consideration are portion sizes, portability, and ease of eating. Because most people eat dinner prior to club meetings, keep portions small. Make sure food can be transferred from house to car without concern and can be eaten easily while discussing the book of the evening.

BEVERAGES White wine, red wine, a small tea and coffee tray with mugs and saucers, a carafe of hot water, a selection of herbal and black teas, a carafe of hot coffee (decaffeinated if the meeting is at night), a bowl of sugar and sweetener packets, a small pitcher of milk, and spoons.

Roasted Eggplant Dip

A warm dip is ideal for noshing on while discussing the book at hand. Serve it with crackers, flatbreads, and sliced vegetables for dipping. This dip can easily be made up to two days in advance and it transports well.

MAKES 3½ CUPS DIP

2 large eggplants (about 2 pounds)

¾ cup extra-virgin olive oil, divided, plus more for drizzling

1 medium-size garlic clove

1 teaspoon kosher salt

½ teaspoon freshly cracked black pepper

½ cup sour cream

Juice of 1 large lemon

1. Preheat the oven to 400°F. Line a large baking sheet with parchment paper and set aside.

2. Slice the eggplants in half and lightly rub each half with 1 tablespoon of olive oil. Bake skin-side down on the prepared baking sheet for 25 to 30 minutes, or until they soften and collapse. Remove from the oven and allow to cool until comfortable enough to handle.

3. Scoop the insides of the eggplant into a food processor and add the garlic, salt, pepper, ½ cup of the olive oil, and the sour cream and lemon juice. Pulse until completely smooth, about five 10-second pulses.

4. Transfer the dip to a decorative bowl, drizzle the top with the remaining 2 tablespoons of olive oil and serve!

Quick Spiced Almonds

These almonds are hugely popular in our group. They don't take long to prepare and can easily be made ahead of time. A handful of this salty nut mix satisfies salt cravings and is packed with protein.

MAKES 6 TO 8 SERVINGS

1 pound whole almonds
½ cup extra-virgin olive oil
1 tablespoon kosher salt
½ teaspoon cayenne pepper

1. Preheat the oven to 350°F. Line a rimmed baking sheet with aluminum foil and set aside.
2. In a large bowl, toss the almonds with the olive oil, salt, and cayenne until they are evenly coated.

3. Spread the nut mixture onto the prepared baking sheet and bake for 8 to 10 minutes, or until the almonds are golden brown and fragrant. Allow to cool slightly and serve.

Note To make these ahead of time, simply allow them to cool to room temperature before storing in a container with a lid. The almonds will stay fresh like this for 1 day. To give them a quick refresh before serving, warm them in the microwave at 50% power for 10 seconds.

Baked Spinach & Feta Dip

Serve this cheesy baked dip with pita chips or tortilla chips. To make it a little fancier, arrange water crackers alongside.

MAKES 2 CUPS DIP

Vegetable oil for dish
1 (10-ounce) box frozen chopped spinach, thawed and squeezed dry
1 (8-ounce) block feta cheese, crumbled
¾ cup low-fat sour cream
¾ cup low-fat mayonnaise
½ cup coarsely grated Parmesan cheese
1 large garlic clove, minced

1. Preheat the oven to 350°F. Lightly oil the inside of a 9-inch pie plate and set aside.
2. In a large bowl, mix together the spinach, feta, sour cream, mayonnaise, Parmesan, and garlic. Scrape the mixture into the prepared dish and smooth the top with a spatula.
3. Bake the dip for 20 to 25 minutes, or until the top and sides are bubbling and the dip is heated through. Remove from the oven and serve warm.

Meyer Lemon Cream Tart

This creamy tart is the perfect sweet treat, especially in midwinter when Meyer lemons are in season. The bright citrus flavor is the best kind of pick-me-up when the days are short and gray.

MAKES 1 (10-INCH) TART

FOR THE CRUST

⅔ cup (1¼ sticks) chilled unsalted butter, cut into pieces, plus more for pan

1¼ cups unbleached all-purpose flour, plus more for pan

2 tablespoons granulated sugar

1 large egg yolk

½ teaspoon kosher salt

3 tablespoons ice water

FOR THE LEMON CURD

½ cup Meyer lemon juice (from 3 or 4 lemons)

3 large eggs

1 large egg yolk

1 teaspoon pure vanilla extract

⅔ cup granulated sugar

¼ teaspoon kosher salt

6 ounces (1½ sticks) unsalted butter, cut into small pieces

½ cup raspberries

1. To make the crust: Butter and flour the inside of a 10-inch tart pan with removable sides and set aside.

2. Place the flour, sugar, egg yolk, and salt in a food processor fitted with a blade and pulse the mixture for 30 seconds. Then add the butter and pulse the mixture until the dough resembles coarse sand. Add the ice water 1 tablespoon at a time through the feed tube, pulsing between each addition, until the dough comes together and forms a ball. Remove the dough and press it evenly into the prepared tart pan. Wrap it in plastic wrap and chill the crust for 2 hours.

3. Preheat the oven to 375°F. Wrap the bottom of the tart pan in aluminum foil to prevent any butter from leaking into the bottom of the oven. Bake the crust for 25 to 30 minutes, or until it turns lightly golden around the edges and begins to pull away from the sides of the pan. Set the pan on a cooling rack and let it cool completely before assembling.

4. To make the curd: Pour 2 inches of water into a large saucepan and bring it to boil. Combine the lemon juice, eggs, egg yolk, vanilla, sugar, and kosher salt in a large, heatproof bowl and set it over the pot of boiling water to make a double boiler. Use a whisk to mix everything together and whisk the mixture continuously for about 8 minutes, or until the curd thickens and a trail is left when you drag the whisk through it.

5. Remove the pan from the heat and set it on the countertop. Immediately add half of the butter pieces and blend them into the curd with a handheld immersion blender. Once they are completely combined, repeat this process with the remaining butter. The curd should be very thick and creamy. Allow it to cool to room temperature before assembling.

6. To assemble the tart: Spread the cooled lemon curd into the cooled tart crust. Arrange the raspberries evenly along the perimeter of the tart just before serving.

Notes

It is best to assemble this tart right before serving. If it is assembled too far in advance, the crust will get soggy. The crust and the curd can be prepared up to a day before assembly. The crust can be stored at room temperature, wrapped in plastic wrap. The curd can be stored in the refrigerator in a bowl covered with plastic wrap. Press the plastic directly on top of the curd to prevent a skin from forming.

If Meyer lemons aren't available then regular lemons can be used.

Dark Chocolate Brownies *with* Chocolate Chunks

Every book club needs a special bite of chocolate on the table. Cut these brownies into small squares and serve them as one-bite brownies. This way everyone can enjoy a bite or two without any guilt.

MAKES 16 BROWNIES

Cooking spray

6 ounces dark chocolate, coarsely chopped

5 tablespoons unsalted butter, cut into pieces

¾ cup granulated sugar

2 large eggs, at room temperature

2 teaspoons pure vanilla extract

½ teaspoon kosher salt

1 cup semisweet chocolate chunks

⅓ cup unbleached all-purpose flour

1. Preheat the oven to 350°F. Spray an 8-inch square baking pan with cooking spray, paying special attention to the corners, and set aside.

2. In a microwave-safe bowl, combine the chocolate and butter. Microwave on high for 45 seconds, then stir. Repeat for 15 seconds as a time, stirring between each interval, until the chocolate and butter are completely melted. Stir the mixture until it is smooth and glossy. Allow to cool slightly before proceeding,

3. Stir in the sugar and eggs until the mixture is smooth. Then add the vanilla and salt and stir well.

4. In a small bowl, toss the semisweet chunks with the flour and stir into the chocolate mixture until the flour is no longer showing.

5. Spread the batter into the prepared pan and flatten the top with a spatula. Bake for 26 to 30 minutes, or until a cake tester comes out clean. Allow the brownies to cool completely in the pan for at least 2 hours. Cut the brownies into 1-inch squares and serve.

Cooking for Friends

There are many occasions when we are called upon to cook for friends. Sometimes it is for a family that has recently welcomed a new baby. Other times it is for a friend going through a difficult time. No matter what the occasion, sending them a little love from your kitchen is always a good idea. Never underestimate the comfort your friends will get from the delivery of a nourishing meal. It will free up their time so they can do important things, such as care for their children, get much-needed rest to heal, or tend to whatever needs their full attention. All it takes is a little communication and planning and you can cook a meal that will transport well, is easy for them to eat, and will sustain them both inside and out.

Your Meal-Packing Strategy

PLANNING Ask your friend whether there are any food allergies or food aversions to consider. This is especially important if a friend is recovering from a medical procedure or a mother is breastfeeding. Inquire whether they are comfortable with warming food, cooking it, or freezing it. Knowing this will help you determine what foods are best for their family table.

PORTIONS If a situation is long term, double a soup or casserole recipe and provide freezing instructions, so they can save some food for later.

BEVERAGES Don't forget the importance of hydration. Include one or two bottles of a noncaffeinated beverage, such as sparkling water or fresh-squeezed juice. A bottle of wine never hurts, either.

SMALL BITES Include some no-cook, small-bite items for grazing. Roasted nuts, dry granola, crackers and cheese, olives, and dried fruits are great to have around the house. They can always be served to visitors and a hungry parent can reach for them during midnight feedings.

ADD-ONS Tuck in a few store-bought items that might be needed at home. A fresh baguette for soup or French toast, a box of favorite tea, or some breakfast pastries. If small children are at home, tuck in a package of their favorite sweet.

CALL IT IN If you can't cook a full meal, call your friend's favorite restaurant for take-out. Grocery store catering departments or specialty food shops can help assemble menus. Add a batch of your fresh homemade cookies to round out the meal and deliver it with love.

PACKING Whenever possible, pack food in recyclable containers, so friends don't have to worry about returning them.

Pesto Chicken Orzo Soup

This soup is a welcome twist on traditional chicken noodle. It is full of fresh garden flavors and vegetables. It is chock-full of nutrients for tired parents and freezes well for later.

MAKES 8 CUPS SOUP

2 tablespoons olive oil

1 small yellow onion, peeled and finely diced

1 large carrot, peeled and finely diced

1 pound fresh chicken sausage, casings removed

1 large garlic clove, finely chopped

¼ cup white wine

6 cups low-sodium chicken stock

⅓ cup fresh basil pesto (thawed if using frozen)

1 teaspoon kosher salt, or more to taste

½ teaspoon freshly cracked black pepper

1 cup orzo pasta

Parmesan cheese, for serving

1. In a large, heavy-bottomed pot, heat the olive oil over medium heat. Add the onion and carrot, and crumble in the chicken sausage. Cook until the sausage is browned all the way through and the onion is translucent and softened, 7 to 8 minutes. Then add the garlic and cook for an additional minute so it is softened but not burned. Pour in the wine, deglaze the bottom of the pan, scraping the bottom to incorporate any browned bits, and simmer for 1 minute, or until the wine is almost evaporated.

2. Carefully pour in the chicken stock, 3 cups of water, and the pesto, salt, and pepper, and bring the soup to a boil. Boil for about 2 minutes, then lower the heat to medium-low and add the orzo. Simmer for 8 to 10 minutes, or until the pasta is cooked through. Allow to cool slightly before pouring into a plastic container with a lid. Pack a separate container of Parmesan cheese on the side, for serving. To reheat, ladle soup into individual bowls and microwave at 50% power for 30 seconds, or until as hot as desired. Or pour the entire container back into a soup pan and warm slowly on the stovetop over medium heat.

Note If you can't find chicken sausage, substitute the same amount of cubed boneless skinless chicken breast.

Freezing Note To freeze this soup, pour it into a glass or plastic container and leave 1-inch headspace at the top to allow for expansion. Seal tightly with a lid and mark the container with a permanent marker so you can identify it in the freezer at a later date.

Lentil Vegetable Soup

When one of my friends was undergoing chemotherapy, we set up a dinner train for her family. One of the things I made for her was this mild, healthy soup. Lentils are a terrific source of iron and the vegetables provided just the right amount of flavor without being overpowering.

MAKES 4 TO 6 SERVINGS

3 tablespoons olive oil

2 medium-size yellow onions, finely chopped

3 large carrots, peeled and cut into ½-inch pieces

3 large celery stalks, cut into ½-inch pieces

3 garlic cloves, finely chopped

2 teaspoons kosher salt

½ teaspoon freshly cracked black pepper

1 (14-ounce) can diced tomatoes with juices

2 quarts low-sodium chicken stock

2 teaspoons fresh thyme leaves

1 pound dried green lentils, rinsed

Freshly grated Parmesan cheese, for serving

1. In a large stockpot, heat the olive oil over medium heat. Add the onions, carrots, celery, garlic, salt, and pepper, and cook until the vegetables are softened and fragrant, about 8 minutes.

2. Pour in the tomatoes and their juices, chicken stock, thyme, and lentils. Bring the soup to a simmer and cook for 45 minutes, stirring occasionally, until the lentils are tender and the flavors are nicely developed. Serve with the Parmesan on the side.

Note For convenience, pack this soup in freezer containers with lids. Leave at least 1 inch of headspace at the top of each jar. This way, your friend can easily place the jars in the freezer to save some of the soup for a later date. The jar presentation makes it easy to only reheat as much as is needed.

Tomato Quinoa Soup

This version of tomato soup is packed with protein-rich quinoa and spinach to give the recipient much-needed energy and strength. When you give this out, include bread and cheese for making grilled cheese sandwiches or just for eating on the side. This recipe makes a large portion and half can easily be frozen for a later date.

MAKES 10 SERVINGS

2 tablespoons olive oil

2 medium-size shallots, finely chopped (about ⅓ cup)

2 cloves garlic, peeled and finely chopped

¼ cup white wine

2 (28-ounce) cans whole tomatoes with juices

5 cups low-sodium chicken stock

⅔ cup uncooked quinoa, rinsed

5 ounces fresh baby spinach leaves, washed and patted dry

6 large fresh basil leaves, coarsely chopped

1 tablespoon granulated sugar

2 tablespoons balsamic vinegar

Parmesan cheese, for serving

1. Heat the olive oil in a large pot over medium heat. Add the shallots and stir until they are very soft but not browned, 4 to 5 minutes. Then add the garlic and cook it for 1 minute.

2. Pour the white wine into the pan and allow it to simmer for 2 to 3 minutes, or until it has almost completely evaporated. Carefully pour in the tomatoes with their juices and the chicken stock. Use an immersion blender to purée the soup until completely smooth. Alternatively, if you do not have an immersion blender, purée the chicken stock and tomatoes together in a blender and then carefully pour it into the soup pot.

3. Bring the soup to a boil, boil for 1 minute, then add the quinoa. Lower the heat to medium-low and allow the soup to simmer for about 20 minutes. At the 15-minute mark, add the spinach leaves and basil and stir until all the greens are completely wilted. Then stir in the sugar and vinegar. Allow to cool slightly before pouring into a plastic container with a lid. Pack a separate container of Parmesan on the side, for serving. To reheat, ladle soup into individual bowls and microwave at 50% power for 30 seconds, or until as hot as desired. Or pour the entire container back into a soup pan and warm slowly on the stovetop over medium heat.

Penne alla Vodka

Pasta is one of the world's best comfort foods. Make a creamy penne dish to accompany a lean protein. A warm bowl makes a soothing lunch or easy meal.

MAKES 4 TO 6 SERVINGS

1 pound penne or similar tubular pasta

1 tablespoon olive oil

6 garlic cloves, thinly sliced

1 (28-ounce) can plum tomatoes with juices

1 teaspoon kosher salt

¾ cup vodka

½ cup heavy whipping cream

½ cup freshly grated Parmesan cheese

1. Cook the penne in salted water according to the package instructions. Drain and set aside.

2. Meanwhile, in a medium pot, heat the olive oil over medium heat and add the garlic. Sauté the garlic for about 1 minute, then pour in the plum tomatoes and add the salt. Simmer the tomatoes for 5 minutes, or until heated through and starting to bubble. Use an immersion blender to purée, or ladle the tomatoes into a blender and purée until smooth.

3. Return the tomatoes to the pan and add the vodka. Simmer the sauce again for about 20 minutes. Then stir in the cream and Parmesan and simmer for an additional 3 to 5 minutes, until the sauce is a uniform pink color.

4. Add the cooked penne to the vodka sauce and toss everything well so the pasta is coated. Serve warm, or pack in a big bowl with a lid to transport.

Easy Herbed Parmesan Couscous

This easy dish is a great stand-alone side or is a good base for serving with easy healthy main courses like broiled salmon or baked chicken.

MAKES 4 TO 6 SERVINGS

2 cups low-sodium chicken stock

1 tablespoon unsalted butter

1 (10-ounce) box plain couscous

¼ cup grated Parmesan cheese

1 tablespoon olive oil

¼ teaspoon kosher salt

¼ teaspoon freshly cracked black pepper

1 tablespoon pine nuts, lightly toasted

2 teaspoons finely chopped fresh parsley

1. In a large pot, bring the chicken stock and butter to a boil. Stir in the couscous, cover the pot, and remove it from the heat. Let it sit for 10 minutes.

2. Pour the cooked couscous into a large mixing bowl or disposable container with lid and fluff it up with a fork. Stir in the Parmesan, olive oil, salt, pepper, pine nuts, and parsley. To reheat, place in a microwave-safe bowl and reheat at 50% power for 1 minute, stirring well before serving.

Broccoli Rabe *with* Garlic

This healthy side dish is a nice change from salad. It also reheats well and leftovers can be stirred into pasta to be extended into a second or third meal.

MAKES 4 SERVINGS

2 bunches broccoli rabe (about 24 ounces)

1 tablespoon good olive oil

5 garlic cloves, finely chopped

1 teaspoon kosher salt

½ teaspoon freshly cracked black pepper

1. Trim the broccoli rabe by cutting off the tough ends. Cut the stalks into 3-inch pieces and place them in a colander. Rinse them under cold water and pat dry.

2. In a large skillet, heat the olive oil over medium-low heat and add the garlic. Sauté for about 1 minute. Then add the broccoli rabe, salt, and pepper and sauté for an additional 8 to 10 minutes, or until the broccoli is soft enough that it can be speared easily with a fork. Remove the pan from the heat and allow to cool to room temperature. Cover the pan with a lid or plastic wrap and transport. To reheat, place on a microwave-safe plate and warm at 50% power until heated through, about 30 seconds.

Roasted Acorn Squash

Wedges of soft acorn squash with a light coating of salty butter are the vegetable version of comfort food. For a touch of sweetness, brush it with a light coating of maple syrup before roasting.

MAKES 4 SERVINGS

1 tablespoon vegetable oil
1 large acorn squash (about 1½ pounds)
Kosher salt
3 tablespoons unsalted butter, melted
Freshly cracked black pepper

1. Preheat the oven to 400°F. Line a large, rimmed baking sheet with aluminum foil and brush the vegetable oil evenly over it.

2. Quarter the squash and remove the core, seeds, and strings. Place it skin-side down on the prepared baking sheet and sprinkle each piece with a small pinch of kosher salt.

3. Roast the squash for 35 to 40 minutes, or until the flesh is tender enough to be speared easily with a fork. Remove the pan from the oven and allow the squash to cool for 5 minutes before handling.

4. Cut the squash quarters into equal-size wedges. Brush each one with a little bit of butter and sprinkle with pepper to taste. Serve!

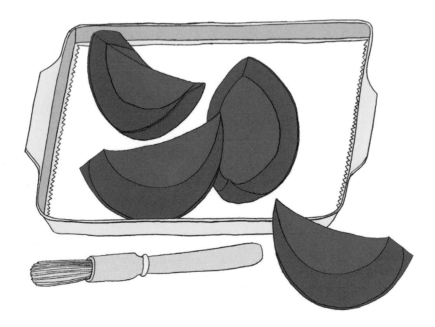

Roasted Root Vegetables *with* Thyme

A fragrant platter of roasted root vegetables is always a welcome alternative to a salad. Serve it in a large bowl and people can try a little of everything. These can also be stirred into grains, such as wheat berries or couscous, and tossed with some dressing for an impromptu salad.

MAKES 4 TO 6 SERVINGS

Cooking spray

8 ounces fingerling potatoes, cut into 1-inch pieces

3 large carrots, peeled and cut into 1-inch pieces

2 large parsnips, peeled and cut into 1-inch pieces

2 turnips, peeled and cut into 1-inch pieces

2 red onions, cut into ¼-inch-thick slices

8 garlic cloves

2 tablespoons fresh thyme leaves

3 tablespoons olive oil

1 teaspoon kosher salt

½ teaspoon freshly cracked black pepper

1. Preheat the oven to 375°F. Spray a 17 x 11-inch roasting pan with cooking spray and set aside.

2. Toss the potatoes, carrots, parsnips, turnips, onions, and garlic in a large bowl. Then add the thyme, olive oil, salt, and pepper and toss well so that the vegetables are evenly coated.

3. Pour the seasoned vegetables into the prepared pan and arrange them in one even layer. Roast the vegetables for 35 to 40 minutes, turning occasionally as needed. Remove from the oven and allow to cool slightly. Serve warm.

Braised Chicken Thighs *with* Artichokes & Olives

A simple pot of steaming chicken is always a welcome dish when one is feeling under the weather. It's all at once fortifying and delicious without being overly rich or decadent.

MAKES 4 TO 6 SERVINGS

2 to 3 tablespoons olive oil

8 boneless skinless chicken thighs

1 teaspoon kosher salt

½ teaspoon freshly cracked black pepper

1 teaspoon chopped fresh rosemary

1 medium-size yellow onion, finely chopped

3 garlic cloves, finely chopped

½ cup white wine

1¾ cups chicken stock

Zest and juice of 1 medium-size lemon

½ cup pitted green olives, drained

8 ounces frozen artichoke hearts, thawed

Cooked long-grain rice or couscous, for serving

1. Heat the olive oil over medium-high heat in a large, heavy-bottomed lidded saucepan or Dutch oven.

2. To brown the chicken, season the thighs with salt and pepper, and add them to the pan in batches, cooking until each side is golden brown, about 3 minutes per side.

3. Transfer the cooked chicken to a plate. Add the rosemary and onion to the pan and sauté until the onion is softened and translucent, about 5 minutes. Then stir in the garlic and cook for 1 more minute. Pour in the wine and deglaze the bottom of the pan to incorporate any browned bits. Cook until the liquid is almost completely evaporated, 1 to 2 minutes.

4. Lower the heat to medium-low, add the chicken stock and the lemon zest and juice, and place a lid on the pan. Simmer for about 15 minutes to reduce.

5. Carefully add the chicken and any chicken juices from the plate, the olives, and the artichokes to the pan and increase the heat to medium-high. Bring the mixture to a simmer and cook for about 5 minutes, or until the chicken is cooked through. Transfer the chicken to a clean plate and simmer the sauce for 3 to 4 more minutes, or until it has slightly thickened. Return the chicken to the pan and serve over rice.

Rigatoni Chicken & Vegetable Casserole

This is the perfect casserole for pasta lovers. It is full of healthy proteins, vegetables, and starches. This dish reheats well and can also be frozen for later.

MAKES 6 TO 8 SERVINGS

Vegetable oil for pan

1 pound rigatoni pasta

2 tablespoons olive oil

1¼ pounds boneless skinless chicken breasts, trimmed and cubed into 1½-inch pieces

Kosher salt

Freshly cracked black pepper

2 medium-size shallots, finely chopped

3 large eggs

1⅔ cups whole milk

3 cups coarsely grated Gruyère cheese

1 (10-ounce) bag frozen quartered artichoke hearts, thawed and patted dry

1 (10-ounce) box frozen chopped spinach, thawed and squeezed dry

½ cup coarsely grated Parmesan cheese

1. Preheat the oven to 350°F. Lightly oil the inside of a 13 x 9 x 2-inch baking dish and set aside.

2. Bring a large pot of salted water to a boil and add the pasta. Cook it until al dente, about 2 minutes less than the directions on the box, drain, and set aside.

3. Heat the olive oil in a medium skillet set over medium heat. Liberally sprinkle the chicken with salt and pepper and add it to the skillet. Cook it for 4 to 5 minutes per side, or just until a light golden brown, turning the cubes as necessary. It is okay if they are not completely cooked through; they will continue to cook in the oven. Remove from the skillet and reserve.

4. Add the shallots to the skillet and lower the heat to medium-low. Cook the shallots for about 5 minutes, or until tender and translucent. Use a wooden spoon to scrape up any browned bits from the chicken. Remove the skillet from the heat and set aside.

5. In a large bowl, beat together the eggs and milk. Then stir in the Gruyère and cooked shallots. Carefully add the pasta to the egg mixture and toss it well until the pasta is completely coated. Then stir in the chicken, artichoke hearts, and spinach.

6. Pour the pasta into the prepared baking dish and flatten the top with a spatula. Then sprinkle the top with the Parmesan. Cover the dish with foil and bake for 30 minutes. Then remove the foil and bake for about 10 minutes more, or until the top is a light golden brown. Remove the pan from the oven and allow it to cool to room temperature. Cover it with plastic wrap and an outer layer of aluminum foil before transporting. To reheat, remove the plastic wrap and warm for 10 minutes in a 350°F preheated oven.

Easy Baked Chicken Enchiladas

This casserole is perfect for Tex-Mex lovers. It carries the flair of a Mexican fiesta with a hint of spice, and it isn't over the top. Pack it with a container of green rice, a side of cornbread, and some fresh guacamole and chips.

MAKES 4 TO 6 SERVINGS

2 tablespoons vegetable oil

1 pound boneless skinless chicken breasts

1 teaspoon kosher salt

1 teaspoon freshly cracked black pepper

1 tablespoon Mexican spice blend

10 corn tortillas

1 (32-ounce) can enchilada sauce, divided

1 (4-ounce) can diced hatch chiles

4 ounces fresh goat cheese, crumbled

1 cup shredded Mexican cheese blend

Sour cream, guacamole, thinly sliced scallions, and sliced black olives, for serving

1. Preheat the oven to 350°F.

2. In a large skillet, heat the oil until over medium-high heat. Season the chicken with salt, pepper, and the spice blend and cook each breast for about 8 minutes per side, or until the chicken is cooked through. Place the chicken on a platter to cool. Then shred it into small, bite-size pieces.

3. Wrap the tortillas in a paper towel and microwave at 50% power for 30 seconds to make them more pliable. Spread ½ cup of the enchilada sauce into the bottom of a 13 x 9-inch baking pan. Pour the rest into a shallow bowl to allow for easy dipping.

4. To assemble the enchiladas, dip a warm tortilla in the enchilada sauce. Then add a large pinch of the chicken, followed by a teaspoonful of the chiles and about 2 teaspoons of goat cheese. Roll up the tortilla and place it seam-side down in the baking pan. Repeat this process with the remaining tortillas, making sure they all fit snugly into the pan.

5. Pour the remaining enchilada sauce from the bowl over the pan and cover the top with the Mexican cheese. Bake for 20 minutes, or until the cheese is melted and bubbly. Allow to cool, wrap the pan in plastic wrap and aluminum foil and transport. To reheat, remove the plastic wrap and replace the aluminum foil on top of the pan. Warm for 15 minutes in a 350°F preheated oven. Pack the garnishes in small zip top bags on the side.

Mustard-Crusted Pork Tenderloin

When my friend Kirsten brought this to us after Garner was born, I thought I had died and gone to heaven. We ate this after a particularly exhausting twenty-four hours and it sustained me through a second rough night of no sleep. She also brought a simple couscous salad, roasted acorn squash, homemade biscotti, and a box of my favorite English Breakfast tea. It was absolutely perfect.

MAKES 4 SERVINGS

½ cup panko breadcrumbs

1 teaspoon dried rosemary

1 teaspoon garlic powder

1½ pounds lean cut pork tenderloin, silverskin
 removed

3 tablespoons brown mustard

1. Preheat the oven to 425°F.

2. In a small bowl, stir together the breadcrumbs, rosemary, and garlic and set aside.

3. Rub the pork tenderloin all over with the brown mustard so that it completely coats the meat. Then place it in a baking dish that leaves at least 2 inches of space all around to allow for even cooking. Sprinkle the breadcrumb mixture over the top and the sides of the tenderloin to make a crust, using your hands to press it down so that it sticks to the mustard. The crust will be fairly thick and you won't be able to see any of the mustard once it is on.

4. Bake the tenderloin for 25 to 30 minutes, or until a meat thermometer inserted into the center of the meat reaches 140°F. Allow it to cool slightly; then transfer it to a cutting board to slice and serve.

Notes If the new parents want to cook it themselves, coat the tenderloin in mustard and place it in a large resealable plastic bag. Prepare the breadcrumb mixture separately and place in a separate resealable plastic bag. Bring both to the new parents with a note attached, containing the following instructions: "Place the pork in a large baking dish. Sprinkle all over with the breadcrumbs. Bake at 425°F for 25 to 30 minutes, or until a meat thermometer inserted into the center reaches 140°F. Slice and serve!"

Dottie's Baked Custard

My friend Dottie in Cooperstown makes the most delicious creamy vanilla custard you've ever tasted. The only problem is that when she makes it for you, it usually means something is wrong! Dottie has made this for countless friends and family members during their times of need, including my own when my father was undergoing emergency medical treatment. It is nursery food of the highest order and every spoonful is the best kind of medicine you could ever want.

MAKES 6 SERVINGS

Butter for greasing the baking dish
2 cups whole milk
4 large eggs, slightly beaten
½ cup granulated sugar
½ teaspoon salt
1 teaspoon pure vanilla extract

1. Preheat the oven to 325°F. Butter the bottom and sides of a 2-quart baking dish and set aside. Place the baking dish in a roasting pan or deep baking pan.

2. Scald the milk by placing it in a small saucepan over medium heat. Cook the milk, stirring a lightly a few times, until tiny bubbles start to form around the edges, but don't allow it to boil. Remove the pan from the heat and allow the milk to cool for 5 minutes, discarding any skin that may form on the surface.

3. Meanwhile, in a large bowl, whisk together the eggs, sugar, salt, and vanilla until combined. Pour the cooled milk into the bowl in ¼-cup increments, whisking continuously as you go, to temper the eggs so they don't cook. Continue adding the warm milk a little bit at a time and whisking continuously until everything is fully combined.

4. Pour the egg mixture into the prepared baking dish. Pour enough water into the roasting pan until it comes 1 inch up the sides of the baking dish.

5. Bake the custard for 1 hour, or until a knife inserted into the center comes out clean. Carefully remove the baking dish from the water bath and allow it to cool to room temperature. The custard can be served warmed or chilled.

Note To fancy this up, make a brûlée sugar crust by coating the top in a thin layer of sugar and placing it under the broiler heated to high until it turns golden brown. Allow the crust to set for 30 minutes before serving with fresh berries. To add different flavors, consider using fresh orange zest or vanilla beans to make it extra rich.

Lemon Cream Cheese Pound Cake

For friends who are sick, the simpler the food, the better. This lemon pound cake is just the right amount of plain and pick-me-up. The bright, citrusy flavor is inviting and comforting, and the dense, spongy texture is easy to take in. There are no bells and whistles, no fancy ingredients on this humble loaf, and that, sometimes, is just what the doctor ordered.

MAKES 2 LOAVES

8 ounces (2 sticks) unsalted butter, at room temperature, plus more for pans

3 cups unbleached all-purpose flour, plus more for dusting pans

1 teaspoon baking powder

1 teaspoon kosher salt

1 (8-ounce) package cream cheese, at room temperature

3 cups granulated sugar

¼ cup freshly grated lemon zest

2 tablespoons freshly squeezed lemon juice

6 large eggs

1. Preheat the oven to 325°F. Butter and flour two 8 x 4-inch loaf pans and set aside. Combine the flour, baking powder, and salt in a mixing bowl and set aside.

2. With an electric mixer fitted with a paddle, cream the butter, cream cheese, and sugar on high speed in a large bowl until light and fluffy, about 3 minutes. Then add the lemon zest and juice and beat until combined, about 1 minute.

3. With the mixer on low speed, add the eggs one a time, beating well after each addition. Then, working slowly, add the flour mixture until it is evenly incorporated, stopping once to scrape down the sides of the bowl.

4. Divide the batter evenly between the loaf pans and smooth the tops with a spatula. Bake for 55 to 60 minutes, or until a cake tester comes out clean.

5. Allow the loaves to cool in the pan for 10 minutes. Then turn them out onto a cooling rack to cool completely.

Note To make this fancier for a friend, pack a container of ice cream and some berries so they can make little pound cake sundaes if they are up to it!

Chewy Chocolate Cookies *with* Sea Salt

When Garner was born, I craved chocolate like nobody's business. However, in my postpartum state I felt gigantic and none of my clothes fit, so I wouldn't let myself have any sweets at all. Finally, I gave myself a break and whipped up these cookies. Having a sweet chocolate nibble on hand can make all the difference after a long day with a newborn!

MAKES ABOUT 3 DOZEN COOKIES

2½ cups unbleached all-purpose flour

¾ cup unsweetened cocoa powder

1 teaspoon baking soda

1 teaspoon kosher salt

1 cup plus 2 tablespoons (2¼ sticks) unsalted
   butter, at room temperature

1 cup granulated sugar

1 cup light brown sugar

2 large eggs, at room temperature

12 ounces semisweet chocolate chunks

2 tablespoons sea salt

1. Preheat the oven to 350°F. Line two rimmed baking sheets with parchment paper and set aside.

2. In a small bowl, combine the flour, cocoa powder, baking soda, and salt and stir with a whisk. Set aside.

3. With an electric mixer, cream the butter and sugars on high speed in a large bowl until light and fluffy. Then beat in the eggs one at a time, mixing well after each addition to ensure they are well combined.

4. With the mixer on low speed, beat in the flour mixture, stirring until just combined with no streaks of flour. Stir in the chocolate chunks.

5. Use a 1-inch cookie scoop to form the dough into balls. Place the balls 2 inches apart on the prepared pans. Sprinkle the top of each ball with a generous pinch of sea salt and bake for 10 to 12 minutes, or until the tops are no longer shiny or jiggling. Allow them to cool for 2 minutes on the pan, then transfer them to a cooling rack to cool completely.

Cinnamon Swirl Bread

This recipe is inspired by my dear friend Julie Van Rosendaal who writes the blog Dinner with Julie. *You can use it for sandwiches, French toast, or toasting with butter for a late-night snack. The warm cinnamon flavors are a little, gentle hug each time you cut a slice.*

MAKES 2 (8 X 4-INCH) LOAVES

2½ cups warm water

2¼ teaspoons (1 packet) active dry yeast

½ cup plus 1 tablespoon granulated sugar, divided

7 cups unbleached all-purpose flour, plus more for dusting

1 teaspoon kosher salt

4 tablespoons (½ stick) unsalted butter, at room temperature, plus more for pans

Olive or vegetable oil for dough bowl

1 tablespoon ground cinnamon

1. With an electric mixer fitted with a dough hook, combine ½ cup of the water, the yeast, and 1 tablespoon of the sugar on low speed in a large bowl. Let the yeast stand undisturbed for 5 minutes, until it begins to look foamy. If foam doesn't form, then it is likely the yeast is dead. Toss it and try again with fresh yeast.

2. Add the remaining 2 cups of water and 3½ cups of the flour and knead on low speed until well blended. Add the remaining 3½ cups of flour, the salt, and the butter and knead with the dough until all the flour is incorporated and the dough begins to develop raggedy edges and pulls away from the sides of the bowl.

3. Transfer the dough to a countertop dusted with flour and knead it a few more times by hand to make sure it is totally smooth.

4. Lightly rub a large mixing bowl with oil and place the dough in it. Cover the bowl with a clean

kitchen towel and let it rest for 2 hours, or until the dough has doubled in size. Butter the inside of two 8 x 4-inch loaf pans and set aside.

5. Punch the dough down and divide it in two. Roll each piece into a 9 x 12-inch rectangle on a lightly floured surface. Sprinkle the surfaces evenly with the remaining sugar and cinnamon. Carefully roll up each rectangle, pinching the ends tight. Place each one roll seam-side down in each prepared loaf pan, tucking the ends underneath.

6. Cover each pan with a towel and allow the dough to rest for 1 hour. Preheat the oven to 375°F.

7. Bake the loaves for 30 to 35 minutes, or until the tops are golden brown and the bread begins to pull away from the sides. Allow the loaves to cool for 10 minutes in the pan and then invert the bread onto a cooling rack to cool completely. Either eat immediately or store wrapped tightly in plastic wrap.

Bourbon Banana Bread

A slice of banana bread is the best kind of comfort food. It is great for new parents to enjoy at all hours of the day. It can also be sliced and packed in lunchboxes for the older children.

MAKES 1 LOAF

4 ounces (1 stick) unsalted butter, at room temperature, plus more for pan

2 cups unbleached all-purpose flour, plus more for pan

1 cup granulated sugar

2 large eggs

3 ripe bananas, mashed well with a fork

2 teaspoons bourbon or bourbon extract

1 teaspoon baking soda

1 teaspoon ground cinnamon

½ teaspoon ground nutmeg

1 teaspoon kosher salt

1. Preheat the oven to 350°F. Butter and flour a 9 x 5-inch loaf pan.

2. With an electric mixer, beat the butter and sugar together on high speed in a large bowl until light and fluffy, about 3 minutes. Beat in each egg one at a time, beating well after each addition.

3. Add the bananas and bourbon to the mixture and beat well until there are no lumps.

4. Stir the flour, baking soda, cinnamon, nutmeg, and salt together in a small bowl. With the mixer on low speed, beat in the flour mixture until just incorporated. Turn off the mixer and scrape down the sides of the bowl as needed to make sure all the flour is mixed in.

5. Pour the batter into the prepared pan and use the back of the spoon to smooth out the top. Bake the loaf for 50 to 55 minutes, or until the top is set and a cake tester inserted into the center of the loaf comes out clean. Allow the bread to cool in the pan for 10 minutes, then invert it onto a cooling rack to cool completely.

Wine & Cheese

*Duncan and I are totally obsessed with wine and cheese parties.
They work any season and are always a hit. The best part of hosting
a wine and cheese party is that there is no wrong way to do it.
Review the following suggestions and then make it into whatever
kind of party you want!*

CREATING A CHEESE BOARD

SERVING SIZE Buy around 3 to 4 ounces of cheese per person.

SELECTING CHEESES It's helpful to limit your cheese selection to six so you have at least one cheese from each category. If you are serving a lot of people or want a wider variety, you can add as many cheeses as you like.

Cheese Categories

SOFT Spreadable fresh cheeses, such as goat cheese, which are generally not aged.

SEMIHARD Creamy cheeses with bloomy soft rinds, such as Brie and camembert.

HARD Firm cheeses, such as Cheddar and Parmesan, which don't squish when you touch them. They have usually been aged and have sharp, salty flavors.

BLUE Fragrant cheeses with soft, crumbly textures and blue veins.

Setting Up the Cheese Board

Arrange the cheeses in categories from mildest to strongest. If they are on one large board, arrange the cheese clockwise in the order of the firmness of the cheeses. If using small boards, dedicate one board to soft cheeses, another to semisoft, one to hard, and one to blue.

CHEESE KNIVES Dedicate one knife per cheese. This way there is no flavor contamination between the cheeses. Use dull-bladed knives for crumbly cheeses, such as blue, and sharp knives for harder cheeses, such as Cheddar and Parmesan. For a soft cheese, such as goat, use a thin, sharp blade or a taut piece of string.

Serving

Cheeses should be served at room temperature. To serve round cheeses, cut them in wedges like pizza. Blocks of cheese should be cut in thin slices from left to right.

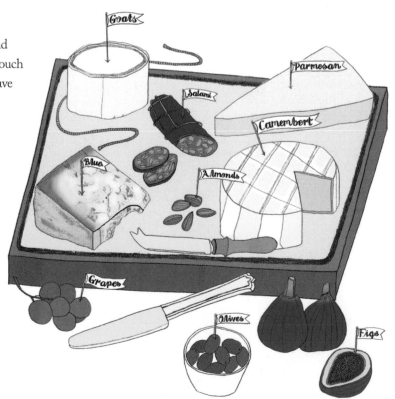

SNACKS TO SERVE *with* CHEESE

Cheeses beg to be paired with all kind of sweet and savory nibbles. Choose things that will complement the cheese, but not overpower it.

SAVORY Cornichons, salami, olives, prosciutto, Marcona almonds, roasted salted nuts, toasted walnuts, crispy salted crackers, toasted baguette rounds, sun-dried tomatoes.

SWEET Dried cranberries, dried apricots, candied pecans, grapes, strawberries, honey, pear or apple slices, fresh figs, dark chocolate squares, quince paste, guava paste.

WINE PAIRINGS

There is no hard-and-fast rule about which wine to drink with certain cheeses. Pairing them is all about creating complementary flavors. For example, an acidic wine will cut sweetness, whereas a full-bodied wine will complement rich, creamy flavors. To discover your favorite pairings, eat an unadorned piece of cheese. Then sip the wine of your choice. Observe how the flavors mingle in your mouth and decide if you like the pairing or not. Here are some guidelines to help you get started:

SOFT CHEESES Pinot Grigio, Sauvignon Blanc, Chenin Blanc

HARD CHEESES Merlot, Cabernet Sauvignon, Zinfandel, Chianti

SEMIHARD CHEESES Champagne, Chardonnay, Prosecco

BLUE CHEESE Riesling, Port, Sauternes, Cabernet

Latke Party

CLASSIC POTATO LATKES   312

—

ZUCCHINI-SHALLOT LATKES   312

—

SPICED BUTTERNUT SQUASH LATKES   313

To throw a festive latke party, fill up a table with platter of latkes and several homemade condiments and let everyone mix and match. Everything can be made in advance and you can spend the evening having fun, not tied to the stove.

Classic Potato Latkes

These are the latkes you grew up loving. If you make the latkes in advance, reheat them on a parchment-lined baking sheet at 400°F until crisp, 10 to 15 minutes.

MAKES 1 DOZEN LATKES

1 pound russet potatoes (about 2 medium-size)

1 small yellow onion

1 large egg, beaten

2 tablespoons unbleached all-purpose flour

½ teaspoon kosher salt

Vegetable oil for frying

Sour cream, for serving

Applesauce, for serving

1. Coarsely grate the potatoes and onion and place in a fine-mesh sieve. Squeeze out any excess moisture and transfer the potato mixture to a medium mixing bowl. Add the egg, flour, and salt and stir until just combined.

2. Heat a thin layer of oil in a large, heavy-bottomed skillet over medium-high heat until almost smoking. Without crowding the pan, add a heaping tablespoon of the mixture for each latke and flatten it with your spatula. Fry the latkes in batches until golden brown, about 2 minutes per side. Transfer the latkes to a paper towel–lined plate to drain. Serve immediately with sour cream and applesauce on the side.

Zucchini-Shallot Latkes

To give latkes a fresh twist, add lots of grated zucchini. The pretty color and enhanced flavor will make them a welcome addition to your table.

MAKES 1 DOZEN LATKES

1½ cups coarsely grated zucchini (about 1 medium-size)

1 large shallot, halved and thinly sliced

¼ cup unbleached all-purpose flour

½ teaspoon kosher salt

1 large egg, beaten

Zest of 1 lemon

Vegetable oil for frying

Crème fraîche, for serving

1. Preheat the oven to 400°F. Line a baking sheet with parchment paper.

2. In a large mixing bowl, stir together the zucchini, shallot, flour, salt, egg, and lemon zest until just combined.

3. Heat a thin layer of oil in a large, heavy-bottomed skillet. Add the zucchini mixture in scant tablespoonfuls, making sure not to crowd the pan. Cook until golden brown and firm, about 1 minute per side. Transfer to a paper towel–lined plate to drain and repeat with the remaining zucchini mixture, adding more oil as necessary. (Note: The latkes can be made up to 2 days in advance.)

4. Right before serving, arrange the latkes on the prepared baking sheet and bake in the oven until crispy, 10 to 15 minutes. Serve the latkes immediately with crème fraîche on the side.

Spiced Butternut Squash Latkes

Let the season inspire you and use butternut squash to complete your feast. The festive warm flavors and pretty color will make this spread a latke feast that is hard to beat.

MAKES 1 DOZEN LATKES

1½ cups coarsely grated, peeled, seeded
  butternut squash
2 tablespoons finely chopped fresh cilantro
2 tablespoons unbleached all-purpose flour
½ teaspoon kosher salt
¼ teaspoon ground cumin
¼ teaspoon paprika
1 large egg, beaten
Vegetable oil for frying
Greek yogurt, for serving

1. Preheat the oven to 400°F. Line a baking sheet with parchment paper.

2. In a large mixing bowl, stir together the squash, cilantro, flour, salt, cumin, paprika, and egg until just combined.

3. Heat a thin layer of oil in a large, heavy-bottomed skillet. Add the squash mixture in scant tablespoonfuls, making sure not to crowd the pan. Cook until golden brown and firm, about 1 minute per side. Transfer to a paper towel–lined plate to drain and repeat with the remaining squash mixture, adding more oil as necessary. (Note: The latkes can be made up to 2 days in advance.)

4. Right before serving, arrange the latkes on the prepared baking sheet and bake in the oven until crispy, 10 to 15 minutes. Serve the latkes immediately with Greek yogurt on the side.

Winter
Ch-Ch-Chili Night

BOURBON SPICED HOT CIDER   315

—

SLOW-COOKER BEEF CHILI IN A BREAD BOWL   316

—

LENTIL CHILI   317

—

CHEDDAR CORNBREAD   318

—

CHOCOLATE CHUNK PRETZEL COOKIES   319

January and February always bring lots of fresh snow and frigid temperatures to Connecticut. During this season we pack in as much sledding and skiing as possible during the day and throw chili parties at night. There is nothing better than setting big pots of bubbling soup on the stovetop, baking up a big pan of cornbread, and sitting around a roaring fire. This chili party menu comes together with ease. Choose one chili recipe, bake the side dishes in advance, and you are all set for your party.

Your Chili Party Strategy

Keep It Casual. It's a great time to haul out the slow cookers and let people serve themselves.

ON THE COUNTER Bowls or bread bowls, plates, ladles for serving.

ON THE TABLE Bowls of fixings, including tortilla strips, diced avocado, shredded cheese, sour cream, guacamole, hot sauce (for the truly brave), squares of cornbread in a warm basket, spoons, napkins.

BEVERAGES A selection of beer and wine, hot spiced cider, mulled wine (page 239).

Bourbon Spiced Hot Cider

For a go-to winter cocktail, buy cider from the store, add a few spices and some bourbon, and you are all set. To keep the cider warm, make it in a slow cooker and keep the setting on low for the duration of the party. Keep a ladle next to the pot so people can serve themselves as they please.

MAKES 1 GALLON CIDER,
ABOUT 10 SERVINGS

1 gallon apple cider
1 tablespoon ground cinnamon
1 tablespoon ground ginger
2 teaspoons ground nutmeg
2½ cups bourbon

1. Bring the cider and spices to a simmer in a large stockpot over medium heat. Lower the heat to low; stirring the mixture occasionally, heat for about 10 minutes. Stir in the bourbon, remove from the heat, and serve.

Slow-Cooker Beef Chili in a Bread Bowl

Make entertaining easier on yourself by cooking your chili in the slow cooker. This gives you more time to prepare for your party and enjoy some time by the fire. To make this one extra fun, get bread bowls at the bakery and set them out for serving.

MAKES 8 SERVINGS

1 tablespoon vegetable oil

1½ pounds boneless round steak, cut into ½-inch pieces

1 large yellow onion, peeled and finely chopped

1 large carrot, peeled and chopped into ½-inch pieces

2 celery stalks, chopped into ½-inch pieces

2 garlic cloves, finely chopped

1 (15-ounce) can red kidney beans, drained and rinsed

1 (14-ounce) can diced tomatoes with juices

1 (14-ounce) can tomato sauce

2 tablespoons tomato paste

1 tablespoon ancho chili powder

¼ teaspoon red pepper flakes

2 teaspoons ground cumin

2 teaspoons ground coriander

1 teaspoon freshly cracked black pepper

1 teaspoon kosher salt

1. Heat the oil in a large skillet over medium heat. Add the beef and brown it on all sides, about 2 minutes per side. Then transfer it to the bowl of the slow cooker. Add the onion, carrot, and celery to the pan, scraping up any browned bits, and cook them for about 5 minutes, or until the onion is soft and translucent.

2. Add the vegetables, garlic, beans, tomatoes and their juices, tomato sauce, tomato paste, chili powder, red pepper flakes, cumin, coriander, black pepper, and salt to the slow cooker. Cook on the high setting for 5 hours, or until the beef is very tender and the flavors are well blended. Keep warm at the low or warm setting until serving.

Lentil Chili

In recent years some of my friends have adopted a vegan diet. I love vegan dishes but used to have trouble coming up with a vegan main course until I made this. It is hearty enough to be the main meal and makes everyone happy. Serve it with a huge platter of cornbread and a buffet with all the fixings.

MAKES 8 CUPS CHILI

2 tablespoons olive oil

1 medium-size yellow onion, finely chopped

3 garlic cloves, minced

1½ tablespoons ground turmeric

1½ tablespoons ground cumin

1 tablespoon ground coriander

1 teaspoon ground chili powder

2 tablespoons tomato paste

2 cups brown lentils, rinsed

8 cups vegetable stock

Kosher salt and freshly cracked black pepper

1. Place a large, heavy-bottomed pot over medium-low heat, heat the oil, and cook the onion for 20 to 25 minutes, or until it turns golden brown and begin to caramelize. Add the garlic and stir for a minute, until fragrant.

2. Add the spices and tomato paste to the pot and stir well. Carefully pour in the lentils and vegetable stock. Taste the soup and season it with a little salt and pepper. Bring the mixture to a boil, and boil for 5 minutes. Then lower the heat to a simmer and cook for 30 minutes, or until the lentils are tender. Taste again for seasoning and add a little more salt and pepper, if necessary.

Tip Rinsing lentils gets rid of any leftover debris or stones that may have made it into the packaging. To rinse them, place the lentils in mesh strainer set over a large bowl. Place this under the faucet and swish the lentils around with your hand until the water coming out of the strainer runs clear. Then pick out any shriveled lentils or stones you find. Leave the lentils in the strainer to drain until you add them to the soup.

Cheddar Cornbread

A big platter of cornbread hits the spot after a big night of celebrating. This easy bread is perfect for sopping up sauces or crumbling into soups. One year, I even took this to Daphne's classroom for its Thanksgiving celebration. I cut it into small squares and the children enjoyed it alongside their fresh applesauce and sliced turkey.

MAKES ABOUT 24 SQUARES

6 tablespoons unsalted butter

1½ cups unbleached all-purpose flour

1½ cups yellow cornmeal

¾ cup granulated sugar

2½ teaspoons baking powder

1 teaspoon kosher salt

2 large eggs, at room temperature

1½ cups whole milk

1½ cups coarsely shredded sharp Cheddar
    cheese

1. Preheat the oven to 350°F. Place the butter in a 13 x 9 x 2-inch baking dish and put it in the oven to melt while the oven preheats.

2. In a large bowl, mix together the flour, cornmeal, sugar, baking powder, and salt. In a smaller bowl, whisk together the eggs and milk. Fold the wet ingredients into the dry ingredients, then stir in the Cheddar until completely combined.

3. Remove the dish from the oven and set on a flat, heatproof surface. Scrape the batter into the prepared baking dish and spread the top flat with a spatula. Bake the cornbread for 28 to 30 minutes, or until the top springs back when touched and a cake tester comes out clean. Allow to cool slightly. Slice and serve.

Chocolate Chunk Pretzel Cookies

A hefty dose of coarse salt takes the flavor of a chocolate chip cookie to the next level. To riff on this idea, one day I added crushed pretzels to our favorite cookies to add both flavor and texture. They tasted even better than a regular chocolate chip cookie with salt sprinkled on top, so these have become a mainstay in our house. They are perfect for serving to friends for a casual dessert. Pile them on a plate in front of the fireplace and enjoy.

MAKES ABOUT 3 DOZEN COOKIES

2½ cups unbleached all-purpose flour

1 teaspoon kosher salt

½ teaspoon baking soda

8 ounces (2 sticks) unsalted butter, at room temperature

1 cup light brown sugar

¾ cup granulated sugar

1 large egg, at room temperature

1 tablespoon pure vanilla extract

1½ cups semisweet chocolate chunks

1 cup crushed salted pretzels (about the size of chocolate chips but not reduced to dust)

1. Whisk together the flour, salt, and baking soda in a small bowl and set aside.

2. With an electric mixer, beat the butter and sugars on high speed in a large bowl until light and fluffy, about 3 minutes. Then beat in the egg, 1 tablespoon of water, and the vanilla until everything is combined.

3. With the mixer on low speed, slowly add the flour mixture until the flour is just combined and is no longer visible. Stop the mixer, scrape down the sides of the bowl, and stir in the chocolate chunks and crushed pretzels. Then dump the dough onto a large sheet of plastic wrap and wrap it up completely so none of it is exposed to any air. Then place the dough in the fridge and chill for at least 6 hours or up to 2 days.

4. Preheat the oven to 350°F. Line rimmed baking sheets with parchment paper. Use a 1-inch cookie scoop to make balls of cookie dough. Place them about 2 inches apart on the prepared pan.

5. Bake the cookies for 10 to 12 minutes, or until the edges turn golden brown and the tops are set. Allow the cookies to cool for 2 minutes in the pans, then transfer them to a cooling rack and allow them to cool completely. Store in an airtight container for up to 4 days.

Note The cookie dough can be baked immediately after it has been prepared, if you don't have time to chill it. However, chilling it deepens the flavor and allows the saltiness of the pretzels to meld with the chocolate chunks, which really makes them taste amazing.

Valentine's Treats for School

WHITE CHOCOLATE HEART LOLLIPOPS 321
—
CHOCOLATE-DIPPED MARSHMALLOWS 322
—
STRAWBERRY ROSES 322

Daphne's classroom always has really fun Valentine's Day celebrations, complete with homemade gifts for the children. To beat the midwinter blahs, we spend a few weeks leading up to the holiday in planning our handout for the year. The key is to think of something sweet and small that is easy to personalize for classmates. Choose one project and double or triple the recipe according to the volume you need.

White Chocolate Heart Lollipops

This superfun activity doesn't require any baking and can be personalized with simple decorations. These can be completely gluten-free and nut-free, depending on the decorations you use. Cover the lollipops with plastic bags and tie them closed with yarn or a ribbon.

MAKES 12 LOLLIPOPS

1 (10-ounce) bag white chocolate chips

1 cup pink or red candy hearts (or sprinkles, cinnamon bites, or any other decorating candy you choose)

12 lollipop sticks

1. Line a large baking sheet with parchment paper or a silicone mat. Place the decorations in small bowls next to it.

2. In a microwave-safe bowl, heat the chocolate chips at 50% power in 20-second intervals, stirring after each interval, until they are melted and smooth.

3. Spoon the melted chocolate into a large resealable plastic bag and snip off a tiny part of the corner. Twist the top of the bag until the chocolate is in the corner with the end cut off and looks like a pastry bag. Place a lollipop stick on the baking sheet and pipe a 2- to 3-inch circle or heart shape of warm chocolate over the top inch of the stick. Then decorate the circle immediately with the candies. Repeat with the remaining sticks and chocolate.

4. Once all of the lollipops are finished, set the sheet in cool, dry place to harden for at least 1 hour. Do not refrigerate immediately or it could cause the chocolate to seize and harden unevenly. After an hour they should be transferred to the refrigerator and chilled for at least 2 more hours. Once the lollipops have hardened and chilled, you can eat them, or wrap the tops in cello bags and tie with a ribbon to give as a gift.

Note These can also be made with semisweet chocolate chips.

Chocolate-Dipped Marshmallows

The simplest Valentine's Day treats are chocolate-dipped marshmallows. I first made these with Daphne when she was just two years old. It is a really easy activity for preschoolers. Wrap them in a waxed paper bag sealed with a decorative sticker.

MAKES 24 MARSHMALLOWS

8 ounces milk chocolate or white chocolate, coarsely chopped (do not use chocolate chips)

24 jumbo marshmallows

½ cup sprinkles or crushed peppermint candies

1. Line a baking sheet or flat tray with parchment paper and set aside.

2. In a microwave-safe bowl, heat the chopped chocolate at 50% power in 20-second intervals, or until it can be stirred smooth.

3. Dip a marshmallow in the melted chocolate so that it goes halfway up the side. Then immediately dip in the sprinkles or crushed candies to coat the chocolate. Carefully place the marshmallow, dipped-side up, on the prepared baking sheet. Repeat with the remaining marshmallows. Allow the marshmallows to cool at room temperature for 30 minutes, then chill in the refrigerator for 2 hours, or until hardened.

Strawberry Roses

This is my favorite prettiest fruit based treat for Valentine's Day. They are creative, easy to make, and the children love them.

MAKES 12 ROSES

1 (10-ounce) bag white chocolate chips

12 large strawberries, washed and patted dry

1 red gel decorating pen

12 large sticks

1. Line a large baking sheet with parchment paper and set aside.

2. In a large, microwave-safe bowl, place the chocolate chips. Heat them at 50% power in 30-second intervals until they are melted and can be stirred until smooth.

3. Dip a strawberry up to the top in the melted chocolate and it hold it in your hand so the tip is facing up. Make a spiral design with the red gel pen from the tip to a third of the way down the berry. Put the lollipop stick in the bottom of the strawberry so the spiral design is still facing up. Place the rose delicately on the parchment paper and repeat with remaining berries. Place the sheet in a cool, dry place away from sunlight to harden.

Valentine's Dinner for Two

Because dinner reservations and babysitters are generally very hard to come by on Valentine's Day, we usually celebrate the holiday with a special meal at home after the kids are asleep. To step up your at-home dinner, focus on these surefire recipes you can execute with ease while you enjoy your evening together.

Valentine's Day Cocktails

For Valentine's Day, I like to break out the bubbly and make something sweet and flirty for myself. Duncan prefers a stronger cocktail made with hard liquor. Here are our favorites.

MAKES 2 SERVINGS EACH

FRENCH 77 2 ounces of St. Germain elderflower liquor, 8 ounces of Champagne. Divide evenly between two champagne flutes. Squeeze the juice from 1 lemon wedge into each glass. Serve.

KIR ROYALE 2 tablespoons of crème de cassis, 8 ounces of Champagne, four raspberries. Divide evenly between two champagne flutes. Serve.

POMEGRANATE MARTINI 2 ounces of vodka, 2 ounces of Cointreau, 8 of ounces pomegranate juice. Place in a cocktail shaker filled with ice and shake well. Divide between two martini glasses and serve.

GINGERED OLD-FASHIONED 4 dashes of bitters, 4 teaspoons of ginger beer, 4 ounces of rye whiskey, two orange slices. Divide the ingredients evenly between two lowball glasses. Stir and serve.

Easy Cheese Soufflé

There is never a better occasion for a soufflé than Valentine's Day. The silky cheese pairs beautifully with Champagne. There also is a wonderful wow factor when it hits the table. Soufflés can be intimidating to the make, but this one never fails and is easy enough for even the most novice soufflé baker.

MAKES 1 (7-INCH) SOUFFLÉ

3 tablespoons unsalted butter, plus more for the pan

1 to 2 tablespoons finely grated Parmesan cheese for the pan

4 large egg whites

3 large egg yolks

3 tablespoons unbleached all-purpose flour

1 cup whole milk

½ cup coarsely grated Gruyère cheese

1. Preheat the oven to 400°F. Butter the bottom and up the sides of a 7-inch soufflé dish. Toss the grated Parmesan into the dish and rotate it gently so the Parmesan covers all the butter. Be careful not to let the Parmesan coat the top rim of the pan, or it will burn. Dump out any remaining cheese. Set the pan aside.

2. With an electric mixer fitted with the whisk attachment, whip the egg whites on high speed in a large bowl until they form stiff peaks, 3 to 5 minutes. While they are beating, place the egg yolks in a small separate bowl and use a whisk to beat until smooth.

3. In a medium saucepan, melt the butter over medium heat, then whisk in the flour until a thick paste forms. Cook for 1 to 2 minutes, or until the roux has turned a light golden brown color. Then pour in the milk, whisking continuously so no floury lumps form. Continue to whisk the milk mixture until it thickens slightly and is smooth, about 3 minutes. Remove the pan from the heat.

4. Working quickly, stir the Gruyère into the hot milk mixture until smooth, then slowly add the egg yolks, whisking continuously so the yolks don't cook. Finally, use a spatula to fold the stiff egg whites into the cheese sauce, carefully folding just until the whites are combined and are no longer visible.

5. Pour the mixture into the prepared soufflé dish and bake for 25 to 30 minutes, or until the soufflé has risen and set. It should no longer be watery looking in the center and the edges should be slightly browned. Remove from the oven and serve immediately.

Coffee-Rubbed Steak

This easy rub is a delicious way to elevate your everyday steak dinners. If the weather is bad, cook the steak on the stovetop grill pan and it will still taste amazing.

MAKES 2 SERVINGS

2 teaspoons ancho chili powder

2 teaspoons instant espresso powder

½ teaspoon ground ginger

1 teaspoon dark brown sugar

¼ teaspoon salt

¼ teaspoon freshly cracked black pepper

1½ pounds sirloin steak, about 1¼ inch thick

1. Heat the grill to a medium flame, or heat a lightly oiled grill pan over medium-high heat.

2. In a small bowl, mix together the chili powder, espresso powder, ginger, sugar, salt, and pepper. Rub the steak all over with the mixture so it is well coated.

3. Cook the steak for 7 to 8 minutes per side for medium-rare, then allow it to sit for about 5 minutes before slicing and serving.

Roasted Rosemary Fingerling Potatoes

These simple potatoes are easy to make and pair so well with steak. I use fresh rosemary plucked from our little indoor rosemary tree, but you can use dried rosemary, too.

MAKES 4 SERVINGS

½ cup extra-virgin olive oil

1 tablespoon finely chopped fresh rosemary, or
    2 teaspoons dried

1 teaspoon kosher salt

½ teaspoon freshly cracked black pepper

2 pounds fingerling potatoes, scrubbed and cut
    into 1-inch pieces

1. Preheat the oven to 400°F. Line a baking sheet with aluminum foil and set aside.

2. In a large mixing bowl, whisk together the olive oil, rosemary, salt, and pepper. Add the chopped potatoes to the bowl and use clean hands to toss them very well until everything is lightly coated.

3. Spread the potatoes evenly on the baking sheet and roast them for 40 to 45 minutes, turning them with a wooden spoon at least once or twice to ensure even cooking. Remove them from the oven and allow them to cool for 5 minutes before serving.

Note To change the flavor of these potatoes, try using different herbs. Dried thyme, basil, sage, or a blend would also taste wonderful.

Salted Caramel Cheesecake

A decadent dessert dripping with caramel is always a welcome way to cap off Valentine's Day. Instead of a chocolate bombe, make this tangy velvet cheesecake topped with a smooth layer of salted caramel.

MAKES 1 (9-INCH) CHEESECAKE

FOR THE CRUST

1½ cups gingersnap crumbs

3 tablespoons granulated sugar

3 tablespoons unsalted butter, melted

FOR THE CHEESECAKE

4 (8-ounce) packages cream cheese, at room
    temperature

1¼ cups granulated sugar

¼ teaspoon kosher salt

1 tablespoon pure vanilla extract

4 large eggs

¾ cup sour cream

½ cup heavy whipping cream

½ cup caramel sauce

Sea salt

1. Preheat the oven to 350°F. Wrap the bottom and sides of a 9-inch springform pan in aluminum foil. Keep the wrapping very tight so no water can get through.

2. To make the crust: In a medium bowl, combine the gingersnap crumbs, sugar, and butter and mix until evenly moistened. Press the crumbs into the bottom and up the sides of the springform pan. Bake for 10 minutes, then remove from the oven and allow to cool. Lower the oven temperature to 325°F.

3. To make the cheesecake: With an electric mixer fitted with the paddle, beat the cream cheese on high speed in a large bowl until smooth and creamy, about 4 minutes. Beat in the sugar until fluffy, about 4 more minutes. Beat in the salt and vanilla. Then beat in the eggs one at a time, mixing well after each addition. Beat in the sour cream until smooth, followed by the cream, scraping down the sides of the bowl as needed. Once everything is beaten together, the batter should be thick and smooth.

4. Pour the batter into the prepared crust and smooth the top with a spatula. Rap the bottom of the pan on a countertop a couple of times to release any bubbles. Set the prepared pan into a large roasting pan or deep baking dish. Carefully pour hot water into the baking dish so that it comes halfway up the sides of the pan. Bake the cheesecake for about 1 hour 30 minutes, or until the center is set and no longer wet-looking. If the top begins to brown too much at the end, tent the pan with aluminum foil. Once the baking is finished, turn off the oven and crack the door open by about 1 inch. It usually works well to place a wooden spoon in the door to hold it open. After 1 hour, remove the cake and set it on a cooling rack. (This helps to prevent drastic changes in temperature, which causes cheesecake to crack.)

5. Carefully pour the caramel sauce evenly over the top of the cooled cake and sprinkle a pinch or two of sea salt on top. Place the pan in the refrigerator to chill for at least 4 hours or up to overnight. This will set the cheesecake and the caramel. When ready to serve, unmold the pan and allow the cheesecake to sit at room temperature for 15 minutes. Slice with a sharp knife and serve.

ACKNOWLEDGMENTS

This book would not exist without the loyal and enthusiastic readers of *The Naptime Chef* and those who stop by my Facebook page to chat every day. Thank you for your feedback, comments, and ongoing support. You've been with me for more than five years and I am eternally grateful for all the time we've spent together.

A special thanks to my agent, Jenni Ferrari-Adler, who helped bring this idea to fruition and encouraged me every step of the way.

Thanks to my editorial team, Kristen Green Wiewora and Jennifer Kasius, for their wisdom, sound guidance, and ongoing support. I also extend my deepest gratitude to Seta Zink, Ashley Haag, and the entire team at Running Press for their seamless execution in the formation and promotion of this book. To the talented Lindsey Spinks for the gorgeous artwork that graces these pages and so beautifully illustrates each and every word.

Writing and testing recipes is always a huge endeavor and this book wouldn't be the same without the professional culinary skills of Helen Johnston, Phoebe Lapine, and Adelaide Mueller. A huge thank-you to my team of at-home testers, including Hilary Burrall, Koren Bradshaw, Emma Bradshaw, Nicole Garwood, Jennifer Giudice, Kirsten Hennigan, Melissa Lawrence, Barbara McLaughlin, Elizabeth Perhac Schmitt, and Char Zola, for lending me their kitchen skills, time, and resources. Their willingness to test and retest any recipe was above and beyond and I am forever indebted to them for their kindness.

A big hug to my crew of cheerleaders for their friendship, including Ellen Genovese, Kerry Gillespie, Jessica Gray, Katie Rothschild, Sarah Turner, and Cassie Walker.

Finally, having a baby and writing a book all in the same year takes a lot of juggling and I never would've been able to do it without my family. An enormous thank-you to my parents, Roger and Carla MacMillan, for their open arms and words of support whenever I needed them, and even when I didn't. To my brother, Will, the coolest uncle on the planet, for his ongoing culinary contributions and gardening expertise. Thank you to my gracious in-laws, Geoffrey and Patty, for respites in Florida and for rooting for me every step of the way. And, finally, a hug and kiss to Duncan, for being my partner in life, love, and parenting. Without you none of this would happen and I am grateful for every single day we have together as a family. To my sweet Daphne, who grows much too quickly and gets even more delicious every single day: I am so proud of the smart, curious, strong girl you've become. And to my little guy, Garner, who arrived just in time for me to start writing this book. Thank you, sweet boy, for ironing out a solid nap schedule early on and enthusiastically eating just about anything I put on your plate. Peering into those baby blues and kissing those chubby cheeks is my favorite way to start every single day.

INDEX

3 1901 05812 2260